SMITTEN

SMITTEN

SEX, GENDER, AND THE CONTEST FOR SOULS IN THE SECOND GREAT AWAKENING

RODNEY HESSINGER

CORNELL UNIVERSITY PRESS
Ithaca and London

First published 2022 by Cornell University Press

Library of Congress Cataloging-in-Publication Data
Names: Hessinger, Rodney, author.
Title: Smitten : sex, gender, and the contest for souls in
    the Second Great Awakening / Rodney Hessinger.
Description: Ithaca [New York] : Cornell University
    Press, 2022. | Includes bibliographical references and
    index.
Identifiers: LCCN 2022010574 (print) | LCCN
    2022010575 (ebook) | ISBN 9781501766473
    (hardcover) | ISBN 9781501766480 (pdf) |
    ISBN 9781501766497 (epub)
Subjects: LCSH: Second Great Awakening. |
    Christianity—United States—History—19th century. |
    Enthusiasm—Religious aspects—Christianity—
    History—19th century. | Sex—Religious aspects—
    Christianity—History—19th century. | Sex role—
    Religious aspects—Christianity—History—19th
    century. | Women in Christianity—United States—
    History—19th century. | Christian communities—
    United States—History—19th century. | United
    States—Church history—19th century.
Classification: LCC BR525 .H47 2022 (print) | LCC
    BR525 (ebook) | DDC 277.307—dc23/eng/20220722
LC record available at https://lccn.loc.gov/2022010574
LC ebook record available at https://lccn.loc.gov/
2022010575

To Norah, Ella, and Quinn

Contents

ACKNOWLEDGMENTS

Finishing a book in the midst of a pandemic presented some unique challenges, but this project began long before that. Seeds of it were actually planted with my first book. As I studied generational tensions in the early republic, I became attuned to the family and gender disruption of enthusiastic religion. As such, the enduring impact of my mentor, C. Dallett Hemphill, whose loss I will always mourn, must first be acknowledged. The wider early Americanist community, which she helped constitute at the McNeil Center for Early American Studies in Philadelphia, proved wonderfully supportive in her absence. Susan Branson was one of the very first people to offer advice and source tips as I began to conceive this project. Jim Green at the Library Company was also a gracious host and guide to Mathew Carey's pamphlets as I was in residence for a fellowship. Dee Andrews provided valuable feedback and support on portions of the manuscript. Bruce Dorsey, who also is working on the intersection of sex and religion in early America, shared ideas and valuable leads. So too did Dan Cohen, who also has tilled this same field. Lucia McMahon, Charlene Boyer Lewis, and Julie Berebitsky have long been supportive sounding boards and friends, great fellow travelers in mapping the gender dynamics of America's past. As the larger project began to coalesce, Sally Gordon at Penn provided invaluable feedback, asking just the right questions to help me formulate the conceptual and narrative framework for this study.

Other scholars, whom I met outside the Philadelphia orbit, also provided helpful advice and leads to sources. Spencer McBride of *The Joseph Smith Papers* helped initiate me into the rich world of LDS scholarship. Seth Bryant, then of the Kirtland Temple, tipped me off to the wonderfully illustrative story of the Mormon mission to the Shakers and also encouraged me to appreciate the distinct influence of Sidney Rigdon on the rising LDS Church. The staff at the Western Reserve Historical Society also further opened doors of the early republic to me, locating rare texts that play key roles in this study. I also want to thank the *Journal of the Early Republic* for allowing me to reproduce much of the content of the second chapter of this book. The staff at Cornell University Press has been great. Michael McGandy first helped me develop larger ambitions for this project, while Sarah Grossman helped me creatively react to reviewer feedback, and Jacqulyn Teoh deftly guided me through the final editing process.

I am especially indebted to my valued colleague and good friend, Kristen Tobey. For the last six years we have taught a pair of linked classes at John Carroll University, mine dealing with spiritual awakenings in early America, hers on spiritual enthusiasm in modern America. Our ongoing dialogue about the dynamics of enthusiastic religion have had a formative influence on this study. Plus, Kristen provided close readings and deeply perceptive feedback on several chapters, suggesting sociological frameworks to help make fuller meaning of my findings.

Finishing a book requires not just scholarly support, but emotional support too. When I left Hiram College and joined John Carroll University, I was leaving behind a close community of friends. While those friendships endure, I was lucky enough to find a new community of friends at JCU. Kristen, as well as Michelle Millet, Margaret Farrar, and Amy Wainwright have been close allies and supportive friends as we have navigated the troubled waters of higher education. My colleagues in the History Department, Anne Kugler, Matt Berg, Dan Kilbride, Roger Purdy, Paul Murphy, Malia McAndrew, Marcus Gallo, Maria Marsilli, George Vourlogianis, and Jim Krukones, were welcoming from the moment I arrived. Since then, I have had the opportunity to work together with them in charting a vision for our students, department, and school. Their collective wisdom and support have made me feel at home.

I am also very grateful to the deans and fellow associate deans I have worked for and with at JCU, each of whom has supported me as I pursued scholarship alongside my administrative work. Graciela Lacueva, Pam Mason, Margaret Farrar, Peter Kvidera, Rebecca Drenovsky, Mike Martin, Lisa Shoaf, and Bonnie Gunzenhauser have helped me keep my sanity, always putting our administrative work in perspective. I also want to thank JCU for granting me the Grauel Research Leave that allowed me to bring this book to completion. Doing this work in a pandemic seemed daunting, but I was saved by the librarians of the world. Their collective labor in building the wonder that is the Hathitrust Digital Library was a true gift. The wealth of early American texts now at all of our fingertips will be a boon to scholars for the years ahead.

I finally want to thank my families. My family of birth, parents Dorothy and Frank, brothers Greg and Glen, and sister Chrissa, helped make me who I am. Their spirit of persistence has always inspired me to push on, and their supportive care and sense of humor also keep me steady. My in-laws, Margaret and Bill Feeny, have been great and supportive neighbors, always happy to share a meal or help with the kids.

My own immediate family, my dear spouse, Norah, and our children, Ella and Quinn, have been the emotional center of my life. Not only has Norah been a partner and loving friend in building a family, she also has read various drafts of the chapters and given much clarifying feedback. Her empathy and devotion are unparalleled. Ella and Quinn, each with their own unique personalities, have opened new ways of seeing the world to me. My book is dedicated to the three of them.

SMITTEN

Introduction

The pursuit of souls in early nineteenth-century America was a volatile endeavor. People were on the move. They were flooding into the cities, canal towns, and newly opened frontier lands. The displacement of Americans created ripe conditions for religious competition. In the midst of the Second Great Awakening, religious seekers by turns could play the missionary and the convert. Competing within an increasingly democratic religious marketplace, preachers had to court converts to flourish. They won followers through charismatic allure and concessions to the desires of the people. As such, the dynamic of religious rivalry inexorably led toward sexual and gender disruption. Preachers aimed for the heart, trying to sweep sinners off their feet. Opening their own hearts to new religious impulses, some religious visionaries offered up radical new dispensations. Their revelations offered new visions of how God wanted them to reorder sex and gender relations in society.

To start our journey into the heart of religious struggle, we will consider the story of a Mormon mission trip to the Shakers on the Western Reserve in Ohio in 1831. This tale begins to suggest the religious and sexual contingency of the Second Great Awakening. The leader of this trip was Sidney Rigdon. Perhaps no figure better captures the early nineteenth-century quest for conversions and religious meaning than

Rigdon. He and his fellow Mormon travelers rode twenty miles from their village at Kirtland to North Union Village (today Shaker Heights) to convert the Shakers.

Rigdon's own earlier winding religious journey to join the Mormons set the stage for this encounter with the Shakers. His spiritual voyage involved sojourns with the Baptists and Disciples of Christ, both of whom appealed to Rigdon's yearning for a more personal and accessible God. Raised in western Pennsylvania and baptized into the Baptist Church in 1817 at the age of twenty-four, Rigdon quickly pursued training to become a minister, receiving a license to preach in 1819. He spent a couple of years preaching across the state line in and around Warren, Ohio, before returning to western Pennsylvania in early 1822, having been invited to take the pastorate of the First Baptist Church in Pittsburgh.

He returned a changed man, however. During the time of his Ohio residency, Rigdon had been won over by Alexander Campbell, one of the founders of the Disciples of Christ movement. Campbell rejected established clerical authority, arguing that every man should be his own theologian. His egalitarian ethos and emphasis on restoring primitive Christianity appealed greatly to Rigdon.[1] While Baptists represented an autonomous strain within the American Christian tradition, they nonetheless found the Campbellite rejection of church hierarchy and doctrine too radical. When Rigdon brought the Campbellite message to the First Baptist Church in Pittsburgh, the congregation was split in two. But before being disowned by the Redstone Baptist Association, the ecclesiastical body to which the Pittsburgh church belonged, Rigdon managed to win most of his congregation to the Disciples cause.[2]

After Rigdon was forced from the Pittsburgh church, he preached to his followers in a courthouse. He supported himself as a tanner, for he and his fellow reformers rejected the notion of a paid ministry. A more secure livelihood than the tanning business became available when Rigdon's father-in-law offered up a landed estate in Bainbridge, Ohio, in 1825. This was an attractive place to move, for reformist Baptists had gained fuller traction on the Western Reserve. Rigdon began preaching a circuit throughout northeastern Ohio, managing to help establish the first recognized Disciples church at Mantua Center, serving the villages of Hiram, Nelson, and Mantua. A larger opportunity became available in 1826 when a congregation offered him a pastorate in Mentor, Ohio, a budding town on Lake Erie.

From Mentor, Rigdon staged a series of revivals. A renowned orator, he visited towns and captured converts throughout the Western Reserve, including, most notably, Parley Pratt, who would later turn from disciple to teacher. Over time, Rigdon wished for an even fuller restoration of the primitive gospel order. He began to chafe at some of the limits imposed by Alexander Campbell. Specifically, Campbell's insistence that the age of miracles ended in the apostolic age, that the Bible was to be studied rationally, left Rigdon cold. Rigdon was convinced that the restoration of the ancient order of things included the revival of apostolic gifts, such as revelations and miracles. In addition, Rigdon went beyond his teacher in wanting to establish a communalism of property as practiced in the early Jerusalem church.[3]

Thus, when Parley Pratt presented Rigdon with a copy of the *Book of Mormon* in late 1830, Rigdon was ready to receive it. On a journey to New York a couple months earlier, Pratt had first discovered the text. He sought out its author, Joseph Smith Jr., but found instead the Mormon apostle Hyrum Smith, Joseph's older brother. Converted by Hyrum to the Church of Jesus Christ of Latter-day Saints, Pratt was soon thereafter directed by Joseph to join a mission to convert the Indians in Missouri. Along the way, Pratt convinced his companions to take a detour to visit his teacher Rigdon. On receiving the book from Pratt and Oliver Cowdery, Rigdon asked for time alone to read it. After days of close reading, subsequent conversations, spiritual struggles, and a personal vision, Rigdon was ready to join the Latter-day Saints. Joseph Smith's testimony of visits by angels, golden tablets, and ongoing revelations was the fuller restoration of the ancient order he had been seeking.[4]

In a short time, Rigdon would become Joseph Smith's scribe and closest counselor. Together they determined to move the LDS headquarters from upstate New York to Kirtland, Ohio, a place where Rigdon had a strong following and the Mormon missionaries had won many converts. Once there, they began to think about how to evangelize the greater Western Reserve. The Shakers seemed like good prospects. Like the Mormons of this era, the Shakers believed in inspired visions, faith healings, and the sharing of property. Plus, a longtime Shaker, Leman Copley, had just joined the Mormons and suggested to Smith that the Mormons might enjoy success in such a venture. Through revelation, Smith directed Rigdon, Pratt, and Copley to visit North Union village.[5]

Rigdon and Copley arrived first, equipped with a copy of Smith's revelation, as recorded in *Doctrine and Covenants* 49. Its purpose was to correct the Shakers in their chief errors. While the Shakers and Mormons shared a preoccupation with the millennium, the Shakers believed that Christ had already appeared again in female frame, as Mother Ann Lee. Smith's revelation reproved them for this, saying that "the Son of Man cometh not in the form of a woman," nor for that manner would he appear as merely a "traveling man." He would instead arrive in celestial glory announced by a shaking earth and an angel's trumpet. In addition, Smith criticized Shaker laws of abstinence, singling out their rejection of both meat and marriage. According to his revelation, one was not to forsake the flesh by chastity, for God had warned, "whoso forbiddeth to marry is not ordained of God." Husband and wife were to be of "one flesh," so "that the earth might answer the end of its creation." Following Genesis, humans were to procreate and live on the abundance of the animal kingdom.[6] While this revelation did endorse monogamy, it is notable that it shared with Smith's later revelation on plural marriage an emphasis on fertility.[7]

To Shaker ears, this would prove profane. Having earlier received copies of the *Book of Mormon* from Oliver Cowdery, they were already familiar with Mormon teachings. Shaker Ashbel Kitchell, leader of the North Union settlement, narrated the Mormon visit in his pocket journal. It is the fullest account we have of this encounter. Seeing Copley arrive in tow with Rigdon, Kitchell was immediately suspicious. He recognized the man who had abandoned them. He said Copley had found in Mormonism an "easier plan," wishing not to live under "the cross," the Shaker term for the life of celibacy.[8] Nonetheless, Kitchell was hospitable to his visitors. Over the course of the night, he reported, "the doctrines of the cross and the Mormon faith were both investigated." According to Kitchell, Rigdon "frankly acknowledged" that the life of "self denial corresponded better with the life of Christ," but he said he could not "bear that cross." Kitchell said he therefore could not look upon Rigdon as a "Christian." Even so, they retired for the night on good terms. At this point, Rigdon had yet to share Smith's revelation directly, saving it for the next day's Sabbath service.[9]

When the morning arrived, the religious discussion resumed. Kitchell turned the tables, offering a missionary message of his own. He first disarmed the Mormon visitors by suggesting that neither side should "force their doctrine on the other." Instead, he asked that their shared "time be spent in feeling of the spirit" at the Shaker service. For a seeker like Rigdon, such a request could hardly be denied. Kitchell added that he hoped Rigdon would be led to discover that the "foundation he was now on, was sandy." It was then that Parley Pratt arrived to join Rigdon and Copley. Pratt was taken aback at what had so far transpired, distressed that Rigdon and Copley had now been "bound to silence" by Kitchell. Pratt told them to "pay no attention" to Kitchell, for the Mormons had together "come with the authority of the Lord Jesus Christ." The Shakers were to hear their message.[10]

The Mormons did sit through the Shaker service quietly, but when it ended, Rigdon stood and asked if he could deliver a message sent by Christ. The Shakers consented. Rigdon then read the revelation in full. Kitchell was not pleased. He said the "Christ" revealed in the revelation "bore on its face, the image of its author." It was guided by a false Christ he once knew as "a boy" but now knew better to be "rid of his influence." He asked to end the community gathering. But Rigdon wanted the congregation to stay and discuss the revelation further. Kitchell relented, allowing his community to address Rigdon directly. They stood firm with Kitchell, saying they were "fully satisfied with what they had" and wanted "nothing to do with either them or their Christ." Rigdon was then ready to have matters end there. Pratt was not. He rose in indignation and shook his coattail at them, saying that he "shook the dust from his garments as a testimony against us."[11]

That was enough for Kitchell. He called Pratt a "filthy Beast," incredulous that he would "presume to come in here, and try to imitate a man of God, by shaking your filthy tail." He demanded Pratt to "confess your sins and purge your soul from your lusts." Kitchell then turned his attention to Copley and called him a "hypocrite," chastising him that he "knew where the living work of God was" but chose "for the sake of indulgence" to "consent to deceive yourself and them." The meeting dispersed and Pratt hopped on his horse, heading back for Kirtland. Rigdon stayed on for supper, seemingly remaining on better terms with his host. According to Kitchell, Rigdon "acknowledged that we were the purest people he had ever been acquainted with, but he was not prepared to live such a life."[12] Perhaps wishing to make some repair with old friends, Copley spent the night.

When Copley returned to his farm, a homestead hosting many Mormon residents, he got a poor reception. According to Kitchell, the Mormons were upset with Copley for leading them to believe they would be able to convert the Shakers. They "rejected him," saying they "could not own him for one of them." Copley was left feeling "very bad," unable to sleep after this upsetting fight. He came back to the Shakers and "begged for union" with them again. After some community deliberation, the Shakers consented to Copley's return. Kitchell accompanied

Copley as he returned to his farm. There, the Mormons and Shakers clashed once more. Copley and Kitchell had a spirited conversation with Mormon elder Newel K. Knight and his father, Joseph Knight. The older man called on Kitchell to repent, warning "at the top of his voice" that he was bound for "*Hell*." In reply, Kitchell said that if his warning had come "from a man of God," they "would have caused my knees to have smote together like Belshazers." But since they came from a "man that lived in his lusts—who gratified a beastly propensity, and often in a manner that was far below the beasts," he disregarded his words. Kitchell then provided a "lecture on the subject of the cross, and a life of self denyal," saying his lecture was well received by his Mormon audience.[13] The mission led by Rigdon and Pratt had failed, with Copley having returned to the Shakers.

While Kitchell's account surely carries some bias, predictably showing the Shakers coming out on top of this religious contest, it is still an illuminating illustration of the sexual and gender dimensions of religious conflict during the Second Great Awakening. We see through Shaker eyes how differences over sexual conduct could define notions of religious difference. The role of Rigdon in this affair also highlights the volatility of religious competition in this era. Having twice converted to new churches, Rigdon had his faith tested again. Whether or not Rigdon "frankly acknowledged" that Shaker chastity was superior to Mormon virility, we can clearly see how he had to weigh the merits of different dispensations on sex. Copley's fluctuations suggest this too. He had to choose whether to accept a female savior, and forego sex and marriage, if he were to join in full union with the Shakers. During the Second Great Awakening, religious disputes went deeper than ordinary doctrinal differences and theological disputes. The shape of social structure and the very ordering of human behavior were at stake as radical new religious visionaries pronounced their messages and founded new churches.[14]

In the early nineteenth century, religious innovation flourished in America. As new sects emerged, religious competition escalated, as witnessed in chance encounters like this Mormon visit to the Shakers. The competition became manifest in print, with pamphlets and books pouring from the presses as church leaders traded heated invectives. Sometimes it went beyond verbal sparring. Physical intimidation tested the ideal of religious pluralism in the young nation. Charges of sexual exploitation and gender disruption helped define these rising religious jealousies. As some churches radically reimagined relations between men and women, opponents accused them of violating the acceptable boundaries of religious liberty. While the phenomenon of religious competition is well known, its rhetorical dimensions deserve more study. This work uncovers how sex and gender were at the center of debates over religion in the early republic.

Religious conflict was particularly intense between and toward new churches. We will soon see Sidney Rigdon, along with Joseph Smith, tarred and feathered by Rigdon's former church, the Disciples of Christ. This episode actually predated Mormon pronouncements on polygamy. Thus, the animosity toward Mormons would only become broader and more intense after plural marriage was revealed. The emergent Shakers similarly inspired controversy with their unusual approach to sex and gender. The Shakers were notorious for embracing universal chastity, empowering women as church leaders, and separating children from their mothers. Shaker critics insisted that the sect violated natural family feelings that God had implanted in all. The evolving ideas of John Humphrey Noyes about free love and complex marriage scandalized his neighbors, for he was striking at a broad American consensus on monogamy.[15] Only once his Oneida Community gave up proselytism would they be left in relative peace. Differentiation between upstart churches and wider American society worked in both directions. While these new groups could use their unique practices as a way to test and strengthen the commitment of believers in their communities, bourgeois Americans could solidify their dedication to middle-class norms of gender and sexual relations by criticizing such divergent faith groups.[16]

Sexually charged conflict happened *within* churches too. Witness the Catholic experience in Philadelphia: there, disagreements about the distribution of power between the laity and clergy merged with a fight over women's involvement in church politics. Catholics, like their Protestant counterparts, had begun to entice followers into their flocks. Needing broad support, church leaders courted women, disrupting the customary gender relations within the church. It was the Reverend William Hogan's reliance on women (who were said to be "set agog" by the power of his "animal magnetism") that opened him to the ridicule of rival priests.[17] When one female follower accused him of sexual assault, the ensuing trial helped expose the intricate gender politics in the church. Its outcome encouraged rising anti-Catholicism. Tentatively invited to join the Christian mainstream during the early years of the republic, by mid-century Catholics were firmly placed on the outside, imagined as imprisoners of women.

These are but examples of a broader pattern in nineteenth-century America. Charges of seduction and gender trouble ignited fights within, among, and against churches. Archival libraries contain a multitude of exposés targeting religious groups. Such criticism began in earnest early in the century, encouraged by religious competition, and remained highly popular deep into mid-century, helping define a broader pan-Protestant rejection of religious passion. Upstart churches like the Shakers, the Mormons, and John Humphrey Noyes's Oneida Community were the subjects of particularly strong attacks, but more mainline denominations were also hit by sexual scandal. Methodist circuit riders, carrying the gospel on horseback, were said to leave bastard children behind them, while outdoor camp revival meetings were charged with unleashing passion in ways that led to sex in the woods.[18] *Enthusiastic* religion, a mode of religious expression that relied on the arousal of believers, was seen as too hazardous. As religious opponents would spar with one another, they used association with African Americans as one way to taint opponents. Imagined as either worldly sinners or religious enthusiasts, Blacks were seen as allowing too much license with their bodies. Whether engaged in loose behavior in urban oyster cellars or leaping into the air in African Methodist Episcopal services, they clashed with bourgeois notions of modest bodily comportment.[19] The broad push for respectability meant embracing modesty and religious decorum.

This study should reorient our understanding of the Second Great Awakening, showing how the spread of religious liberty foundered on worries about sex and gender. While benefiting from the many excellent social histories of religious groups of this era, it will focus on the public perceptions of enthusiastic religion as revealed in print.[20] In newspapers, pamphlets, and books, religious rivals and skeptics exposed the sexual liabilities of fervent religion. At first inspection, these various religious groups might seem like strange bedfellows. Groups like the Shakers and the Oneida Community seem to fit the sociological paradigm of new religious movements (NRMs), more than they do that of evangelical Protestants. But they did, in fact, carry forward important dynamics and ideas from their evangelical heritage. Methodists, Baptists, and Presbyterians seem to fit more neatly into the classic evangelical mold, and yet they also, like NRMs, reimagined family, sex, and gender relationships for their members. Mormons are famously hard to define. One can reasonably classify them as evangelicals, as restorationists, or as an NRM.[21] Catholics definitionally are entirely outside of Protestantism, yet we will see that they reacted to the religious marketplace in ways that were quite consistent with their Protestant rivals. Like Protestants, Catholics conceded to democratic pressures, placing more authority in women and local congregations.

No matter how they are classified, there is one thing adherents to these faith groups shared in common in this era: a style of religious engagement here referred to as religious *enthusiasm*. While sometimes used by critics as a term of derision, I will use religious enthusiasm in a phenomenological manner, capturing the unique character of these churches as sensed by my own historical actors. Whitney Cross's foundational work on the Second Great Awakening, *The Burned-Over District*, explicitly framed his book as a study of *"Enthusiastic Religion."*[22] While I will push the geographical boundaries of Cross's study into northern urban and frontier terrains, I think he rightly recognized the benefits of considering a diverse array of churches together under the umbrella of enthusiasm. Perhaps the best modern scholarly parallel concept is religious "maximalism" as developed by Bruce Lincoln in *Holy Terrors*. Religious enthusiasm, as with religious maximalism, connoted in the minds of observers a form of religion that did not observe the boundaries that had been raised by the Enlightenment.[23] It referred to religious expression that violated ordinary norms of religious decorum. Religion in this mode spilled out of churches, traversing the emerging spatial and temporal boundaries separating the secular and sacred in early America. William Hogan's Catholic followers were accused of zealotry, just as much as Methodist camp meeting converts or Shaker devotees. Whether believers were invading the family circle to win converts or pressing parishioners in the streets to join a cause, religious enthusiasts were known for their pushiness.

Religious enthusiasm is ultimately more about commitment and comportment than any particular theology or ecclesiastical form. It fits both NRMs and schisms within long-established churches. In the pages to follow, one can witness the tension between the enthusiasts and their critics, the religious minimalists and maximalists. While Mormons craved a restoration that captured "the fulness of the gospel," Disciples leader Alexander Campbell sharply criticized those who would allow revelation to overtake reason.[24] Methodists at camp meetings saw the boundaries of time and space collapse, inhabiting a sacred space that discomfited middle-class observers. Critics of William Hogan, whether inside or outside the Catholic Church, lamented how women had become "ardent and enthusiastic" in their support of this "zealous" priest.[25] The proselytism of the Shakers, which threatened to break apart families, inspired their critics to enforce new legal and extralegal boundaries around the Shakers, helping isolate them in their own sacred realm. Being smitten was more than simply being converted by a charismatic preacher; it was about being fully captivated and committed in the cause of religion.

Each of the enthusiastic groups in this study reimagined gender and sexual relations in their churches. If we step back to observe the social landscape of the early republic, we can better appreciate the exceptional manner of how gender operated within enthusiastic churches. Political and legal institutions proved more limiting to women than ecclesiastical structures. While women made their voices heard in venues such as parades and parlors, they were denied the opportunity of full citizenship in the body politic. Similarly, real legal empowerment for women lagged for decades following the Revolution. Against this backdrop, churches offered more space for women's voices. Why might this be? I believe that the religious market established an inescapable dynamic. People had to make a choice about whether to accept the terms of salvation; individuals had to decide which church to join. And once they joined, new opportunities for social activism and even missionary ventures greeted women. To be certain, patriarchal dimensions in Christianity were persistent, and some new churches, like the Latterday Saints, even strengthened theological notions of patriarchy. Nonetheless, a husband or father could not morally account for his wife or daughter in religion the same way he was expected to before the bar and legislature. This had important implications for both femininity and masculinity. Rather than contemplate women as empowered converts, most religious critics chose to portray them as smitten by preachers. Male pastors, in turn, were imagined as possessing enough charismatic allure to seduce both men and women.

While evangelicals in the South followed a different journey, more slowly gaining success as they forsook their social radicalism, across the North, both in rural and urban locales, the social challenge of religious enthusiasm was more pronounced.[26] We can now better appreciate that the North's Second Great Awakening was not limited to New York's Burned-Over District. In places as different as the rural frontier of the Western Reserve and the cities of Philadelphia and New York, churches made great gains.[27] As they did, they challenged sex and gender relationships. The very act of evangelizing was fraught with sexual tension. Religious enthusiasts appealed to the hearts, more than the heads, of their listeners, causing members of their audience to swoon. Fathers and husbands, in particular, worried about losing their daughters and wives to insurgent churches. When stories of actual clerical sexual seductions emerged, it greatly inflamed such fears. Reverend rakes made manifest the danger of opening one's heart to a preacher.

In addition, because religious experimentation went so deep during the Second Great Awakening, some churches looked to reimagine the relations of women and men under the gospel. Americans would have to stave off the sexual challenges of religious radicals like Lucy Wright, Joseph Smith Jr., and John Humphrey Noyes. While Wright preached Shaker celibacy and shared female leadership, Smith introduced Mormon polygamy, and Noyes introduced a plan of sexual communism, joining an entire community into a system of complex marriage. Presented with such provocations, many northern Americans lost their passion for religious enthusiasm. By the middle of the nineteenth century, they began to contain and distance the religious movements that had roiled their communities. This study reveals the sexual disruptions and subsequent domestication of religion during the Second Great Awakening.

We will begin with the Latter-day Saints. By looking at the Mormons before and after the public revelation on plural marriage, it will provide conceptual bookends for the study. The reader will see the sexual tensions simmering beneath the surface in the contest for souls, followed by a more targeted rejection of Mormon ways of courting women into polygamy. Notions of religious and sexual consent blurred in fights over Mormonism. Joseph Smith was accused of seducing both converts and plural wives. From this perspective, Mormon pledges were gained on false pretenses, by playing on emotions rather than reason. Charismatic preachers tested the idea of consent in the young nation. The first chapter begins by exploring the debates that led to the tarring and feathering of Smith and Rigdon in Ohio. It next analyzes narratives concerning "spiritual wifery" and polygamy, showing how Mormon families were imagined as a heresy against the companionate marriage ideal.

The next chapter takes us into other dimensions of the sexualized fears unleashed by heart religion, this time in an urban and Catholic context. Cutting a particularly strong figure with women, the firebrand priest William Hogan became an enemy of the established clergy in Philadelphia. When Hogan was accused of rape, the ensuing trial opened a debate on the sexual dimensions of both enthusiasm and Catholicism.

This chapter explores women's forays into the public sphere and reactions to clerical celibacy. Hogan had tried to democratize the American Catholic Church, inviting trustees to elect their own pastors. His later excommunication convinced Protestant observers that Catholicism robbed its followers of voice and volition. Tales of female captivity in convents, such as Maria Monk's *Awful Disclosures*, would give fullest expression of these fears.

The third chapter considers reactions to the Shakers. While Shaker celibacy provoked concern, the sharpest reaction against Shakers concerned their seeming violation of maternal love. Shaker opponents like Eunice Chapman conjured scenes of physical distress caused by women losing children to the Shakers. Whereas in the high fertility culture of colonial America, the womb had been the locus of motherhood, in this new literature, the breast, as a site of nurturance, came to define women. Shakers were said to be so cruel as to rip children away from the bosom of women. Shakers would react to this criticism by reimaging their founder, Ann Lee. They defended her motherhood by stressing the loving care she showed followers. But even more so, Shakers hearkened back to older maternal ideals. In this celibate sect, Lee was described and even drawn (in Shaker spirit drawings) as a fruitful mother.

Fears about particular ministers and faith groups coalesced in the 1830s and 1840s into a larger fear of religious enthusiasm, as described in the fourth chapter. From John Maffitt to Arthur Dimmesdale, preachers, both real and fictional, were charged with preying on their flocks as the nineteenth century progressed. The figure of the "reverend rake" was first popularized in trial reports. Starting with the case of William Parkinson in 1811, an unrelenting series of publicized trials tarnished the standing of ministers. While each trial had its own unique elements, some larger themes emerged. Repeatedly, ministers were accused of deception and hypocrisy, using heart religion to gain inappropriate intimacy with their female followers. By the 1830s the notorious cases of Ephraim Avery and the prophet Matthias produced a broader indictment. Conservative critics insisted that enthusiastic religion, anchored in the insecure foundation of emotions, was inherently prone to manipulation, mixing carnal and religious feelings.

The final chapter looks at the containment of the boldest religious sexual experiment of the Second Great Awakening, the perfectionist community of John Humphrey Noyes. Once men and women were reborn, Noyes insisted, they were incapable of sin. Rejecting both secular and religious law, Noyes crafted a system of "complex marriage." In theory, each member of the perfectionist community could have sex with one another, as long as the pairing was vetted by respected elders. Monogamy was strictly prohibited, for it encouraged jealousy and possessiveness. But the initiation of this system came at a significant cost, a self-imposed isolation from the outside world. Once safely settled in upstate New York, Noyes and the Oneida Community forsook proselytism. A series of critics had forced this settlement. Noyes's antinomian theology, his insistence that one should follow the spirit rather than ground one's religion in scripture and reason, they said, was his fatal flaw. In addition, they insisted this sect endangered young women, threatening to seduce them into a dangerous commune. Facing heated criticism, the Oneida Community would make peace with its neighbors by publicly declaring that their door was shut to new members.

While the Mormons had escaped to Utah, keeping the specter of religiously inspired sexual disruption alive, by mid-century the Second Great Awakening had been tamed and contained. Americans became convinced that the guard rails of scripture, reason, and social norms were necessary to protect their families and society from the danger of sexual and gender disorder brought by enthusiastic religion. For their part, religious outliers found that safety was best achieved in separatism. Ashbel Kitchell's summons to Sidney Rigdon to only listen to the "feeling of the spirit" proved too much to ask.

CHAPTER 1

"Fanaticism Can Wield Such a Mighty Influence over the Female Heart"

The Evolving Rhetoric of Anti-Mormonism in the Early Republic

The Mormon prophet Joseph Smith Jr. was tarred and feathered by a mob in Hiram, Ohio, a village on the Western Reserve, in March 1832. Smith and his scribe Sidney Rigdon were drug outside under the cover of a cold night. The two and their families had been staying on the properties of John and Elsa Johnson, converts to the Mormon faith (see figure 1.1). The crowd first violently assaulted Rigdon, dragging him so roughly on the ground that he was knocked unconscious. They then turned to Smith. According to Luke Johnson, son of John and Elsa, the mob "dragged Joseph out of bed by the hair of his head." They "stretched [him] on a board" and tore off his clothes "for the purpose of emasculating him." A local physician, Dr. Dennison, was on hand to perform the procedure, but when he "saw the Prophet stripped and stretched on the plank, his heart failed him, and he refused to operate."[1] Smith later recalled hearing voices during the episode: " 'Simonds, Simonds, *where's the tar bucket?*' 'I don't know,' answered one, *'where 'tis Eli's left it.*' " Presumably, Smith refers here to Mormon apostate Symonds Ryder, but the Eli figure is less certain. He continued: "They tried to force the tar-paddle into my mouth; I twisted my head around, so that they could not; and they cried out, *'G[od] d[amn] ye, hold up yer head and let us giv ye some tar.*' " Being stripped of all except his "shirt collar," he notes, "one man fell on me and scratched my body

FIGURE 1.1. Unattributed photo of Johnson Farm (built 1828). It was on the grounds of this farm where Smith suffered a mob attack and near-castration at the hands of Disciples rivals. © Intellectual Reserve, Inc.

with his nails like a mad cat!" After the tarring, Smith struggled back to the Johnson farm. His wife Emma fainted at the site of his battered body.[2] Smith's violent stripping, scratching, and near-castration evokes the sexualized contest for power between churches during the Second Great Awakening.

This incident, which plays prominently today as an instance of colorful local lore at Hiram College, deserves scholarly attention for a number of reasons. It is a peculiar episode because it does not fit neatly into the accepted narrative of American religious pluralism. Historian Chris Beneke has argued that by the late eighteenth century, Americans had moved beyond mere tolerance to a positive embrace of pluralism.[3] Scholars, including Beneke himself, have certainly recognized some significant exceptions, most notably Catholics and Mormons, to the broad experience of toleration in the early American republic.[4] The suggestion has been that such anomalies were enabled by imagining targeted religious groups as something other than mere dissenters, as social pariahs rather than heretics. With specific reference to the Church of Jesus Christ of Latter-day Saints, Terryl L. Givens has shown how there was in fact a "dissociation of Mormonism from religion."[5] Mormon persecutors cast Latter-day Saints as a peculiar quasi-ethnic group with distinct and disturbing social customs, most notably polygamy, as an effort to reconcile bigotry with an "ideology of Jeffersonian religious toleration and pluralism."[6] The problem with the Hiram episode is that it predates the revelation of most of the socially subversive and scandalous aspects of Mormonism. As J. Spencer Fluhman has argued, Mormonism was testing the American commitment to disestablishment even before the most socially subversive aspects of the church unfolded.[7] By the Missouri, Illinois, and Utah years, anti-Mormon mobs could rally rioters by trumpeting Mormon theocracy, polygamy, or purported abolitionism.[8] While Smith had been threatened with violence previously in New York, the Hiram attack was the first time a crowd had fulfilled their warnings. We need to better understand what provoked this assault.

It should not be terribly surprising that retrospective accounts of this episode would take on the colorings of later anti-Mormon campaigns, emphasizing Smith's wanton ways. Most notoriously, one account from the late nineteenth century framed the mob assault as an orchestrated effort by Eli Johnson to preserve the honor of his sister, Nancy Marinda Johnson. That would suggest a motivation for castration. Purportedly, Eli was upset with Smith's attempts at seducing Marinda.[9] But there does not appear to have been a Johnson son called Eli. Nonetheless, we know the Johnson family had been split by Mormonism, with mother, father, and some children, including Marinda, converting, but others not.[10] While two separate mid-nineteenth-century accounts also describe the effort to castrate Joseph Smith, these particular retellings notably fail to mention anything about Joseph's attentions to Marinda.[11] The story of Smith's near-castration and that of his advances on Marinda were only later conflated by Fawn Brodie into a singular tale of an attempt to rescue female honor.[12]

While this tale of rescuing Marinda cannot be conclusively denied, it fails to persuade. The first, and only, nineteenth-century account that specifically links the attack to Smith's forward behavior toward Marinda was voiced by Disciples of Christ minister Clark Braden. While Braden was publicly locking horns in debate in 1884 with E. L. Kelley, a leader of the Reorganized LDS Church, he strived to prove that Smith always possessed a lecherous disposition, even before embracing polygamy. In his telling, Smith's wayward disposition had deep roots, for his father had run their home as a "perfect brothel." He reported that the "entire money hunting gang" connected to the Smith home consisted of "low men surrounded by lewd women." It is in this context that Braden mentions Joseph's advances on Marinda. Braden correctly reports that Marinda "afterwards married Orson Hyde," the Mormon apostle. He next suggests that "Brigham Young, in after years, twitted Hyde" with stories of Smith's early intimacy with Marinda, driving Hyde to leave his wife.[13] But Braden seems to blur one story here with another. Smith had later pursued Marinda, but this was after she had married Hyde, with Smith taking her as a plural wife in 1842. And perhaps Brigham Young did later taunt Hyde about this relationship. But there is no documentary evidence to suggest that a romantic bond between Joseph and Marinda dated back to the time in Hiram.

Agreeing with a number of previous scholars, Richard L. Bushman in his authoritative biography of Smith links the Hiram attack to a series of nine letters published by the Methodist minister and Mormon apostate Ezra Booth in the *Ohio Star*, a newspaper published just down the road from Hiram in Ravenna.[14] If one contextualizes these letters in the conflict unfolding on the Western Reserve between the Disciples of Christ and the Mormons, it does seem obvious that Booth's letters helped inflame local passions. As such, these letters deserve a closer reading than they have heretofore been given. As I proceed, I will explore the tensions between pluralism and committed faith displayed in Booth's letters, hoping to capture something of the sentiment on the ground in northeastern Ohio. In Booth's rendering, tolerance seems only possible for those religious rivals who are not so bold as to assume the miraculous powers of the apostles. These letters exacerbated a wider set of conflicts that had been unfolding as two upstart churches battled for adherents in Ohio country. In many ways, the battle over the souls of Sidney Rigdon and Symonds Ryder would represent, in miniature, the battle between the Disciples and the Mormons for converts on the Western Reserve.[15] But what these letters also reveal is that conversion itself was a sexually loaded prospect. Swooning into the arms of the prophet could happen to both men and women. As I next turn to anti-polygamy texts produced after the open admission of polygamy, we will see an intensification of this blurring between sexual and religious fears. Women who were lured into polygamous marriages were much like the early settlers in Ohio, vulnerable to being smitten by charismatic Mormon preachers.[16]

In publishing the letters by Ezra Booth, the *Ohio Star* clearly felt compelled to make some gestures toward American religious pluralism. They noted their previous silence on the upstart religion, suggesting

they had deliberately wanted to remain "blameless" of "giving it notoriety, or of interfering [with] the faith of those who honestly embraced
it." Here they try to have it both ways. They felt that the publicity of
"newspaper opposition" would only backfire, attracting more converts
to the faith; nonetheless, they seemingly defend the Mormons by criticizing "most of the stories which have found their way into the papers,"
which they assumed were "about as extravagant in their details, as mormonism itself was false in its pretensions."[17] In this commentary they
show a rather savvy appreciation of the sensationalistic strain developing in the American press of the day.[18] They published Booth's letters,
they insisted, because they offered a reliable inside account of the workings of the Mormon Church, calling it "a kind of official exposition of
the fraud; authentic and incontrovertible, by one who has enjoyed every
opportunity of learning it by sad experience."[19]

Booth's letters critique the early Mormon Church leaders from several different angles. Like later critics, Booth does point to some seemingly secular difficulties with the church, exposing, for example, Mormon attitudes toward property and Native American relations, but he
invests his greatest energy in exposing what he sees as the divine postur-
ing of Joseph Smith, insisting that "the revelations which come from
him, are something short of infallible, and instead of being the production of divine wisdom, emanate from his own weak mind." In this
he was following the lead of Thomas and Alexander Campbell, leading
lights of the Disciples of Christ Church, who had in preceding months
used the *Painesville Telegraph,* a paper from a neighboring county, as a
forum for assaulting Joseph Smith.[20] Like the Campbells, Booth ham-
mered away at the Mormons as religious enthusiasts beholden to a "delusion."[21] But Booth himself had been subject to this delusion, making
his task of distinguishing truth from fiction more difficult to the discerning reader. Nonetheless, he insisted the "testimony of [his] senses"
had provided him "evidence so clear" that he now had awoken to the
real state of things.[22] In essence, Booth tried to show the Mormons as
badly out of step with an emerging post-Enlightenment age, revealing
how leaders had falsely claimed to suspend the laws of nature. Unlike
Alexander Campbell, however, Booth could not as easily declare the
age of miracles over; in fact, for Booth, it was Smith's failure to deliver
a consistent round of miracles that called the Mormon religion into
question.[23] Booth was rejecting religious fraud more than he was religious enthusiasm. Such a distinction would have been less salient to
many of his readers.

According to Booth, the Mormons' failures were threefold: they could not reliably perform faith healings, convincingly speak in tongues, or accurately predict the future. Furthermore, they had back-tracked from earlier scenes of wonder, wishing to sweep under the rug dramatic possession scenes that might bring the scorn of a skeptical public. It was the awkwardness and inconsistency of their performance that undermined his faith. While Alexander Campbell would argue his case against the Mormons on purely theological grounds by showing how *The Book of Mormon* contradicted the Bible, Booth would play to the religious skepticism of the wider public, presumably leaving the question of heresy aside.

Booth reported that in the heady days of 1831 when the Mormons first established themselves in Ohio they anticipated that the "work of miracles" would soon begin. A June conference was the scene of numerous notable failures. For example, Smith seized the hand of one elder, saying, "Brother Mordock, I command you in the name of Jesus Christ, to straighten your hand," while "endeavoring to accomplish the work by using his own hand, to open the hand of the other." According to Booth, the transparent attempt "proved unsuccessful," but Smith "again articulated the same commandment, in a more authoritative and louder tone of voice." While barking the order, Smith tried to straighten out Mordock's hand, "but after all the exertion of his power, both natural and supernatural, the deficient hand returned to its former position, where it still remains." This failed faith healing paled in comparison to a much more spectacular botched attempt to raise the body of one who had died two or three days previous. Despite being "commanded" to "wake into life," the deceased, Booth reported, "bid defiance to the puny efforts of the Mormonites."[24]

The phenomenon of speaking in tongues was similarly mocked by Booth. At early gatherings members "articulated sounds, which but few present professed to understand; and those few, declared them to be the Indian language." Responding to this cue, "they would, at times, fancy themselves addressing a congregation of their red brethren; and mounted upon a stump, the fence, or from some elevated situation, would harangue the assembly, until they had convinced and converted them." "These actors," Booth continued, "assumed the visage of the savage, and so nearly imitated him, not only in language, but in gestures and actions, that it seemed the soul and body were completely metamorphosed into the Indian." Witnesses were thus persuaded that this was "an extraordinary work of the Lord" that was "designed to prepare those young men for the Indian mission." However, the lie would be exposed, for "many of the principal actors" had "since apostatized."[25] Moreover, Booth would lay witness to the failures of the mission to the Lamanites when he accompanied Mormon leaders to Missouri. Those on the trip assumed that "when we commenced our journey for Missouri," "an 'effectual door' would be opened, to proclaim the new system of faith, in that region; and that those who were ordained to the gift of tongues, would have an opportunity to display their supernatural talent, in communicating to the Indians, in their own dialect."[26] However, such hopes were dashed. After Oliver Cowdery was confronted by the US Indian agent for crossing over the border into Indian Territory without permission, a *"comparative nothing"* in Booth's estimation, he quickly forsook the Indian mission, his principal charge on the Missouri trip.[27]

But this setback little mattered, for Native Americans had received Mormonism coolly anyway. Booth insisted that "the truth is not an individual [Indian] had embraced it when I left that place, nor is there any prospect they will embrace it." To the extent that Native Americans had shown any receptivity to Mormon overtures, Booth attributed the interest to Mormons' willingness to pander to the worst instincts of the Indians. After telling Native Americans that "the Great Spirit designs, in this generation, to restore them to the possession of their lands," Mormons promoted visions of the Lamanite destruction of the Gentiles. This, Booth insisted, was "a fair specimen of the method adopted in the Book of Mormon." "Mormonite teachers" were "ingratiating themselves with the Indians," Booth warned, and "should success attend their endeavors; and the minds of the Indians become inflamed with that enthusiastic spirit which Mormonism inspires, they may be inclined to try the experiment," seeking to discover "whether 'by the shedding of blood,' they can expel the white inhabitants, or reduce them to a state of servitude; and by this means, regain the possession of the lands occupied by their forefathers."[28] Presumably Indian minds were more vulnerable to the enthusiastic tendencies of the Mormons, but they, like Booth, had been left unimpressed.

Booth's disillusionment with the abandoned Indian mission was closely related to his larger disappointment with Mormon prophecy. The Missouri trip had sealed in his mind what seem to have been percolating doubts about his new religion. Booth suggested that "the first thing that materially affected my mind, so as to weaken my confidence, was the falsehood of Joseph's vision." He reminded his ostensible correspondent, the Reverend Ida Eddy, that "Joseph had, or said he had, a vision, or revelation, in which it was made known to him by the spirit, that Oliver had raised up a great Church in Missouri." This proved far short of the mark, for "this great Church was found to consist of three or four females." Even more frustrating to Booth was the way in which Smith's prophecies proved a moving target. If things did not go as anticipated or if he faced new obstacles, he just adjusted his visions accordingly. For example, after facing rough waters aboard a canoe on the return trip, Smith, Cowdery, and Rigdon received a new revelation that they should travel by stagecoach while the others were to stick to the cheaper transport of canoe. So easily, Booth noted, had they forsaken earlier pretensions of equality: "let these men never again open their mouths, to insult the common sense of mankind, by contending for equality, and the community of goods in society, until there is a thorough alteration in their method of proceeding." Booth concluded from this experience that "they turn and twist the commandments, to suit their whims, and they violate them when they please with perfect impunity." As a result, "they can at any time obtain a commandment suited to their desires, and as their desires fluctuate and become reversed, they get a new one to supersede the other, and hence the contradictions which abound in this species of revelation."[29] The tarring and feathering that happened in Hiram could in fact be seen as a perverse test of Smith's powers as a prophet, for according to one newspaper at the time, Smith had predicted that anyone who dare lay a hand on him would be struck down by an avenging God.[30]

The seeming malleability of the Mormon faith, Booth feared, could open the door to endless abuse. He explained that "the relation in which Smith stands to the church, is that of a Prophet, Seer, Revelator and Translator; and when he speaks by the Spirit, or says he knows a thing by the communication of the Spirit, it is received as coming directly from the mouth of the Lord.—When he says he knows a thing to be so, *thus* it must stand without controversy."[31] Perhaps with prophetic vision of his own, Booth glimpsed where this might lead: to sexual violations. Already one convert had been encouraged to take a wife among the Lamanites, even though he was still married to a woman in New York. Similarly, Booth insinuated that Smith had courted and even entered a "matrimonial contract" with a woman before he betrayed her and became the "gallant" of Emma.[32] But no whiff was here yet of charges of polygamy against Smith, nor even of an affair with Nancy Marinda. Nonetheless, Booth must have sensed the real potential of sexual scandal as a means to raise popular passions. And he also likely sensed the inherent sexual power invested in a persuasive prophet like Smith. Consequently, Booth warned that a man possessing unchecked powers like Smith could, like David in the Bible, choose to "'get another man's wife,' and commit adultery; and 'by the shedding of blood, seek to kill her husband.'" So as long as "he retains the use of his tongue, so as to be able to utter his jargon," no one would question his conduct. Such a man "can continue as long as he pleases in the bed of adultery, and wrap himself with garments stained with blood, shed by his own hands, and still retain the spotless innocence of the holiest among mortals; and must be continued in the office of revelator, and head of the Church."[33] Thus, the talk of polygamy that began to surface several years later could only have been received by Mormon opponents as a confirmation of their worst fears.

Perhaps the choice of tar and feathers was a knowing reference to revolutionary-era fears of tyranny, of power concentrated in a single man. Booth did, after all, frame Smith as a "despot" who sought to "allure the credulous and the unsuspecting into a state of vassalage."[34] The record is frustratingly opaque on why this punishment was chosen. What is clear is that Booth played up the image of Mormons as fanatics, deluded witnesses to underwhelming miracles. This emphasis makes perfect sense if one considers Booth's own personal history: he had converted himself after witnessing the faith healing by Smith of Elsa Johnson's rheumatic arm.[35] In penning his exposé, Booth presumed his audience possessed more skepticism than he once possessed himself, for Booth was a religious seeker who had fallen "victim" to this "delusion."[36] Perhaps the Enlightenment had made enough inroads that Booth could imagine a broad pan-Protestant skepticism toward scenes of religious enthusiasm. Yet the growing commitment to religious freedom could easily undermine the deployment of a charge of fanaticism. Booth doubled his bets by turning to fearmongering on Indian affairs and sexual exploitation, suggesting he sensed the limits of a purely religious critique in his pluralistic age.

The little-noticed letters that *followed* Booth's in the *Ohio Star* provide an important final piece to this puzzle of the Hiram assault. Booth's letters had entered a playing field where a bitter contest for souls was being fought on the Western Reserve. Sidney Rigdon, who we must remember was assaulted that same night along with Smith, was a critical religious figure in the Western Reserve. Recall that in 1827 he had established the very first Campbellite congregation in Ohio. A celebrated orator, his Disciples church grew propitiously after it was established in Mantua, a congregation, it should be noted, that included the village of Hiram.[37] In other words, when Smith and Rigdon moved onto the Johnson farm, they brought Mormonism into what Rigdon himself had established as the symbolic heart of the Disciples movement on the western frontier. It was no coincidence that the likely central mover in the mob attack, Symonds Ryder, was a popular Disciples preacher in Hiram who had been drawn into Mormonism by Ezra Booth, later abandoning it as Booth did.[38] Not surprisingly, then, Booth's letters were followed by a spate of barbs traded between Ryder, a leading Disciples preacher and Mormon apostate, and Rigdon, a leading Mormon preacher and Disciples apostate.

Rigdon laid down a challenge to Booth to appear for a public lecture by Rigdon in which he would review and refute Booth's *Ohio Star* letters. Rigdon added to this, however, a special personal challenge to Symonds Ryder to debate him in Hiram. Rigdon, who had left the Disciples on poor terms after Campbell rejected his notions of apostolic gifts and communal property, seemed to save special venom for his Disciples rival.[39] He invited Ryder to correct him if he had proven "deluded in receiving" the Book of Mormon as a "revelation from God."[40] Ryder saw the invitation for what it probably was. He would not take Rigdon's bait. In his response, Ryder stated: "That Mormonism is a base imposition, I most certainly believe." Nonetheless, a public debate would prove a spectacle, not an educational opportunity. He said of Rigdon, "if he really is anxious that I should teach him the truth, and correct his errors, it does appear to me that a private interview would be much more convenient and much more to his profit, as our dwellings are but about sixty rods apart." If he were instead "to undertake to correct him of his errors before the public," Rigdon's "irascible temper, loquacious extravagance, impaired state of mind, and want of due respect to his superiors, I fear would render him in such a place, unmanageable."[41] In other words, he didn't want the verbal equivalent of a barroom brawl.

Or perhaps even more so, he did not want to afford Rigdon the opportunity to win more converts. In a new revelation, Joseph Smith had called for a fresh preaching campaign in Hiram and its environs.[42] Ryder surely recognized the danger. He accused Rigdon of seeking a chance to save a "sinking cause," suggesting nearby residents had been leaving the Mormons in earnest after word had returned from the Missouri trip. To him, "Sidney Rigdon's challenge" was "one of the last throes of expiring Mormonism."[43] Such taunting evokes a deep rivalry, and we should reserve some doubt as to whether Mormonism was really on the ropes. There is no need to tar and feather a man while he is down. Soon after this, the *Ohio Star* refused to publish any more letters, presumably not wanting to get in between warring neighbors.

When the mob appeared at the Johnsons' door, one can only assume Ryder was there, though he and his son would later claim he had been at home in bed sick.[44] But I do not want to overstate his importance. The crowd, which Luke Johnson would later put at forty or fifty men, was reportedly composed of men drawn from three different villages.[45] The personal animosity of Ryder for Rigdon, or, for that matter, the fear of the Johnson sons for the future of the family farm or the honor of their sister, might have animated the leadership, but the crowd surely drew most of its inspiration from Booth's letters.[46] That said, these letters simply painted on a broader canvas what both Ryder and Booth experienced personally. In the contest for souls on the Ohio frontier, they felt duped. In the preface to his public letters, Booth openly admitted that his conversion had exposed his "own weakness." He had "fallen a victim" to Smith's wiles. This was, he said, a "humiliating truth." While admitting this truth was "*humbling*" to him, he hoped it would prove beneficial to others.[47] This feeling of humiliation surely had more to do with the sexualized nature of the attack on Smith than any anger over a purported seduction of Marinda. Seen in the light of the fictional portrayals of women seduced into Mormonism that would proliferate at mid-century, portrayals to which I now turn, being duped as a religious seeker amounted to a seduction, a swooning into the prophet's arms. Smith had embarrassed Ryder and Booth, endangering their manhood by fooling them with staged scenes of wonder. Thus, castration would have seemed a fitting penalty for his imposture.

If the tarring and feathering episode in Ohio suggests the sufficiency of religious rivalry to provoke mob violence, the later revelation of plural marriage would nonetheless greatly exacerbate tensions between the Mormons and wider American society.[48] In the Illinois years, rumors of Mormon polygamy would play a critical role in the mob attack that ended in Joseph Smith's death in a Carthage jail. Starting in 1842, Mormon apostate John C. Bennett began publishing scandalous accounts of plural marriage in newspapers and a book exposé.[49] His most important contribution to later rhetoric on Mormon anti-polygamy was his charge of "spiritual wifery." In essence, Bennett described a system where Mormons were encouraged to find their soul mates for the hereafter, whether or not this search caused them to violate existing legal marriage vows. Because Bennett was a wholly unreliable narrator, most likely himself involved in attempted seductions, not much attention has been paid to his rhetoric of spiritual wifery. Nonetheless, we will see that this concept does provide a key to wider-held concerns with the Mormons. Rumors of polygamy were brought closer to home for Joseph Smith when they were aired in a newspaper founded by a splinter faction of Mormons in Nauvoo, Illinois. When they published their charges in the *Nauvoo Expositor*, Smith called for the destruction of this newly founded newspaper press, leading to his fateful imprisonment and then murder in Carthage.[50]

While Smith had entrusted a revelation on polygamy with church leaders in 1843, it was not until the open announcement and endorsement of plural marriage in 1852 in Utah that anti-polygamy writings emerged as a significant new genre in American writing. A series of apostate memoirs and anti-polygamy novels would help crystallize influential and enduring criticisms of the Mormon faith, alienating Mormons from American society and the body politic. Within a few short years, five important texts would emerge: Alfreda Bell's *Boadicea, the Mormon Wife* (1855), Orvilla Belisle's *The Prophets or Mormonism Unveiled* (1855), Maria Ward's *Female Life among the Mormons* (1855), Metta Fuller's *Mormon Wives* (1856), and John Hyde Jr.'s *Mormonism: Its Leaders and Designs* (1857).[51] These books attracted wide attention (Ward's book, for example, sold forty thousand copies in its first week) while also exerting decisive influence in the halls of Congress and the White House, where legislative and military action against the Mormons was enacted.[52] There have been a number of important scholarly treatments of these texts, but fuller attention to the gender work accomplished within them is still needed. Historian Terryl Givens concentrates on how these texts cast Mormons as distinct ethnic others, with polygamy serving as a way to imagine Mormons as akin to Eastern sultans ruling over harems. Legal historian Sarah Barringer Gordon considers gender more directly, showing how fears for women entrapped in Mormon polygamous marriages informed reconceptualizations of the federal state. The emergent Republican Party would insist that polygamy was one of the "twin relics of barbarism," with both it and slavery demanding more federal intervention in the states and territories.[53]

Scholarly works on gender relations in the early republic and on women's experience of Mormonism still offer additional interpretative opportunities. Scholars such as Rosemarie Zagarri and Lucia McMahon have shown that a revolutionary settlement was reached in gender relations at the turn of the nineteenth century. Women were granted new cultural power in the young nation, enjoying the right to choose their own marriage partners and live as "mere equals" with their husbands. A revolution against patriarchal authority had occurred. Marriage was to be a full partnership, with husbands looking to wives as intellectual and emotional companions. This reconceptualization of marriage, most fully realized in middle-class families, was accompanied by a rapid expansion in educational opportunities for women, allowing companionship to flourish. But while there were real gains for bourgeois women in forming marriage and pursuing education, the door was shut in other areas. Divorce and property rights largely remained unchanged (thereby undercutting marital equality), while women were also excluded from suffrage and involvement in political campaigning.[54]

The innovations in gender relations introduced by the Mormons would reopen gender questions that seemingly had been settled for half a century. Such challenges also appeared inconveniently at the very moment the women's suffrage campaign was emerging on the national stage. At first blush, the Mormons would not seem to offer much to women seeking freedom or power. Historians, echoing the original anti-polygamy texts themselves, have demonstrated the particular appeal of Mormonism for men who were yearning for restored patriarchal powers.[55] But Laurel Thatcher Ulrich, in her commanding new exploration of women within the LDS Church, *A House Full of Females*, challenges some of our underlying assumptions about Mormonism and polygamy. While not denying the very real patriarchal dimensions of the early LDS Church, Thatcher is able to reveal that Mormons offered many opportunities for female liberation. She shows that women were as liable to flee *to* the Mormons, escaping abusive or neglectful husbands, as they were to flee *from* Mormonism. She insists that the early adoption of female suffrage in Utah was no paradox, for Mormons had granted women a significant voice and freedom of action within their communities.[56]

How, then, does the rhetoric of the antebellum texts fit with the reality of women's lived experience? These works do, in fact, offer some acknowledgment of the subversive liberation available to women in Mormonism. In particular, the rhetoric of spiritual wifery within them suggests women's ability to escape unhappy marriages. In addition, some of the tales display strong female characters who take full advantage of what Mormonism has to offer. Ultimately, however, these authors chose to refute Mormonism by concentrating on its patriarchal dimensions. In particular, they portray the revolution against patriarchal authority as being rolled back within Mormon marriages. Equal companionship was denied in various ways: husbands distributed their attention across many wives; old men married weak girls; parents bargained away their daughters; and men held on to the keys to salvation. But this emphasis on patriarchy left a troubling question for these authors to answer: why, then, *did* women choose to join the Mormons? By a small margin, they actually outnumbered men in Utah.[57] In answering this question, writers had to engage larger questions about the nature of consent. Why did people choose to join a new heretical church? Why did women choose to marry men who were already married? To answer these questions authors had to challenge the great American fiction of consent granted freely. Women and religious seekers were posed as victims, either duped or coerced into consent. In essence, these writers were left in the same position as the early Disciples leaders in Ohio two decades previously, trying to explain why they or others they knew had been seduced into Mormonism. In these tales, where women were most often the victims, doubts about women's ability to make choices were thereby sown. While women were seemingly most vulnerable to coercion or manipulation, one also had to wonder whether consent itself was a reliable foundation for the nation.[58]

The term "spiritual wifery" was attached to Mormonism by John C. Bennett, but the concept had not begun with him. In fact, its earlier incarnations (including its appearance in seventeenth-century Rhode Island among the Immortalists) may have influenced Joseph Smith's thought on plural marriage.[59] Nonetheless, the term took on a particular cast in the hands of anti-polygamy authors. Bennett had emphasized the way Smith could use the idea of spiritual wifery as a way to steal away wives and daughters from fellow Mormons, a thought that appears in the later anti-polygamy texts too.[60] Thus, the character Ellen in Maria Ward's tale relates how Smith had chosen to "receive [her] as his spiritual wife, for a time." This, he did, "the same as he received Irene and those foolish women, who have abandoned their homes for him." Such unions were ephemeral: "when he tires of her, she will be cast off, or given to someone else."[61] But anti-polygamy authors also showed how women might be enabled to follow their own hearts under this doctrine. Orvilla Belisle has a Mormon missionary in Europe extoll the benefits of Mormon thinking on marriage to a young woman. He comments on the limits of current society. He tells this woman that she might wish to join with a man who would provide the "pleasure, happiness, nay the very acme of [her] life." Yet she cannot be with him, for "custom does not sanction such a tie." As such, she will go through life "lonely and cheerless." Broaching polygamy more directly, he notes that a man and woman in love might be denied happiness simply because the man is married to another: "A man may wed a wife, and though he retains all his affection for her, if he encounters another, he loves equally as well, and is loved in return, he is forced to relinquish her affection, while she may go down life's way alone, uncheered by the voice that could smooth her path, because another loving him no better than she, calls him husband."[62] While Belisle certainly was not intending to endorse such thinking, her character nonetheless reveals how the rules of monogamous marriage limited the expression of love.

Metta Fuller's character Sarah most fully suggests the liberating potential of Mormon thinking on marriage for women, linking Mormonism explicitly to the free love and socialist doctrines of Stephen Pearl Andrews.[63] Sarah, rather than any man, was the chief culprit for the woes of the female protagonist, Margaret. Though a lifelong friend of Margaret, Sarah longed to unite with Margaret's husband, Richard. Richard was first seduced into Mormonism by hopes of great wealth in Utah, but he rejected their teachings on marriage. Sarah, in contrast, had been lured by Mormon ideas on love from the start. She was not a real villain, for she had been orphaned as a child, never receiving the proper guidance growing up. Left thus vulnerable, she allowed herself undisciplined thoughts. Under Mormon influence, she came to believe that she should join with Richard, for she loved him most of all. She rejected an offer of marriage by Harry, Margaret's brother, for her heart belonged to Richard. Imagining that a bond with Richard was possible, she followed the married couple out to Utah. She eventually won Richard over to polygamy. After they had built a second house for her in the wilderness, she celebrated how they could now enjoy their freedom: "Here, free from the cold bonds, the chilling orthodoxies of the world, with a love-breathing, kindly, fascinating religion, and lavished by the indulgent hand of nature all about us, why cannot our souls revel in life as it was designed to be? Why cannot we be free as the winds, bright as the flowers, happy as the birds?"[64] Of course, this victory was not to stand. Richard's heart soon moved to another woman, and Sarah comes to regret her ways. Standing at Margaret's graveside (for Margaret had perished in grief), she repented: "It was for *me* to say that she could live with half the heart of her husband, to take away from her her rights, because I weakly, wickedly coveted what was not mine. You are no true woman, Sarah Irving; you have debased yourself below the level of your sex."[65] Sarah's late redemption had been secured, but not before she had exposed the limits of conventional marriage.

The fluidity of marital ties expressed (and rejected) in these texts was not as far removed from the reality of the Mormon experience as we might first have supposed. Laurel Thatcher Ulrich has shown that Joseph Smith Sr. performed blessings for women who had deserted their husbands to join the Mormons. Lydia Goldthwaite, for example, had fled her husband for Canada. There she met Mormon missionaries and, with the sanction of Joseph Smith Jr., married Newel K. Knight. Joseph Smith Sr. looked past her bigamy, saying that the "Lord loves thee and has given thee a kind and loving companion for thy comfort."[66] Perhaps in the early years of Mormonism, when there was a special emphasis on gaining new converts, it made more sense to grant women such freedom. Maria Ward suggests this possibility, having one character note that she "don't hear anything about spiritual wives, as I used to." Mrs. Brandish replies, "That's done away with," since the model now was the "example of the patriarchs" in the Bible.[67] And while the revelation on polygamy undoubtedly tilted power toward men, Mormons did retain a greater flexibility toward marriage than wider American society, forming and dissolving unions in ways that discomfited Mormon observers.[68]

More than spiritual wifery, then, it was patriarchy and polygamy that garnered the greatest attention in these works. In describing patriarchal and polygamous unions the authors emphasized that companionship was denied to women. One variant of this theme were depictions of young women being forced to marry against their will.[69] This looked to be a reversion to patriarchal patterns of the colonial era. There was, in fact, a quickening toward youth-directed courtship and marriage in the decades following the American Revolution. In truth, however, youth had always seemed to, at the very least, hold a veto power over proposed matches. Nonetheless, arranged marriages had been a familiar foil in revolutionary-era literature.[70] Mormons were accused of resurrecting a practice that a previous generation had put to rest. For example, Alfreda Bell relates the story of a cruel father, Boisrouge, "as veritable a rascal as ever lived," who forced his daughter into a marriage with a Mormon. His "villainous plotting" included depriving her of fashionable clothing, beating her, and spiriting away her true love. He was determined to make the match, for her prospective husband had "agreed to pay her father a certain sum for her person."[71] Similarly, John Hyde Jr. relates a story of George B. Wallace, a Mormon missionary who converted a father and his family in England. After paying for their passage to Salt Lake, Wallace insisted he be compensated. Following the "counsel" of Brigham Young, the father "gave him his three daughters, to all of whom he was married." They were all found "living with Mrs. Wallace, proper, in a little two-roomed house."[72] Maria Ward also links Mormonism and the loss of female will in marriage. Her character Mrs. Brandish promises that Mormonism will restore women to "their primitive condition," being put in a "state of utter and entire dependence on their male relatives." Such men "will have the power of disposing of them in marriage as they see fit." The husband "will bestow a gift on her parents or guardians, which will be handed over to the church."[73] It was clear these women, forced to marry men not of their own choosing, would not find companionship or love.

Similar to this accusation of arranged marriages was the charge of marriages lopsided in age. Historically, proximity in age between husband and wife has accompanied a growing emphasis on companionship.[74] An old man taking a young wife connoted, and likely produced, a power imbalance in marriage. Mormon apostate John Hyde Jr. explores this theme, noting that he had "seen old men with white hair and wrinkled faces, go hunting after girls." These old men used various means to capture these women, "deceiving them with all sorts of professions and promises" or "using the terror of Brigham's name and threatening the penalty of excommunication," so as to "induce them to marry them." Seeking only sensual gratification, they soon left the young women "despoiled and degraded, either to the obloquy of divorce, or to the incurable sorrows of a grieved and wrung heart."[75] Thus, the tropes of seduction fiction lived on in anti-polygamy fiction. Maria Ward offered up similar testimony, when the character Mr. Melton tried to force his daughter, Henriette, to marry Mr. Weldy. The father said he would take Henriette "to the alter in chains," if necessary. But his daughter insisted she would "never by word or deed signify her assent to the contract," for Weldy sought to "make [her] a slave." She asked her father why he would ask her "to marry that hideous old man, who looks like an ogre and acts like a fool."[76] Clearly, this was no companionate match for Henriette.

Once within marriage, Henriette's fears about such matches seemed to be confirmed. Mormon husbands were depicted as cruel tyrants, abusing their wives and forcing them to compete for affection. Alfreda Bell suggests physical abuse, narrating the story of Mary Maxwell. Her husband had decided to bring a second wife home. Mary had "rebelled against this," but he drove her "from the house with blows." In case anyone doubted this, Bell noted that the "bruises upon her hands and arms, as well as her shoulders, attested the truth of her assertions."[77] Maria Ward similarly describes Mormon households where patriarchs and even fellow wives administered secret punishments including whippings and imprisonment in cellars.[78] Obedience became the expected posture for women in such households. Orvilla Belisle shows how the character Arthur reorients his treatment of Margaret once they moved to Utah. Deciding he was now to take a second wife, he addressed Margaret in an "imperious tone, which of late months had often grated on her ears." He instructed her, "I am sorry to be under the necessity to remind you that, it is a husband's place to command, and a wife's to obey." He had too long tolerated her self-assertions; now his "God forbids [him] allowing it longer," and from that point forward he would "command and expect that obedience" that she is "duty bound to give."[79] Maria Ward summarized this call for obedience, saying that among the Mormons women "are decidedly inferior beings, created to minister to the wants and passions of men."[80] There were no republican wives, nor companions; women were to accept their lower status within patriarchal households.

As suggested in the quotes above, polygamy was perhaps the key ingredient in creating such unequal unions. These writers insisted that polygamy was forced on women against their will. According to Orvilla Belisle, Joseph Smith had imposed such arrangements on Emma Smith, saying that polygamy was his patriarchal privilege. When Emma fought Smith about taking additional wives, he warned her, "If you do not silently submit, your life is in danger!" He asked whether she supposed that "a paltry woman" would be allowed to "thwart a scheme that makes men and women by [the] thousands do us homage, and pours wealth into our coffers, while we are worshipped as superior beings." He tells her that "the leading men" had now "gone to the plurality system." Whether she "liked it or not," he would "marry as many women" as he wanted; she would have to accept it "without a word of dissent!"[81] John Hyde Jr. similarly puts such callous words in Mormon apostle Heber C. Kimball's mouth. Hyde first describes how Mormon men kept their various wives in separate sleeping compartments, saying such men lost all "decency and self-respect" and "degenerate into gross and disgusting animals." Kimball, he said, "does not scruple to speak of his wives, on a Sabbath, in the Tabernacle, and before an audience of over two thousand persons, as 'my cows!' " Such rhetoric, he said, was received by Kimball's audience with laughter.[82]

One of the cruelest elements of polygamy, these authors claimed, was the way it engendered jealousy among women.[83] Women, who were thought to be the reservoir of affection and compassion in the family, instead turned vindictive. Maria Ward discusses one Mormon household where "blows were not infrequently exchanged, hair flew by handfuls, and many a face was bruised and battered till it bore little resemblance to the human countenance." The wives "hated and disliked each other," acting as "spies on each other's conduct."[84] The source of these difficulties was the way they had to compete for the affection of their husbands. These texts dwelled on how women could not possess the hearts of their husbands alone.[85] Metta Fuller has Margaret explain this point to Sarah: "How could *you*, with all your pride, consent to occupy an inferior, secondary situation, and have the heart of your husband divided up among a dozen others."[86] John Hyde Jr. alone, as the only male author (and former Mormon), expressed some small measure of sympathy for the men in these situations. He said they had to avoid expressing affection for women, because it would be construed as favoritism: "jealousies the most bitter, reproaches the most galling and disgusting, scenes without number, and acrimony without end, are the inevitable consequences of the slightest partiality. It is impossible for any man to equally love several different women." Therefore, he is forced to become "equally indifferent about any number."[87] Affectionate companionate marriages were therefore impossible among the Mormons.

To drive the contrast home for readers, these authors took the time to wax poetic about the beauties of monogamy. Before Richard fell to Sarah's seduction, he was held back from polygamy by his faith in the bourgeois romantic ideal. Metta Fuller noted of Richard: "He could not so suddenly abandon the holiest and sweetest institution of Christianity and civilization, and all that there is pure and saving in the midst of the selfishness of man: one abiding love, one hearth, one home. His Margaret was all-in-all to him—his wife—the other part of himself; upon whose union with him depended the perfection of his being."[88] He would have to learn the hard way why it was a mistake to abandon his "one love" with Margaret for polygamy. Alfreda Bell has the same sentiments expressed by Boadicea, who said that "heaven has rightly ordained that one woman shall belong to one man, to one man alone." This was to be a lifelong match, and within such a marriage only could one find "perfect love, harmony, and happiness."[89] In renewing a commitment to possessive monogamy, these anti-polygamy texts were performing a key cultural function, that of boundary maintenance, for wider American society. Sociologists of religion such as Kristen Tobey and Stephen Taysom have shown how minority religious groups enact religious boundaries to strengthen the convictions of the faithful. From this perspective, the enactment of polygamy served the Mormons, by allowing them to suffer a purifying persecution from wider American society.[90] But the contrast between polygamy and monogamy served Mormon opponents too. These writers were reconsolidating an American commitment to monogamy and notions of companionship within marriage.[91] Simultaneously, they were inscribing a justification for prejudice toward the Mormons.

According to these writers, Mormons denied not only marital equality but religious equality too. During the course of the Second Great Awakening women had gained greater opportunities for making independent choices and action. With the proliferation and splintering of churches, women had expanding opportunities to join new churches (sometimes against the will of their parents or husbands), get involved in church-affiliated social action, perform missionary work, and sometimes preach.[92] These writers showed Mormons going against this religious tide. In addition to introducing plural marriage, Mormons had endowed men alone with priesthood powers. Women were to seek salvation by attaching themselves to a man in celestial marriage. These writers would distort Mormon notions of celestial marriage to fit their wider case for gender inequality within Mormonism.

Laurel Thatcher Ulrich suggests women had real benefits to gain in celestial marriage, seeking sisterhood with sister wives, as much as celestial glory with a husband. Nonetheless, it was, in fact, the case that women achieved higher status in the hereafter by attachment to a Mormon husband.[93] These writers insisted that salvation was used as leverage against women, forcing women to marry men they otherwise would not have.[94] Alfreda Bell had *Boadicea* state it baldly and loudly: "According to the Mormon creed—I repeat—no woman can enter heaven on her own merits—that is, without a man to take her there!!!!!!!"[95] Metta Fuller tried to expose how notions of celestial marriage worked together with polygamy to entrap the mind of her character Sarah. In love with Richard, she had no choice but to marry him, even though he was married to Margaret: "She could not go to heaven except as the wife of some man—she could not be the wife of any man whom she did not love—she could not love any man but Richard Wilde."[96] Sarah therefore plunged forward in her efforts to capture the heart of Richard. She discovered that he had always harbored a love for her too but had denied himself this feeling so as to preserve his marriage.

As this last example suggests, these writers seemed to recognize that their model for marriage (lifelong monogamy) had constraints too, but constraints they felt were wise and necessary. Thus they were forced to admit that their ideal of romantic companionship was perhaps not natural. Love was too mercurial to be neatly contained within monogamous unions. Sarah should have settled for Harry, not pursued Richard. The love these authors advocated, at times, was a practical, not a romantic, love. Love left unbounded could be dangerous. Alfreda Bell offers up such a warning. In the beginning of her story, Boadicea mistakenly placed too much trust in her husband Hubert and in the enduring power of love: "Each was under the influence of the wild, blind faith in happiness, and in each other, which is the fanaticism, as well as the religion, of love"[97] (see figure 1.2). This quote, conflating notions of marriage with "faith" and "religion," hints at the way fears about religion and marriage could amplify one another. Fearing heart-based decisions, these authors pulled back from notions of romantic love. Enthusiasm

HUBERT WITH THE MORMON WOMEN LEAVES BOADICEA.

FIGURE 1.2. Stereotype plate image from *Boadicea; The Mormon Wife* (New York: Arthur R. Orton, 1855). Courtesy of Western Reserve Historical Society.

was dangerous in both courtship and religion. If practicality sometimes trumped romance, these authors did seem convinced that the sacrifice was worth it. Mormon marriage was no substitute, for it denied women the equality they might enjoy in companionate marriages.

Having criticized the patriarchal character of Mormon marriages, these writers left themselves a problem: why had women chosen to join the Mormons? The fundamental answer was to deny that women had chosen it at all.[98] These narratives showed women's will being manipulated or forced into submission. Mormon preachers and Mormon husbands alike had the power to seduce women. Mormonism was framed as dangerous because it interfered with rational consent by playing on people's emotions.[99] Orvilla Belisle shows Joseph Smith bragging about his powers of seduction. He talks about how he would like a chance to work on the wife of a new man in their ranks: " 'I have a fancy for converting his wife, myself, and if I could get her to listen to me, I think she would not object giving in to our faith—you know I usually have success in that line,' returned the quondam Prophet, with a complacent leer."[100] Maria Ward works hardest to explain the emotive allure of Mormonism. Ultimately, she decides that Smith had discovered the powers of mesmerism, which he picked up from a German peddler. At first she was at a loss, for in earlier years she was "ignorant of the power of mesmeric influence." Smith used these powers to pull off false miracles and manipulate the emotions of his audience. He was, she says, one of the "earliest practitioners of ANIMAL MAGNETISM." A former convert, Ellen, speaks of the power he once possessed over her: "It is true that, hearing continually the praises of Smith, and witnessing the exhibitions of his power, astonished and filled me with awe and veneration." He was like a "basilisk," wielding "mystical magical influence" over her, denying her the "unrestricted exercise of free will."[101] These authors portrayed Mormons as imposters, using various ploys and deceptions to trick followers into joining their churches.[102] It yielded, John Hyde Jr. insisted, a delusion or form of fanaticism: "when persons give themselves up, blindly and enthusiastically, to the directions of other and designing men, imagine they are invested with God-given powers, and endowed with a God-given sagacity, it is inevitable that they run into the wildest vagaries that lunatics could rhapsodize, or fanatics believe."[103] With emotions and the senses so prone to manipulation, it was dangerous to trust the heart, whether in religion or love.

Some were less easily manipulated. For them, force was used instead. When Brother Howard failed in his attempts to seduce Boadicea into marriage, he turned to threats on her life. She relates how she was about to run away from him in "indignant horror," but "he angrily rose and detained me." If she were not to listen to his "peaceful and kind proposals," she would discover that her "life is not one moment safe."[104] In an extended debate between Brigham Young and a young Emily, Maria Ward suggests that Young used religious and legal power to bully women. Emily expresses her desire to marry a man of her own choosing, but Young suggests that he possesses "the control and supervision of every female among us." No marriage, he says, can be "consummated among our people without my consent." Emily bemoaned how Young tried to exploit her "unprotected situation," forcing her "to a connection [her] soul abhors." Emily vows to bear the consequences of Young's "wrath," preferring that to the "state of vilest concubinage" with him that he has in mind for her. Standing up for the companionate ideal, she says Mormon marriage is "without love, without sympathy, without congeniality of mind, or appropriateness of age." Young replies that such "sympathies and congenialities of which you speak" are the product of the "distempered fancy of silly young women." He reminds her that she needs a "husband to protect and support you." While she does avoid being bound to Young in marriage, she nonetheless is killed by Mormon avengers in her escape to California.[105] Thus the prospects for female marital equality seemed grim.

As the exchange between Young and Emily suggests, women were particularly (but not solely) liable to seduction and coercion by the Mormons. Authors worked with the assumption that women were more easily physically overpowered and more readily persuaded by ploys on their emotions. Half a century earlier, seduction fiction had explored fears about women who were enjoying new freedoms on the courtship market. Parental anxiety about male predators helped produce a new emphasis on female chastity, yielding a sexual double standard.[106] Anti-polygamy fiction served a similar function with respect to religious choices for women. Women seemed too weak to handle the responsibility of consent. In addition, when women saw their husbands take additional wives, they did not stand up for themselves; instead, they collapsed and even perished under the emotional stress.[107] Maria Ward's bold character, Mrs. Bradish, would voice an unconventional comment on these sentimental tendencies, noting that she had "no pity for these weak, silly women, who cannot take care of themselves, but sit down and cry, baby-like, over wrongs and inflictions."[108] While highlighting the polyvocal potential of novels, Mrs. Bradish's authority is continually undercut by her mannish manners and her misguided faith in Mormon leaders.

Ward and others ultimately show women who are easy prey for the Mormons. Sometimes they commented explicitly on this vulnerability. A surgeon in Ward's tale noted that Smith's "greatest success is among the women." This, he insisted, was "always the case," for "fanatics of every class and character find their devotees in that class of the community." No matter how "contrary to common sense" a religion might be, "women will be smitten with it." Many, he said, are "weak enough to abandon comfortable homes and situations in order to follow some mad fanatic."[109] While his tone is less sympathetic than that established within these sentimental novels more generally, his judgment of women's susceptibility was representative. While Ward and others did show men also falling under Smith's spell, it was women's victimization that stood for the fate of the larger whole of seduced converts. John Hyde Jr. also noted how "fanaticism can wield such a mighty influence over the female heart." One explanation he offers is that Mormons played on a woman's "strong love for her children." This was "a chord that can be played upon," creating "deep vibrations in her heart." Since salvation could be secured for children brought into the Abrahamic covenant, Mormons chose to take advantage of motherly love, "that delicate fiber of the female heart."[110] Alfreda Bell explicitly linked a woman's liability to her trusting heart: "there is nothing more confiding than a woman's heart, when she loves,—no confidence more blind." While "experience ever teaches that such faith belongs to God alone," it was hard for women to fight their very nature.[111]

It is only from this perspective that one can make sense of the very odd ending to Metta Fuller's *Mormon Wives*. After Sarah had abandoned Harry in pursuit of polygamy with Richard, Harry found a way to recover and find himself a new wife. His choice was Minnie, a character who is so weak that she seems hardly able to support her own airy weight. Their first meeting captures her well. He saw her first through the window of a boardinghouse: "it was the countenance of a very young girl, pure and innocent as a child's, yet with an anxious expression of doubt and sorrow." Drawn to her when he heard her sobbing, Harry found her "standing timidly" in a doorway. She looked at him "wistfully, but not daring to bid him enter." Harry said she "seemed to be in distress." He reassured her: "I was afraid that you needed a friend, and I hoped that you would not doubt me, when I said that I was just as willing to protect and help you as if you were my sister." She confided that she

was in fact "quite alone" and that she did "indeed need a friend." She
was an orphan, having lost her father on an ocean journey to California
and her mother before that. "Poor child," he reassured her, "you shall
not be uncared for."[112] Ultimately, he provided fatherlike protection by
marrying her! Harry here seems almost like a stand-in for the writers of
these texts, who offered up gentle paternalism to protect women from
the threat of seduction, exploitation, and patriarchal domination.

But many men had also been seduced into Mormonism. In fact, respected ministers, including Ezra Booth and Symonds Ryder, had fallen
under the sway of Joseph Smith and his apostles. So the fears expressed
for women in these anti-polygamy texts also spoke to deeper fears about
Mormonism and religious enthusiasm more generally. In the course of
the Second Great Awakening, established churches and families were
at risk of losing members who were awed by the spectacular signs of a
coming millennium. Women and men abandoned their spouses and
their parents to join the Mormons. As such, churches and families had
to find ways to protect their own. Alexander Campbell drew a line between the Disciples and Mormons by declaring the age of miracles and
revelations over. Smith had pushed him into making such pronouncements. The irrational and emotional appeal of Mormonism did not fit
the spirit of the Enlightenment that informed Campbell's upbringing.
But the Enlightenment was not only tested by faith healings and golden
tablets. The Enlightenment had also bequeathed to America a trust in
consent grounded in rational choice. Now Americans saw this basis
for consent tested by heart religion. As converts swayed to enthusiastic
preaching, they lost their consciousness and their ability to grant consent. In marriage too, lovers could sway under the spell of romance. The
rhetoric of spiritual wifery helped expose how monogamous marriage
placed limits on the operations of the human heart. Anti-polygamy
texts helped Americans clarify their commitment to monogamy, showing that companionship might sometimes have to be more a matter of
practicality than romance. Orderly monogamous marriages and rational religion would be a bulwark against the chaos of enthusiasm.

CHAPTER 2

"A Base and Unmanly Conspiracy"

The Hogan Schism and Catholicism in a Gendered Religious Marketplace

For the better part of two weeks in April 1822, Philadelphia mayor Robert Wharton had presided over the trial of William Hogan. This charismatic and controversial priest had been charged months earlier with an attempted rape and an assault of Mary Connell, a loyal member of Hogan's St. Mary's Catholic parish. Clearly agitated by the time spent on and the civic strife caused by the case, Wharton's court recorder, Joseph Reed, used his concluding charge to the jury to comment on the religious contest gripping the city. He took particular notice of the gender disruption caused by the disputes at St. Mary's. This long-embattled church had finally broken into open warfare when the trustees resisted the bishop's efforts to remove Hogan from his pastorate. The recorder first apologized for his "animadversion" to matters not "immediately connected" to the charges against Hogan, but then he launched into a stern lecture against women's political involvement in church affairs. He lamented how this "unhappy dispute" had exerted an undue influence on the "minds of the witnesses," particularly so the "females, who are generally ardent and enthusiastic, but especially so in religious controversies." Adding sexual overtones to his portrayal, he noted women were most likely to get involved in church disputes "when a favourite, zealous, and I may say youthful, clergyman is concerned." Reed concluded: "In controversies of this kind, they move out of their proper sphere, and lose (as we have seen many of them in this case) the softness, the mildness and moderation appropriate to their sex."[1]

Women such as Mary Connell had become deeply embroiled in a fight over the distribution of power in the Catholic Church. We should chart their involvement in the so-called Hogan Schism as part of a larger effort to map women's political experience in the early republic. Historian Rosemarie Zagarri suggested a conceptual shift that has moved us beyond the all-or-nothing terms of debate that long plagued the historiography of separate spheres. Rather than work with either overly expansive or restrictive definitions of the public domain, she asked us to "examine more closely when—and under what circumstances—the notion of women speaking in public came under attack."[2] Considering Mary Kelly's important investigations of female education and citizenship, we now know that women could in fact sometimes safely enjoin the middle ground of "civil society," voicing opinions on public affairs in salons and in print. Numerous others have documented women's forays into public spaces such as conventions, parades, workplaces, reform groups, and religious gatherings.[3] Nonetheless, we know too that as the nineteenth century unfolded, women were criticized as they took up controversial causes, such as sexual reform, abolitionism, and suffrage, even as they often did so under the cover of domesticity.[4] If female education in an academy might have purchased entrance into civil society, such benefits seem to have been out of reach of women like Connell, a newly arrived Irish immigrant, who picked up work as a seamstress and domestic servant. To the court recorder, the female witnesses before the mayor's court failed to qualify for such privileges, especially in a controversy as hotly contested among men as this one.[5]

That women had become so involved in this controversy suggests something about the democratic dynamics at play in Catholicism in this era. When William Hogan, an Irish émigré, arrived in Philadelphia in 1820, becoming pastor at St. Mary's, he quickly fell out of favor with the local clergy. Hogan first upset the priests by flattering the laity with notions of their own religious power, confirming their right to choose their own pastors. Because Hogan enlisted women to his cause, it is no surprise that rumors of sexual indiscretions soon followed, only intensifying the conflict. When Henry Conwell arrived from Ireland to assume the post of bishop in Philadelphia, he sprang into action. The local clergy gave him a primer on Hogan and the democratic notions of his supporters. Conwell suspended Hogan, deeply upsetting the trustees of the church and setting in motion a schism that rent the Philadelphia church for nearly a decade. It was not until 1829, with a nationwide provincial council of bishops and the intervention of Rome, that a lasting resolution of the schism was reached. Hogan's trial for the assault of Mary Connell proved an important opportunity for the contending parties at St. Mary's to carry their disputes into the civic sphere.

While Hogan was clearly controversial, he also brought to a rolling boil a conflict that had long simmered at St. Mary's and in many other Catholic congregations: trusteeism. Many parishioners had been fighting to vest more powers, including the control of finances and even the election of the clergy, in the hands of an elected board of trustees. Trusteeism should be seen as one of a series of Catholic responses to the religious marketplace of the early republic. Catholic consumers of religion desired an ecclesiastical structure consistent with their political convictions. Church leaders split over how fully to meet this expressed desire, opening a space for religious competition. Hogan parted with the Philadelphia clergy in siding with the popular desire for a more democratic church. In addition, his ministry revealed other responses to the religious marketplace. A captivating preacher, Hogan clearly energized the laity with his populist preaching style. It was his popularity with female parishioners in particular that upset his critics. In addition, Hogan shared spiritual power with followers, encouraging them to engage in charity work and teach the gospel in Sunday schools. In these ways he was very much like Protestant evangelical preachers of the era who were similarly reshaping religion.[6]

The religious market became manifest in the pamphlet warfare surrounding Hogan's tenure as priest, as his proponents and opponents battled for popular sympathy in the public sphere. Competing authorities and allegiances created a fluid environment that proved challenging to the incipient American Catholic hierarchy. The bands of patriarchy proved hard to maintain in the midst of religious competition. As competing churchmen fought for adherents, they turned to women to aid their efforts. When William Hogan was charged with the attempted rape and assault of Mary Connell, a former Hogan devotee, the ensuing trial helped inspire a larger dialogue about the gender dynamics of religious conflict. Women had been both pulled into and pushed out of the conflict. Whether or not church matters fell within their "sphere" proved a hard issue to settle. Previous scholars have revealed the ideological, ethnic, and class strains at play in this dispute and in trusteeism more generally, but they have not given proper attention to gender strife in the conflict.[7] We need to resist the teleological pressure that can be exerted by awareness of the nativist hysteria of the late antebellum era; anti-Irish sentiment was present, but it did not have the determinative power it would acquire later in Catholic history.[8]

Kathleen Kennedy's investigation of Hogan's court trial for assault represents an important step in documenting the gendered history of this episode.[9] However, I want to broaden our purview so as to simultaneously witness the controversy of trusteeism, as made evident in pamphlet warfare, next to Hogan's trial for assault. By immersing ourselves in the pamphlet literature, we can see not only how fears about sexual disruption were crucial during the trial but also how they were a consequence of the schism more generally. Even more importantly, we need to contextualize the Hogan Schism and trial in the history of the Second Great Awakening, emphasizing the market and gender dynamics associated with religious enthusiasm. In its religious dimensions, the Hogan Schism has been seen primarily as an internal factional dispute between Catholics. The wider religious environment, if considered, has been imagined as mostly inhospitable to Catholics, with nativism only reinforcing the insular nature of the conflict.

Religious competition bred gender disruption: in a volitional religious market, when followers had to be courted, sexual improprieties were a real danger. When Hogan at one point charged his opponents with an "unmanly conspiracy," he was venting frustration with a private campaign to besmirch his character run by his opponents.[10] Rather than debate him over church doctrine, they tried to alienate the affection of his followers. This fight proved troubling to manhood in other ways too. Hogan would resent the seeming deployment of a woman, Mary Connell, to bring him down. Yet Hogan himself had relied on Connell to advance his cause. In fact, women proved important players in the larger contest for power at St. Mary's, actively joining the debates over Hogan's ministry. In addition, Hogan's magnetic personality and fancy dress brought worries about his sexuality. As a Catholic priest, his purported allure was particularly troublesome, for it called attention to the unique sexual dimensions of Catholicism. Lawyers in Hogan's trial would expose how the clerical vow of celibacy tested American notions of manhood. These concerns about gender would eventually find their way into antebellum nativist rhetoric, with Hogan himself capitalizing on his own troubled past. Thus, in both literal and metaphorical fashion, the Hogan Schism represented an "unmanly" fight within the church.

The struggles at St. Mary's were fought in a brisk and multifaceted pamphlet war. One can almost imagine opponents handing out the freshly printed pamphlets in the pews, as they tried to win adherents (see figure 2.1). Luckily, the famous printer Mathew Carey, who himself wrote and produced many of these pamphlets, saw fit to compile them for posterity. A veteran of the political battles of the 1790s, Carey understood well the business risks associated with bitter partisanship.[11] Thus, Carey initially tried to stand above the fray at St. Mary's, but he would still find himself dragged deeply into the center of the Hogan dispute as he sought to mediate it. Putting undue trust in a republic of letters as a venue to sort out this dispute, Carey only exacerbated the market dynamics of religious competition.[12] The pamphlets that he and others produced intensified factional conflict, as each group fought to win support. The rapidly expanding popular press was emerging as one of the central depots in the American religious market. Ready access to print, when combined with the ideal of religious freedom, as established in the First Amendment, made every pamphleteer a vendor in an expanding marketplace. During the course of the Second Great

FIGURE 2.1. Lithograph, the Catholic Church of St. Mary, Philadelphia. Drawn on stone by W. L. Breton (ca. 1829). Built in 1763 to add capacity for the nearby congregation at St. Joseph's, it became the first Catholic cathedral in Philadelphia in 1810. Courtesy of the Library Company of Philadelphia.

Awakening, the Catholic clergy, much like their Protestant brethren, would lose their monopoly over religious speech.[13]

Catholic leaders had to court parishioners if they wished to survive. Lacking state sponsorship enjoyed in much of the Old World, Catholic churches, like all others, depended mostly on the largesse of the laity, collected primarily by means of pew rents.[14] Under such conditions, it is no surprise that an activist spirit entered Catholicism. Revivalism and its attendant controversies have for too long been portrayed by most American historians as a wholly Protestant affair.[15] The Hogan Schism was a fight that bore important similarities to feuds in other denominations, especially the Presbyterian Church, which was centered in Philadelphia.[16] There was opportunity for influence. The early republic provided an interlude of cultural rapprochement between Catholics and Protestants.[17] While the colonial period had been host to powerful expressions of anti-Catholicism, fanned by fears of the French menace on the border, the antebellum period would witness a revitalized sentiment of anti-popery fueled by large-scale Irish immigration. But in the decades following the revolution, the ideal of religious tolerance, professed by Protestant politicians and preachers alike, when coupled with republican overtures by Catholic leaders such as John Carroll and John England, produced a climate in which Catholicism was left open to many of the same religious dynamics as Protestantism.[18] And certainly Philadelphia's Quaker heritage of religious tolerance may have further served to keep Catholics out of religious isolation.

Hogan was well suited for this host environment. He was born in Limerick, Ireland, in about 1791. He had studied for the ministry at St. Patrick's College in Maynooth, Ireland, though it is uncertain whether he completed his degree. After serving as a priest for several years in his home country, he embarked for America in 1819. Initially stationed as a missionary in the upper Hudson valley of New York, Hogan stopped in Philadelphia on a trip to Baltimore. Seemingly unsatisfied with his appointment in New York, he managed to find himself a new post. During his stay in Philadelphia he impressed enough churchmen to gain an appointment as a pastor at St. Mary's, though the nature of that agreement would later be disputed.[19] He quickly won friends within the St. Mary's community, easily mixing with a wide range of parishioners, from children to weighty trustees. Within a short time, Hogan was gaining wider notice for himself and St. Mary's. Hogan was attuned to the democratic religious marketplace, projecting a dynamic persona that attracted a loyal following. He also proved responsive to the laity by taking the popular side in the cause of trusteeism.

Hogan increased Catholics' presence in the religious marketplace of Philadelphia. He became known for his engaging piety, packing the pews for services long neglected, such as daily vespers. In addition, he empowered ordinary believers by involving them in voluntary association activities. Women and men alike joined Hogan, bringing newfound energy into charity drives and Sunday school instruction.[20] On a broader and deeper level, voluntarism had been taking hold in churches across the city and America.[21] At this very moment evangelist James Patterson was rapidly expanding his Northern Liberties Presbyterian ministry just blocks north of St. Mary's, sowing schismatic dissention in that denomination. The Sunday school movement, headquartered in Philadelphia, was also coalescing. The phenomenon of religious enthusiasm yielded an activist impulse manifested in a multitude of ways. Hogan was happy to call attention to the ways he harnessed laity power, insisting his success had excited the jealousy of his fellow clergy. In fact, Hogan, who would serve for less than eight months in Philadelphia before being suspended by Bishop Conwell, was convinced this envy had produced his suspension. Whether his opponents felt jealousy or not, it is sufficiently clear that Hogan's innovative and sometimes confrontational approach to the ministry was divergent enough from established Catholic practices to disturb the bishop and produce his suspension.

The fight between Bishop Conwell and Hogan was nearly inevitable. On his arrival from Ireland, the seventy-two-year-old Conwell clearly did not appreciate the American religious climate as his countryman Hogan had. Conwell had come to America only when political maneuverings in Rome had denied him an episcopacy he fully expected to inherit in Ireland. Trained as a young man on the Continent, Conwell drank deeply from ultramontane streams of thought, bringing to America a strong commitment to church hierarchy, a stance bound to alienate many American parishioners. Surely compounding the problem was Conwell's noted lack of rhetorical power, suffering by contrast with Hogan.[22] Various commentators noted Conwell's tin ear for the United States, suggesting a clash between Old World and New World Catholicism.[23] Mathew Carey, who was willing to chastise Hogan for his "headlong temper," nonetheless found Conwell's faults more troubling. According to Carey, Conwell supported an "arbitrary exercise of power," which sprang from "an overweening idea of the extent of episcopal authority"; such doctrine "might be received or submitted to in Ireland," but it was "not suited to this meridian."[24] Considering that Carey was a proud Irish immigrant, such criticisms should not be misconstrued: they were fundamentally indicative of an ideological dispute, not an ethnic one. To Carey, Conwell was prejudiced against American notions of authority.

Conwell suspended Hogan less than two weeks after his arrival. Ostensibly, the catalyst for the suspension had been an angry sermon that Hogan delivered against Vicar General Louis de Barth; however, the fight between Hogan and the local clergy had already been well established. In one pamphlet that Hogan himself addressed to the congregation of St. Mary's, he aimed to expose the "unmanly envy" (coding jealousy as a feminine passion) he imagined had driven the bishop and his allies to suspend him. Hogan gave particular attention to the reaction to his efforts at organizing Sunday schools. Hogan boasted that in less than six weeks' time he had managed to assemble somewhere between six and seven hundred children who were instructed by a "society of ladies and gentleman." Additionally, instruction was delivered to two hundred indigent children on Sundays. Rather than responding as men of "real piety," his clergymen rivals at St. Mary's "refused even to go to see the children at catechism." As Sunday schools staffed by the laity did in fact represent an infringement on traditional pastoral prerogatives, it would not be surprising if Hogan's colleagues did give these institutions an icy reception. Hogan reported he was soon treated by the Reverend William Vincent Harold with "repeated indignities." In addition, Harold sought to undermine Hogan by visiting "privately" with a number of the "most respectable families" of the congregation who had become fast friends with Hogan, telling them to no longer accept Hogan into their homes because he was a "bad and dangerous man." This Hogan saw as clear evidence of the "baseness and unmanliness" of his enemies, who would use gossip to bring him down. "Envying the attention" paid to him "since [his] arrival in this city," Hogan said his opponents had "entered into a base and unmanly conspiracy against him." This pamphlet not only reveals Hogan's religious activism; it provides a glimpse of his messianic and provocative style, which contributed to the mounting tensions at St. Mary's.[25]

Hogan's charisma was noted by his friends and detractors alike. He won an especially strong following with his female parishioners. This fact readily lent itself to derision from opponents. One pamphleteer, Francis Roloff, pastor of Holy Trinity in Philadelphia, who assumed the pseudonym "A Sincere Catholic, and no Traitor," highlighted the dangerous sway Hogan had over female minds. Five months after Hogan was suspended by the bishop, he resumed the pulpit without official leave, prompting Conwell to then excommunicate him. In response, Hogan insisted that it was the bishop who had thrown *himself* out of the church by violating church canon. Roloff said this questionable proposition was credulously lapped up by female parishioners. "No sooner had he made an impression with his mock-*cannons*," declaring victory atop the "ramparts of defeated episcopacy," than did Hogan by a "stroke of legerdemain" throw the "chain of excommunication around the neck of his episcopal captive." Hogan's "chorus of female attendants," the pastor sneered, responded "as if set agog by the power of animal magnetism," together proclaiming "the existence of a self-excommunicated bishop." Fighting against this spellbound (perhaps even sexually smitten) crowd, he insisted proponents of the bishop needed to speak up against Hogan's "deluded multitude" of followers.[26]

This enchanted crowd carried their purported delirium to the printing press. Commenting on the pamphlets pouring into the streets in Hogan's favor, Roloff questioned the integrity of Hogan's followers. He declared their pamphlets to be the "effusions of the inmates of grog-shops, and frequenters of brothels." Moreover, he suggested that the pamphlets might be the "language of females, nay ladies, who even now continue to dance at the door of this worthy idol of theirs!" If the rhetoric instead was the "language of gentlemen," he hoped these men would soon be released from what he hoped was a "momentary phrensy."[27] Here he deliberately blurs male and female followers, suggesting both had swooned before this dangerous and infatuating man. Bishop Conwell would also agree that Hogan had cultivated a popular following, suggesting that pandering to the laity had been one of his chief errors. According to the bishop, Hogan actively supported the false notions of his followers, telling them, "Bishops could not exercise authority in this country, from the nature of the Constitution of the United States." Furthermore, Hogan indulged the crowd by letting them believe that the clergy's financial "existence depended on the laity." The bishop attributed the "confusion" in the church to such "speculating adventurers among the clergy," who "made it their chief study to court popular favour" and "to excite a revolutionary spirit among all ranks in society."[28]

In this and other pamphlets, simmering beneath the charge of playing to the crowd was an insinuation about Hogan's sexual appeal. While the bishop was quite reluctant to publicly assign reasons for which he suspended Hogan, in one personal interview he singled out Hogan's penchant for fashion. After first chastening Hogan for using "highly disrespectful language" in the pulpit regarding Louis de Barth, Conwell urged Hogan to "leave off his dandyism." [29] This was not a new charge. Before Conwell arrived, the local clergy had already been publicly criticizing the "dapper" Hogan for his dandyism, one opponent styling him as "the fop who made himself a priest"[30] (see figure 2.2). To be called a "dandy" or "fop" in early nineteenth-century America was to be accused

FIGURE 2.2. Portrait, William Hogan of St. Mary's. Simon Gratz autograph collection [collection 250A]. Hogan was known for his striking looks and fancy dress. His elaborate vestments, for which his accuser Mary Connell had raised money and provided stitching, seem consistent with that reputation. Reproduced with permission from the Historical Society of Pennsylvania.

The cotillion Party.

FIGURE 2.3. "The Cotillion Party," in Waln, *Hermit in America* (1819); courtesy of Library Company of Philadelphia.

of paying undue attention to one's appearance. The rough male counterpart of a coquette, dandies were assumed to be sexual libertines, for they puffed up their appearance to attract the gaze of others. Sometimes carrying homoerotic and sometimes heteroerotic overtones, a dandy was a recognized figure in the Philadelphia urban scene of this era. One Philadelphia satirist in 1819, Robert Waln, mocked dandies as "ambitious 'fashion mongering boys'" who added "pads" to their shoulders and breasts and "corsets" to their waists (see figure 2.3). Waln also spoke of fashionable fops who spent their time engaged in frivolous conversation laced with "liberties" and *"double entendres."*[31] Soon pressured into speaking more publicly about his misgivings on Hogan, Bishop Conwell added more sexual overtones to his characterization of Hogan. In a letter to the congregation he insisted he had a "great deal more charges" against the reverend, but he would not state them explicitly because he was too "delicate and ashamed to mention them." He did suggest, however, that the charges were so "shocking" that he "would not think it safe" to allow any of his "young girls into the same Room with this person."[32]

While Hogan's supporters most certainly would have rejected characterizations of themselves as smitten enthusiasts, they did agree Hogan had drawn attention to himself, marking it instead a boon to their

Catholic congregation. To all parties involved, there was a clear appreciation of how the religious playing field in America differed markedly from the European continent.[33] Hogan's admirers were delighted that he had begun to win them a larger market share. In one letter written in support of Hogan's ministry, church members identified the key dynamic in play: "The success of catholicity in a country where religious toleration is established," they noted, "must depend on the clergy." Catholicism can become an "object of admiration and devotion" if the "medium through which it is conveyed" proves "pure and resplendent." They found Hogan such a medium, noting the contrast with his predecessors under whom the "fire of faith burnt feebly."[34]

Hogan's popular appeal was deeply bound up with the cause of trusteeism. As the people's favorite, it was only natural that he would support the idea that the laity, not the bishop, should choose pastors. In other words, he proved to be a democratic preacher in both style and substance. The trustees and church hierarchy clashed over the distribution of power in the church.[35] Unlike previous conflicts, however, both sides broadened the purview of the debate, arguing about the place of Catholicism within the American republic. The trustees framed this as a transatlantic struggle for self-determination. Perhaps some trustees still burned with the democratic sentiments of the United Irishmen, but clearly the American host environment had proved encouraging. The trustees repeatedly noted the contrast between American political institutions and Catholic practice. A committee of St. Mary's penned a letter to the "brethren of the Roman Catholic Faith throughout the United States" about how to "reform" the "sundry abuses" they saw as endemic to the American church. One proposed reform was that all future bishops be both locally grown and nominated. They maintained that the "arbitrary and unjustifiable conduct of certain foreigners" proved them to be "hostile to our institutions and completely ignorant of our country," bringing "disgrace to our religion, to us, to themselves, and to those who send them." They asked that all future bishops be nominated and selected by "pastors from our own citizens." They did not see this as an extraordinary request; in fact, they insisted Rome did not even exercise the prerogative of appointment in the Old World. There the pope allowed home rule or at least serious input from local governments when appointing European bishops. Also, they called for laity control over the appointment of priests. In Europe the "recommendation and influence of respective congregations" determined pastors, with bishops deferring to local wishes. They felt it a "shame" and an "insult" that "in this enlightened age and country" Catholics would be "placed on a more degraded footing."[36]

A key issue was the colonial status of the American church. Pro-trustee proponents resented Rome's position that American Catholics were to be ruled under the direction of the Propaganda Fide, an institution created for the "propagation of the catholic religion in those countries where the gospels were unknown, or where the government acknowledged a different religion." They chafed at the notion of them being a "missionary colony," putting them on equal footing with "the nation of Cherokees or Choctaws, or the natives of the coast of Africa."[37] Trusteeism was in part an expression of American Catholics rejecting their colonial status.

Rev. William Vincent Harold, who emerged as the most vocal and strident voice supporting the church hierarchy, bristled at such attempts to assume authority by the trustees. A veteran of previous battles at St. Mary's, once having even stoked democratic fires against Bishop Egan, Harold was much more eager to publicly debate church doctrine and to engage the so-called Hoganites in pamphlet warfare than Conwell. Harold now insisted that the settled doctrine of the Catholic Church, in whatever clime, was that "the government of the church appertains exclusively to the hierarchy." He rebuffed notions of shared governance as mere "pretensions of the trustees." The trustees were to have neither voice in the appointment of their pastors nor a say in cases of discipline. He declared it was the goal of the trustees to "overturn all the exclusive rights to govern and decide," powers that "rightfully belonged to the church hierarchy." Instead of accepting the bishop's divinely appointed rule, they misguidedly fought for the "broad principle of democracy" within the Catholic Church.[38]

William Hogan added fuel to this fire of a debate over the distribution of power in the church by rebuffing Harold. Hogan mocked one pamphlet written by Harold as a "crude, meagre production" that contained "little more than *wind*." Hogan could not find blowing through the letter that Harold wrote "a *single* sentence, which does not diminish the respect I had been taught to feel for you, or that shows you possess an enlightened or cultivated mind." While Harold advocated deference to church hierarchy, Hogan advanced claims for a return to the democratic practices of the "primitive ages of the church." Citing a tale from the Bible regarding the apostle Matthias, he took note of how votes were cast to determine Matthias's inclusion among the apostles. Sounding much like contemporaneous democratic preacher Alexander

Campbell, Hogan suggested the apostles were certainly well qualified, if anyone ever was, to "appoint a fit person for the ministry," and yet unlike Bishop Conwell, they "did not arrogate to themselves any such prerogative." Such abuses crept into the church only with the arrival of the "dark and superstitious ages, when the few fragments of literature, which survived the wreck of ages" were "confined to a few friars and monks, who to flatter the Holy See" advanced the claim that "Popes had a *divine right* to appoint Bishops to benefices, and perhaps, of course, Pastors." He insisted the "march of the human mind" had now caught up with "YOUR *pious frauds*." Drawing later in the same pamphlet on the memory of the Reformation, Hogan reminded Harold of Pope Leo, who "possessed as little piety, as your bishop does erudition." He likened Harold to those friars of his own order who had supported Leo "in that most shameful traffic of INDULGENCES, and in his pretensions to infallibility." Hogan protected his Catholic credentials by insisting Luther was "impious and selfish." Nonetheless, he drew selectively and critically from the history of Catholicism to support the cause of trusteeism.[39] If ever reconciliation had been possible, it certainly disappeared as a possibility as such barbs were traded.

In the course of this pamphlet warfare, women mostly appeared as depicted by others: misguided devotees who swooned at the feet of the fashionable Hogan. But there was at least one pseudonymous "Lady" who managed to speak for herself in print. Not surprisingly, it was Mary Clarke Carr, the writer and publisher, whose career historian Susan Branson has brought to light. In fact, Branson credits the schism as a major turning point in Carr's career. Witnessing the wide interest in the dispute, Carr turned to publishing more sensational material.[40] The publishing market was clearly evolving. While Conwell never warmed to the idea of defending himself in print, a woman like Carr saw an opportunity to build her career. Taking tentative steps into this dispute, she simply signed her piece "Mary"; nonetheless, Carr did reveal her identity as a woman. She started by trying to distance herself from those "other females" who have "with a levity, I hope not ill designed, endeavoured to excite a laugh, on the subject of your dissentions with your congregation." Perhaps Protestant women were more prone to smirk than swoon. Carr claimed "higher" objectives, wishing not to mock Conwell, but telling him she wished to "wring tears of compunction from you." If this really was her aim, it was bound to fail, for she goes on to accuse Conwell of seeking "his own" over "his Master's glory." Conwell had found in Hogan a man who was "rich in zeal, in talents, and in piety," characteristics that "entwined" him "in the affections of the people." Rather than work this to his advantage, Conwell had chosen to "disdainfully cast" Hogan away merely because he had a bad temper. Such "malicious" behavior, Carr stated, would sit against Conwell on the "day of judgment." Ostensibly, this communication was first penned as a letter. In her conclusion, Carr says she would give Conwell a week to mend his ways. If he failed to respond, she would go public with her concerns: "at the expiration of that time, if no alteration has taken place, I will, by making it public, enter my protest against conduct that threatens a death blow to religion, by exciting contempt for the clergy."[41] Most certainly, such a letter was received as an astonishing example of how the American market served to erode the authority of church leaders. As a woman, Carr was only exceptional in carrying her concerns to print. As we turn to the trial, we will see women had been busy voicing concerns in their streets and homes.

As both sides were becoming more entrenched in their positions, Hogan prepared to resume his station at St. Mary's. Supported by a newly elected slate of sympathetic trustees, Hogan took over as pastor at St. Mary's in April 1821, and the bishop moved himself to the neighboring church of St. Joseph's, the smaller and original seat of Catholicism in Philadelphia. Both sides made various bids for control of St. Mary's. Annual elections for the board of trustees were hotly contested, even once producing a riot on the grounds of the church (a riot that purportedly saw men and women exchanging blows).[42] There were also two failed attempts to recharter the congregation heard by the Pennsylvania Supreme Court.[43] But the most deeply pitched battle proved to be the trial of William Hogan for the assault of Mary Connell. While Hogan was initially charged with attempted rape and assault, the rape charges were dismissed by the grand jury. Nonetheless, the trial itself still very much dwelled on the prospect of rape and on the gender disruption caused by Hogan's ministry. As in Protestant congregations of the era, the religious allure of charismatic preachers became entwined with notions of sexual power. The reverend rake was known to enthrall his followers in troubling ways. From the perspective of those who opposed religious enthusiasm, appeals to the heart over the head could open up a well of uncontrollable emotions.[44]

The defense team for Hogan, led by Charles and Joseph Ingersoll, represented some of the most respected lawyers in Philadelphia. Undoubtedly, wealthy Hoganite trustees financially contributed to the effort. Connell's counsel, led by the elite Philadelphia lawyer George

Dallas (later to serve as Philadelphia mayor and then vice president of the United States), was equally impressive. That poor Connell could afford such representation naturally led observers to assume that her case was being bankrolled by the bishop's proponents. From the vantage point of today, such an assumption still seems justified, though it need not impugn the credibility of Connell's case. In the courtroom, support or opposition for Hogan fell into the predictable ideological patterns established by the schism; in other words, trusteeism too was on trial. Historian Dale Light has shown how coalitions of class were disrupted by the schism. Therefore, it is not surprising that stable class alliances proved illusory in the trial; rich and poor were called to play roles for both sides.[45] Nonetheless, class prejudices were marshaled by both legal teams, each trying to turn class-based resentments to their advantage.

The prosecution told the story of a privileged man who assaulted a poor woman under his employ. Connell, who did occasional housework for Hogan, was caught wholly off guard while sweeping the floor. In Connell's own words: "Mr. Hogan moved over where I was, and caught hold of me. . . . [He] said I was a very nice woman, and (*smiling*) he wanted to kiss me badly. Not in that words, but in a more indelicate manner, which is not necessary to state."[46] When she resisted, Hogan responded violently, stabbing Connell in the arm with a sword. For many hours following, Hogan's roommate, the Reverend O. A. Hannan, helped detain Connell in the house against her wishes, beating her as necessary to trap her in the home. The prosecution drew on the testimony of the watch and other witnesses, who were able to testify to Connell's wounds, but the account of the assault itself relied entirely on Connell. To bolster her credibility, then, the prosecution brought in a series of respectable ladies, bourgeois women who had employed Connell as a servant or seamstress and could therefore testify to her trustworthy character.

For its part, the defense team took a predictable course in presenting its case. First, they tried to account for Hogan's whereabouts that night, bringing forth a series of witnesses who saw him, leaving him little time to assault Connell. In addition, they pointed to the dearth of witnesses to the crime. They raised doubts in the jury by suggesting such a crime would surely have been noticed in the cramped alley where Hogan lived. To counter the prosecution's clear evidence of Connell's battered body, they blamed Hogan's Black servant, Edward, with assaulting Connell. Their greatest efforts, however, were dedicated to establishing the character of the two contending parties. They slandered Connell's reputation in various ways, painting Connell as a drunk who consorted with African Americans in oyster cellars. They strongly assailed Connell's sexual character, suggesting she was a strumpet who most surely would have welcomed any sexual advances from Hogan. In stark contrast, they portrayed Hogan as a chaste martyr to a noble cause. He had led a justified fight against an overreaching bishop. In their telling, his opponents had bought off Connell to bring him down. Simultaneously, even at the risk of casting doubt on Hogan's character, they boldly asserted he was simply too important a man to be brought down by such a lowly woman.

We know little of Connell beyond what appears in the court transcripts. Still, there are facts provided in the testimony that seem reliable, either because they are corroborated by witnesses on both sides or because they are left uncontested. A few years before the trial Connell arrived from Ireland, having left behind three children and her husband. Opposing sides sharply disagreed as to why her husband stayed behind, but it is clear she emigrated in a state of financial distress. She arrived with one child in tow. Placing her child in what the defense would call a situation "worse than [an] orphanage," she moved from home to home, performing work as a seamstress and servant.[47] It was in this capacity, and as a fellow parishioner, that she came to know Hogan and the trustees. She supported the Hoganites both in her labors and in her political activity. Campaigning for Hogan in the streets, she also swept his home. Their physical proximity and political entanglement were important preconditions in the purported assault.

Whether Hogan was guilty is impossible to determine. Both sides, for reasons we can only speculate, failed to call on Reverend Hannan, whose testimony was vital to the case. Based on a close reading of the testimony, it does seem a strictly legal verdict of "not guilty" was in order, for enough reasonable doubt had been raised by the defense team. The fact that Connell had to be forcibly removed from Hogan's house by the night watch several hours after the assault surely hurt her credibility with the jury. Whether Hogan actually committed the crime, of course, is another question entirely. Here the evidence is decidedly mixed and insufficient to settle the matter. But what should command our attention most in discussing the trial is not Hogan's culpability but rather the way both sides used the prospects of gender disruption and religious turmoil to aid their arguments. With that view in mind, let us look more closely at the arguments tendered by each legal team.

Both sides agreed that Hogan had once relied on Connell in his fight against the bishop. Both therefore presented a tale of betrayal. For the prosecution, it was Hogan who repaid Connell's loyalty with wanton lust and violent assault. In her testimony Connell described her shock in the face of Hogan's attack: "Oh, Mr. Hogan, I often heard your *mask* would fall, but it is down now." Noting his perfidy, she added: "Is that the way you treat me, Mr. Hogan, for all my exertions? I have walked the streets of Philadelphia at all times, to procure you votes, and to procure money to make your vestments." Here one can see some ways women's support was operating in this church dispute. Such active lobbying in a factional battle might seem to have strained the boundaries of acceptable female conduct, but when pressed, Connell proudly embraced her partisanship. She reported that the "respectable" trustee John Leamy had asked for her help in procuring votes, and she was happy to oblige. She claimed she got twenty-seven or twenty-eight signed pledges of support for Hogan, sometimes pretending to be a so-called bishopite to ferret out parishioners' sentiments. She pressed both men and women for their votes. Both were eligible to cast ballots. She similarly took pride in how she had "put every stitch in Mr. Hogan's manacles and most of his vestments," going door to door to collect money to support these efforts. Furthermore, she announced she had "quarreled with every other priest" she saw, arguing "as hard as ever" she could on Hogan's behalf.[48] From the perspective of the "Sincere Catholic," here was one of the "chorus of female attendants" set "agog" as if under the sway of "animal magnetism." But from Connell's perspective, it was Hogan's treachery, not her gullibility, that was to blame for her eventual alienation. Her trust, hard labors, and lobbying had been repaid with violence.

For the defense, it was Connell who was the ingrate. In their telling, Connell became dissatisfied when the trustees denied her paid work, specifically, the task of cleaning the church blinds, which some trustees had offered to do for free. This left her easy picking for the bishop's followers, who had already been trying to slander Hogan's sexual reputation. Thus, when they offered Connell $300 for her testimony, she was happy to accuse Hogan of sexual assault. As the defense summarized in opening their case, they wished to prove that Connell burned with a "feeling of hate and determination of revenge" after experiencing dissatisfaction with the "treatment she had received from the trustees." From the moment of her turn, she developed a "deadly hatred against the Rev. Mr. Hogan and trustees," planning for his "destruction."[49] In examining the relationships between Connell, the trustees, and Hogan, we cannot determine who was most unfaithful, but all accounts do agree on one matter: Connell was a very active agent in the church dispute. One male defense witness chastised her for her efforts, saying it did not "become her as a female" to be "so officious in business that did not belong to a woman to meddle with."[50] Nonetheless, her efforts were not atypical, simply better recorded, as suggested by the recorder's lecture at the trial's end, which chastised the various female participants for moving out of their sphere.

In its case against Hogan the prosecution conscripted gender to its cause by invoking notions of Hogan's masculinity and sowing doubts about the female gossip brought before the bar. From their perspective, Hogan's assault flowed naturally from frustrated lust. He was, they said, only a man. In an era when many saw men, including reverend rakes, as sexually dangerous, such a proposition could be posited.[51] Hogan's supporters, they insisted, had unrealistic expectations. Having risked their souls for his cause, they needed him to be something more than an ordinary man; they required a saint. They had "pledged themselves to support him, at the risk of life and fortune." If this priest, whom they "idolized," was proven guilty, their "humiliation" would be "complete." Thus, they were compelled to see him as "pure, perfect, and immaculate."[52] Anticipating the anti-Catholic rhetoric of the antebellum era, which critiqued celibacy, the prosecution insisted Hogan was giving vent to blocked sexual impulses, despite the growing emphasis on male chastity that was rapidly rising among some Philadelphia reformers in this era.[53] Voicing some early version of the repressive hypothesis, the prosecution insisted Hogan was "mortified by [the] priestly duty of abstinence and retention," leaving him "most liable" to a "gust of passion."[54]

But such a violent burst, the prosecution maintained, had not been Hogan's intention. Rather, he expected Connell would receive his attention favorably. Since he had been dutifully served by Connell, he probably expected "his advances would be met half way." He had, in fact, entered the room in a "smiling and conciliating manner." George Dallas played the scene in the jury's mind: "The course and gradual steps, of similar frolics are probably known to most of you—and I do not fear to ask your common sense, whether this be not the mode usually practiced in order to surmount the coyness and shy modesty of feminine resistance to personal familiarities?" Downplaying the notion of rape, the counsel thus appealed to the all-male jury: "Let any man for a moment figure himself in the situation of this defendant. Imagine yourselves, that calculating on the facility of approaching a woman, kind, and complying, as you suppose, you would meet with such a rebuff, as the reverend received?" Such must have been a "desolating" moment for Hogan. When he found himself "so egregiously mistaken" in his presumption, his desire quickly turned to rage. He foresaw the shame that would befall him and his cause. In his "situation as Catholic priest, bound by the most solemn vows to chastity, as well as *obedience*," such a lapse would be seen as "deplorable and disastrous." Connell's lawyer insisted that Hogan was so distraught over how his "enemies" would "triumph over" him that he violently attacked Connell.[55] In essence, Connell's counsel tried to gain a conviction by making Hogan's crime seem more accessible, if still unlawful. It was a risky strategy, for why not excuse Hogan all together as a victim of a flirtatious woman and unrealistic Catholicism?

In addition to this appeal to pan-male lust, the prosecution worked to raise doubts about certain female witnesses. The defense had drawn on age, class, and ethnic peers of Connell to testify about her drinking and carousing. In response, the prosecution questioned the character of such witnesses, countering them with respectable employers of Connell who vouched for her character. From the perspective of the prosecution, the young single women who slandered Connell were highly unreliable, little more than gossips. In his closing, George Dallas addressed the jury thus: "I will seriously ask you, as men of sense and experience, whether you ever saw vamped up, in a Court of Justice, for the purpose of exculpation, so contemptible a mass of frivolity, or puerile incident and female tittle-tattle?" Similarly, in questioning the testimony of her Irish shipmates aboard the *Aurora*, the prosecution mocked the "testimony of Elizabeth Welsh, Mrs. O'Neil, Mrs. O'Brien and all the 'O's' and 'Macs' that composed the living freight of the good ship Aurora." Connell, they insisted, was twice assaulted; now that Hogan was done with her, she was held up for scorn before the jury and audience. As she "told of her personal miseries and tortures," one could hear in the courtroom "a malignant fiendish laugh of exultation and delight!" Both male and female Hoganite witnesses were so "zealous" and "infatuated" that even while placing their hands on the Bible they evinced "snarls, sneers, and looks of immitigable hate towards this unfortunate female."[56]

The prosecution's prejudiced criticisms of the defense witnesses, however, paled in comparison to the vicious characterizations of Mary Connell by the defense. While the prosecution mostly deployed gender to make Hogan's sexual appetites seem natural, Hogan's defense team utilized gender conventions to make Connell appear sexually aberrant. While the prosecution strategically deployed misogyny against certain character witnesses, the defense unleashed patriarchal rage against Connell. The court recorder, Joseph Reed, blocked the defense from questioning witnesses about Mary Connell's sexual history. Reed had to be heeded, because he was the presiding legal official in the court and a man of some eminence in Philadelphia (he was former attorney general of the state and the son of a famed revolutionary-era politician).[57] Hogan, Reed reminded the defense, was on trial for assault, not rape. Consequentially, much of the defense questioning ended up centering on Connell's temperament, purported dishonesty, and drinking habits.[58] Nonetheless, they exploited some central moments in the presentation of their case to drive home the image of Connell as sexually deviant.

Overall, it was a scattershot approach to Connell's character, the defense bringing forward tales both credible and dubious. One damaging line of testimony concerned her comportment when crossing the Atlantic.[59] Connell clearly had alienated her fellow passengers aboard the *Aurora*. The hostility toward Connell makes sense, for she had been one of the only travelers to side with the captain when passengers staged a mutiny aboard this ship. Two matters were given particular attention: her drunkenness on the ship and the abandonment of her husband. According to Connell, her husband had been aboard the ship, but he disembarked to run some errands when the ship was delayed in port by revenue officials. Her husband had yet to return when the ship was again set to sail. Fearing they would be detained again, the captain pressed on. Despite Connell's explanation, the defense used her separation from her husband as a mark against her, implying she was either unfaithful or such a shrew that her husband wished to abandon her. Given the emphasis on motherhood among the rising bourgeoisie, it surely did not help her case that three of her children had remained in Ireland, living with relatives.[60] According to one hostile witness, while on the ship Connell had so alienated fellow passengers with her boisterous disposition that they threatened to throw her in the ocean.[61]

Mary Connell's employers, who were called to the stand by the prosecution, insisted she had no strong attachment to the bottle, saying she could "take a drink" or "leave it alone."[62] But the defense did their best to portray her as a confirmed drunkard.[63] All parties agreed she had been drunk on the night of the assault. The prosecution maintained that Reverend Hannan had forced this alcohol on her to quell her after his colleague's assault. In contrast, the defense tried to use reports of Connell's drinking to connect her to a working-class underworld of moral turpitude. They contended that Connell did not spend nights quietly with her employers; instead "she was to be found night after night carousing among Negroes in Oyster Cellars, exhibiting her habits of drunkenness and intoxication." One Irish witness, when she first saw Connell emerge from a cellar, assumed she was a "decent woman" and engaged her in polite conversation. Recognizing by her accent that Connell was, like her, from Munster, Ireland, she then tried to warn her of the true character of the place she had just visited. But the conversation was interrupted when a passing Black woman "clapped [Connell] on the shoulder in a friendly manner" and the two then shared a hearty laugh. It was clear to her that Connell knew and reveled in the mixed-race environment of the streets.[64] At a time when the white identity of the Irish was still being negotiated, association with African Americans was a dangerous slur. For bourgeois Philadelphians, the street culture of working-class African Americans was dangerously raucous and disorderly.[65] We have seen how the prosecution also wielded ethnic prejudice in its case. Both sides were willing to exploit and reinforce stereotypes to advance their case.

Having tried to establish Connell as a "habitual drunkard," as well as a "confirmed liar," the defense wondered aloud how anyone could trust her. Even if the prosecution were to "plaister and decorate and bedizzen her in the gorgeous trappings—the furbelows, and finery of their professional wardrobe," it would only "render her more odious and disgusting." It would be like the proverbial lipstick on a pig: "like the rouge on the sickly and sallow cheek of the harlot; instead of exciting our admiration by its beauty, it rather invites our attention to those deep and deadly ravages of vice, which it was its chief object to conceal."[66] As this quote begins to suggest, the defense worked its hardest at conjuring up images of Connell as sexually wanton.

The defense first slandered Connell's sexual character when presenting their arguments for admitting sexual testimony in the first place. David Paul Brown asked rhetorically whether evidence proving a woman to be "an abandoned prostitute," which "in a great measure she is," was not "sufficient ground" to question the credibility of her testimony? Indulging in more colorful imagery, he asked his audience to "suppose a woman comes all reeking from the stews" and then "charges a respectable individual" with an assault with intent to rape. In such a case would not the justices allow the defense to demonstrate that Connell was "so far from" resisting sex but rather "was in the habit of throwing away and lavishing her favours on every one, and was just as lawless in her appetites, as 'the bawdy wind, that kisses all it meets'?"

Honesty, they insisted, was impossible in an unchaste woman. Any "fe-male who surrenders her chastity" thereafter "relinquishes all the other virtues," losing the "very jewel of her soul" and becoming "only the taw-dry, empty casket, worthless and contemptible."[67]

The defense most strongly assaulted Connell's sexual reputation in their marathon closing statement. Neither the recorder nor the mayor stepped in to prevent this. Hogan's lawyers redoubled their negative imagery of Connell to leave the jury with an enduring image of impu-rity. They insisted that any attempt to vouch for Connell's character was "an attempt to purify a charnel house." It was a lost cause: "All the rivers of Damascus, all the waters of Israel, would not make her clean." She had long ago tossed away the "bright jewel of her sex" (her chastity) and therefore had become a "whitened sepulcher, a moving mass of liv-ing corruption." Much like the increasingly suspect working-class pros-titutes housed in Philadelphia's Magdalen Asylum, Connell had slid down a slippery slope of sin.[68] Even if "reformation" were possible, it was hardly the "work of a moment," especially in one who has made her-self "free as the air and common as the ocean." Surely she could not "in a single instant" turn back "the resistless tide of habit and of passion," reversing the "whole current of a lascivious life back on itself." And yet, to tie Connell to the bishop, they insisted this inner corruption had been hidden beneath a mask of loveliness. The bishop's proponents had "hunted among the stews, and discovered her in the cellar of a brothel." They found there a perfect "instrument who was calculated to effect a wicked purpose," for she was a "female of no inconsiderable beauty," possessing an "insinuating and plausible" comportment and "win-ning address." She had "smiles and tears" at her very "command" to manipulate everyone she encountered, including the jury. They called on the jury to peer beneath her "artifice" and recognize her "malicious" character. There was some tension between this portrait of Connell as a cool and sinister actor and the defense's larger arguments about a con-spiracy hatched by the bishop. She was "a puppet that is danced upon wires," but a force to reckon with on her own.[69] The defense wanted to have it both ways, using gender conventions to their advantage while channeling popular resentment of the bishop.

The controversies at St. Mary's were repeatedly brought into the trial.[70] Nearly every witness brought to the stand was asked whether they were a Hoganite or bishopite, the implication being that their partisanship would irreparably bias their testimony. Hogan's coun-sel, working with the assumption that popular opinion rested with them, invoked the church dispute most fully. They presented William Hogan as a persecuted man who had stood up to an episcopal tyrant. The courtroom, the *"Temple of Justice,"* had to be a "refuge" from the "storms of persecution" that swirled around Hogan. "Let ecclesiastical anathemas float upon the air and defile the face of Heaven— Let mitred despots brandish the threatening crosiers in one hand," Hogan's counsel intoned. "Within this sacred temple Justice sits unawed, and smiles serenely amid this sacrilegious war." This trial represented something much more than the accusation of one woman against one clergyman. In fact, the question of the assault was of "little consequence" and not worthy of the time of the jury. Instead, Ingersoll insisted this was a "struggle on the part the enlightened and liberal" whose aim it was to "shake off a load of bigotry and intolerance," a prejudiced church hierarchy "that refuses all compromise, and will be satisfied with nothing but passive obedience and absolute submission." Invoking popular anti-Catholicism to the advantage of their client, Hogan's counsel insisted he suffered under the "darkness and ignorance" that enveloped the church. Church leaders might "delight in their superstition, their starving, their stripes, their inquisitions and their gridirons," but Hogan's followers had fought to "break these chains."[71]

The prosecution in turn argued against such notions of a conspiracy devised by the bishop. They agreed that the courtroom had to be a refuge, but for them it had to be a sanctuary from popular passions, not from an overreaching bishop. To the jury Connell's counsel argued that "the defenders of Mr. Hogan were resolved that your verdict should not be the results of an exercise of judgment"; rather, Hogan's lawyers wished to "play upon your feelings" by making an "impassioned appeal" based on the "alleged characters and circumstances of that religious dispute." Rather late in the trial, Joseph Reed stepped in, actually taking sides on this matter. He suggested there was no evidence linking the bishop to Mary Connell, urging Hogan's lawyers to leave him out of their case (though to little avail). Connell's counsel used this ruling to their advantage. So why, they asked the jury, had you heard "this word *conspiracy* rung in your ears?" The defense did this "in the very teeth of the Court's suggestion" with the hope that "you will permit your judgments to be directed and swayed by prejudices which are known to exist out of this building."[72] Connell's lawyers sought to buffer her case from such popular pro-Hogan sentiments. Rendering a verdict in a political vacuum, however, was nearly impossible.

In starting the closing argument on behalf of Hogan, David Paul Brown noted Hogan's eminent status, contrasting it with that of his accuser. He used dark class-bound and misogynist imagery to conjure up Mary Connell as so much muck beneath a pond. During "storms and tempests," he noted, the "masses of rottenness and corruption which have long lain weltering at the bottom of the deep" are pulled to the surface, spoiling the once "wholesome atmosphere." Such was Connell: "in times of tranquility and peace, [she] had sunk to her proper sphere—the dregs and sediment of society." Such commentary suggests the class limits of female political advocacy, for here the notion of spheres is limited by rank, not gender. When the blasts of an "unholy war blew in her ears—when the children of meek and dove-eyed religion were converted into ravening vultures, rioting in each other's blood, and glutting themselves on the bosom of their common parent"—at that tempestuous moment, Connell appeared "in all her *awful glory*," displaying her "busy, restless, turbulent spirit."[73] As we saw at the start of this essay, the recorder would soon broaden, if somewhat soften, the application of this perspective, linking it to all the women who had been drawn into this battle. While we might be impressed by the strenuous effort to put women back in their place, we would do well to remember that people like William Hogan and John Leamy had first called Connell into action. It was only when her support for the Hoganites faltered (whether because of Hogan's assault, feelings of betrayal, or promises of reward) that she was reimagined as a woman who stepped out of her sphere. In fact, such complex testimony confirms that "separate spheres" was not a set of lived gender relations, whose rise and fall easily can be charted, but rather an enduring ideological construct available to be summoned at certain moments to suit particular political needs.[74]

The jury only deliberated for five minutes when it returned its verdict of "not guilty," much to the delight of the packed courtroom, which erupted with cheers. Surely the instructions delivered to the jury by Joseph Reed hastened the decision. He tried to deliver a balanced assessment but ultimately landed squarely in Hogan's favor. Assisting Connell, he condemned the female character witnesses, who were "partisans of Mr. Hogan," because their statements before the court were "deeply tinctured with the religious controversy." To his mind, they spoke "too much under the influence of their church feelings." He also dismissed notions of a wider conspiracy, suggesting it was beneath the bishop to engage in such activities. He suggested the charge against the priest was both highly serious and improbable, considering Hogan's elevated station in the world. Why, he wondered aloud, would Hogan risk so much for such a base gratification on a lowly object?[75] Furthermore, Connell's drunken aspect and failure to escape from Hogan's home made her testimony too unreliable.

This verdict was an important victory for William Hogan, but not a lasting one. While he would hold on to the pulpit at St. Mary's in the short term, he would leave Philadelphia by the end of 1823, squeezed out by the gyrations of an attempted settlement between the bishop and the trustees.[76] The democratically minded laity fared little better. After Hogan was gone, they would find new champions for their cause and even reach a temporary satisfactory settlement with Conwell. But historians of trusteeism have shown that a definitive turning point in American Catholicism was reached in 1829 when American bishops collectively renounced trusteeism at their first provincial council, insisting pastors were to be appointed and removed solely by bishops. Rome offered its support for this position, confirming that the era of trusteeism had come to a close.[77] This decision of the bishops to close ranks against trusteeism was a renouncement of the demands of the religious marketplace, but it proved a risk that Catholics could afford, for the number of Catholic immigrants would soon be rapidly swelling.

The Hogan Schism exposed the dependency of all churches, including the Catholic Church, on the laity during the Second Great Awakening. This dependency left the clergy vulnerable in various ways. William Hogan might have resented the "unmanly" means by which his clerical foes purportedly deployed Mary Connell against him, but he had left himself open to such an attack by his reliance on her and other women. Hogan's masculinity was bound up with religious competition in other ways too. His pose as a dandy was perceived by his foes as part and parcel of his appeal to a popular audience. We need not accept the judgment of bishop allies that parishioners were swooning before Hogan, but clearly sexual appeal was seen as a way to gain notice in the religious marketplace of the early republic. Finally, the prospect of Hogan's sexual urges toward Connell brought forward a critique of Catholicism that some Protestants would use to compete with their Catholic rivals. From this perspective, clerical celibacy distorted human nature, stopping up passions until released in destructive bursts.

Historians who have concentrated on the political dimensions of this conflict have noted how episcopal resistance to trusteeism helped feed nativist rhetoric in the antebellum era; that is, critics of Catholicism took the rebuke of trusteeism as confirmation of the incompatibility of

Catholicism and republicanism.[78] Similar observations should be made about the gender rhetoric of this conflict. The prosecution team raised criticisms of Catholic gender practices that would deeply resonate in antebellum American culture. In Hogan's trial, as in later nativist works, Catholic celibacy served as a site for exploring notions of male lust. The agency of women within church life also proved contested terrain in both the trial and in later anti-Catholic writings. There was a widespread antebellum Protestant fixation with Catholic gender relations. The burning of an Ursuline convent in Charlestown, Massachusetts, in 1834 and the enormous popularity of the faux "escaped nun" narrative of Maria Monk were simply the most famous and dramatic examples of this phenomenon.[79] We know that the Hogan Schism and trial garnered both local and national attention in an array of newspapers, pamphlets, and books, so it seems fair to suppose that they helped build nativist critiques.[80] But the most direct link that can be drawn between the Hogan Schism and later nativist writings is through William Hogan himself.

Hogan would go on to deliberately aid Protestant campaigns against Catholicism in several ways. In 1824 he began to deliver anti-Catholic sermons in Protestant churches and formally renounced his ties to the Catholic Church. Later, he would join the Episcopalians and twice marry, providing important fodder for those who called into question the wisdom of celibacy.[81] Most importantly, Hogan would gain national attention as an author of unrelenting exposés of Catholicism. Hogan's parting shots at the Catholic Church are well worth reviewing for two reasons: they provide some tantalizing, if inconclusive, final pieces of evidence about the gendered dimensions of the Hogan Schism; in addition, they show most clearly the resonance between the trial and later nativist anxieties about Catholic gender practices.

In a work titled *Auricular Confessions and Popish Nunneries*, Hogan explicitly engaged with the topic of sexual abuse within the church. He described how priests used the opportunity of confession to seduce young women (see figure 2.4). Claiming the authenticity of a former confessor, that is, a priest who had received confessions, he portrayed prurient tactics practiced, and even institutionally encouraged, by the Catholic Church. He begins his description of confession by setting the stage with the players involved: "a young lady, between the age of from twelve to twenty, on her knees, with her lips nearly close pressed to the cheeks of the priest, who, in all probability, is not over twenty-five or thirty years old." He then describes how the priest uses this opportunity to ask immodest questions as a means of implanting impure thoughts in the mind

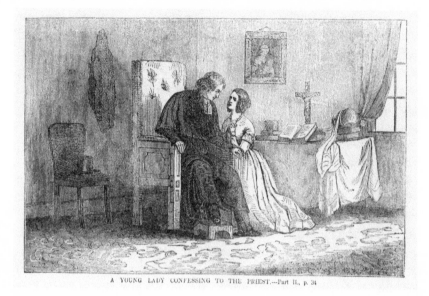

A YOUNG LADY CONFESSING TO THE PRIEST.—Part II., p. 34

FIGURE 2.4. Stereotype plate image in William Hogan, *Popery. As It Was and Is; also, Auricular Confessions and Popish Nunneries* (1853). Hogan describes such a confession as a highly sexualized encounter. Courtesy of the *Journal of the Early Republic.*

of his victim: "in this strain does this reptile confessor proceed till his now half-gained prey is filled with ideas and thoughts, to which she has hitherto been a stranger." The priest then invites the young woman back for repeated visits until he achieves mastery over her. By such means, Hogan asserted, the "Romish confessor debauches his victims."[82]

While Hogan wanted to cash in on his insider status in penning such an exposé, surely he did not intend to admit that he had played this part precisely. But his next comments about the young male confessor betray a sympathy that borders on familiarity. The priest, he insisted, knew the "secret of a woman's soul" and her "every half formed hope" and "dim desire," giving him so much power that he could "move her with his own will" and shape her "according to his own fancy." And this very same priest was "doomed to celibacy." Hogan lamented the resulting trial of the body and soul: "he is a man, but is bound to pluck from his heart the feelings of a man." Those young priests lacking faith would surely become drunk with their power and abuse it, but even those who were "sincerely devout" would have to "struggle with their passions" and there would be a "perilous chance of his being defeated in that struggle." Drawing on a fellow anti-Catholic writer, Hogan imagines the temptation as almost irresistible: "You are young, sir, or you have been so," and the priest too is "only a man." Even if he valiantly strives to serve God alone, as a man possessing natural sexual desires he will develop an attachment to one or more young female members of his flock. And when such a "young woman kneels down at his knees, before him whose heart leaps and palpitates," the result was predictable. Talking in a low murmur to one another during confession, "their lips approach each other, and their breaths mingle."[83] Could a young priest be held liable for his actions if he succumbed? Had Hogan himself once felt such intimacy? Was it for Mary Connell? Of course, he did not broach these final two questions, but one can't help but marvel at the imaginative license he gives himself in conjuring up the predicament of the young man charged with female souls.

Hogan is not to be trusted in his representations. The virulent tone of his later anti-Catholic screeds most certainly contained the anger of a spurned man; and surely the charismatic preacher also appreciated the popular market for moral sensationalism.[84] Nonetheless, the anti-Catholic works of the antebellum era clearly resonated with many readers. And this resonance cannot merely be explained by the fear produced by the massive arrival of Irish immigrants. This resonance would have, at least in part, been derived from a perception of a shift in Catholicism. The end of the Hogan Schism represented an observable turning point in Catholic history. The door to a more democratic church was then shut. Much of the antebellum rhetoric on anti-Catholicism gave vent to fears of unchecked power. One might take the tales of imprisoned nuns or young women entrapped by their confessors as literal or metaphorical representations, but either way it is clear that there was a gender dimension to the maintenance of church hierarchy. Starting to move in the same direction as evangelical Protestant denominations, inviting ordinary followers into church affairs, the Catholic Church moved to constrict laity power. At this same moment many Protestant churches were conscripting women into reform causes and catering to women in religious services. As Ann Douglas has famously argued, Protestant denominations were moving toward a *feminization* of church worship; as such, the Catholic decision to halt democratization in the 1820s would have made the forged fate of someone like Maria Monk more imaginable. Women would stand as both a symbolic and literal representation of the Catholic laity in its struggle with the church hierarchy. Mary Connell seemed to land on the losing side of the battle, but Protestants would nonetheless appropriate the figure of the wronged woman as an emblem in their crusade against Catholics.

CHAPTER 3

"The Fruits of Shakerism"

The Embodiment of Motherhood in Debates between Shakers and Their Rivals

In 1810 Colonel James Smith described a harrowing scene that was sure to get a sympathetic response from readers of his pamphlet. His daughter-in-law, Polly, had lost her children to the Shakers. James's son had become a Shaker convert and tricked his wife into Shaker captivity. While Polly escaped, her children remained trapped behind. With the intervention of friends, Polly eventually earned permission to visit her children. Done under close watch, the visit ended in sorrow when it was time for mother and children to be separated again. When about to leave, "her eldest son laid hold on his dear mamma, and wept bitterly." Smith narrated the scene: "I there beheld the tender child forcibly wrested, by the iron hand of a despotic Shaker, from the arms of an affectionate and weeping mother! The feelings of my heart, I cannot describe. To see my kind daughter treated with savage barbarity, and her heart-rending sorrows made a subject of mock and exultation; my dear grandchildren forced into despotic bondage, which tends to ruin both soul and body, was too much for human nature to bear. These are the fruits of Shakerism."[1]

Appearing first in a pamphlet by Smith and then reprinted in a compendium of testimonials by Mary Marshall Dyer, this scene carries a series of pictures that became stock images for anti-Shaker writers in the early nineteenth century.

In their published exposés of the sect, opponents of the Shakers were able to both exploit and reify emerging ideals for the middle-class family. The gender and sexual practices of the United Society of Believers challenged bourgeois norms in many ways, most famously by asking all followers to forsake sex and monogamous marriage. In addition, the Shakers lived communally, separating children from the direct care of the parents. This was a species of religious enthusiasm that ran roughshod over the family. When mothers failed to convert, they lost all access to their children. Because the Shakers broke up the nuclear family thus, they were accused of denying natural maternal urges, wresting children from "affectionate and weeping mother[s]."

Shakers rejected this formulation. In direct dialogue with Shaker critics like Smith, they would insist that children were not done harm by the Shakers. In fact, Shaker children themselves would be enlisted to rebut opponents. As mobs were raised to rescue children, the young rejected such help, defending their loyalty to the Shakers in print. Over the longer term, Shakers would react to these charges of denied motherhood in more creative ways, insisting that maternity was given full expression within the Shaker faith. This stands in contrast to their unaccommodating stance on celibacy. Shakers never reformulated the distinguishing boundary between themselves and outside society on the matter of sex between men and women, but they did work to accommodate the American orthodoxy on motherhood.[2] Shakers would insist that maternity was central to their religion. But they did not simply affirm dominant ideas about motherhood. Instead, they reimagined motherhood by returning to their holy mother, Ann Lee.

There is no denying that notions of maternity were problematic when applied to the Shakers. By the 1820s the Shakers had fully implemented their unusual living arrangements, separating the sexes in their own dormitories and children from their parents. These patterns of segregation were also replicated in Shaker worship services. The nuclear family, as nineteenth-century Americans understood it, simply did not exist among the Shakers. This was a real liability in a time when sentimental notions of motherhood were gaining increasing cultural sway in wider American society. To counter these difficulties, Shakers insisted that Mother Ann Lee had been a nurturing and loving mother, promoting domestic values among her flock. Yet the Shaker desire to reject wider society and its values prevented them from completely embracing middle-class ideals. Thus, the Shakers would reach back to older biblical notions of maternity, where fruitfulness, not gentle care, was the hallmark of motherhood. Mother Ann Lee would be pictured as the "Tree of Life" that had given birth to a new prosperous church. We will later return to this creative reimagining of Ann Lee, but first we must witness the criticisms that inspired this creative reaction.

To capture the criticism of Shaker motherhood I will concentrate on the writings of the two most famous Shaker critics of the early nineteenth century: Mary Marshall Dyer and Eunice Chapman, both of whom had lost their children to the Shakers. Their campaigns against the Shakers drew wide notice, attracting attention and action by the media and state legislatures.[3] In their writings one can see coalescing notions about maternity and about the nuclear family more generally. From their perspective, any faith that separated husband and wife, and especially mother and child, had to be blind to the natural order established by God. This rhetoric exploited and contributed to a larger cultural shift in America, helping to reimagine the roles of parents and children in the nuclear family. Ironically, their focus on sentimental bonds could even inspire violence. In places such as Union Village, Ohio, the prospect of children estranged from their mother was used to raise anti-Shaker mobs.

The novelty of this rhetorical positioning needs to be more fully appreciated. It was no longer the fruitfulness of a woman who bore many children that confirmed her obedience to the natural order. Instead, it was by showering affection on a few cherished children that a woman staked claim to natural motherhood. As Susan Klepp has made clear, the early nineteenth century was an era when women were changing conceptions of their bodies, taking more ownership over decisions about childbearing. Gone were the images of a time when the primary reference points for pregnancy were "agricultural and botanical," with women being described as "flourishing," "teeming," "lusty," "breeding," and "fruitful." Eighteenth-century portraits of women had often highlighted women's fertile potential by having them carry a basket of fruit or flowers near their womb (see figure 3.1). In place of this emphasis on fertility, pregnancy came to be imagined as an alien condition to the female body with mothers giving birth to "little strangers."[4]

Simultaneously, this was a time when evangelical mothers were reconceptualizing the mother-child bond in sites such as maternal associations and sentimental literature. In these places they claimed precedence over men in parenting skills, insisting that women's affectionate modes of nurturance were the best way to lead children to salvation.[5] Considering that Shakers forswore childbearing altogether, the focus

FIGURE 3.1. Portrait of Mrs. John Stevens (Judith Sargent, later Mrs. John Murray, 1770–72). While Murray would later be famous as a writer, here she is presented as were other young women in this era. Women holding fruit or flowers near their wombs was a common motif of portraiture in the early to mid-eighteenth century. Courtesy of the Terra Foundation for American Art, Daniel J. Terra Art Acquisition Endowment Fund, 2000.6.

of anti-Shaker writings is quite telling. Shaker violations of norms of child-rearing drew more attention than their denial of heteronormative procreation. To be sure, scholars have revealed criticism of Shaker celibacy. And this criticism did have formative power. Stephen Taysom, for example, explores how Shakers used outside criticism regarding celibacy to strengthen their own sense of righteousness and religious community.[6] But this distinction was more meaningful internally than it was externally. Kara French has recently unearthed fuller criticism of Shaker celibacy, but she also found that Shaker critics often denied its practice. They displaced unspoken fears of celibacy by claiming it was a cover for secret violations, such as seduction and spiritual wifery.[7] There were good reasons why it was hard to mount a direct attack on celibacy. Its practice sat relatively comfortably within a society that upheld chastity as an ideal for women and put increasing strictures on male sexual self-expression.[8]

When Shaker critics singled out the sect for denying maternal urges, they most often talked about denied opportunities for child-*rearing*, not childbearing. Similarly, Shakers were condemned for their cruelty to children, for whipping them and driving them to work. The bodies of women and children became the site where new notions of the family were naturalized. In essence, whereas the former locus of maternity had been the womb, it now became the bosom. Drawing on eighteenth-century notions of human sensibility, as well as an emerging emphasis on breastfeeding, anti-Shaker writers displayed the woes of Shaker victims in scenes in which children were ripped from mothers' breasts and mothers were left with empty arms shaking. From this perspective, human nature itself demanded that both milk and affection flow from the female breast.

Eighteenth-century European moral philosophy had helped create new notions of human nature that were promoted in the sentimental literature of the late eighteenth and early nineteenth centuries. Writers such as Adam Smith and David Hume had insisted that all human beings had a natural tendency to sympathetically experience the distress of others.[9] Known as a "moral sense," or "sensibility," other writers and thinkers helped map these tendencies onto the bodies of those who felt or witnessed suffering. Whether experiencing pain oneself or merely receiving the sensory impression of pain through one's eyes, wounded and worried feelings were transported by the nerves throughout the body. Quivering and swooning were just as much a symptom of wounded feelings as were tears.[10]

Mary Marshall Dyer and Eunice Chapman both repeatedly explored how Shakers violated human sensibility, thereby wreaking havoc on the human frame. In addition, they wished to call the sensibility of their readers to action, hoping to inspire others to help them in their quest for the return of their children. In her exposé of the Shakers, Eunice Chapman tried to evoke sympathy by comparing her own childless fate to that of a widow. All, she assumed, would naturally react to a woman who lost her husband: "The cries of a bereaved widow pierce the ears of the human part of our world," causing "their hearts [to] expand with the keenest sensibility." People watching such a woman in distress would be sure to "administer consolation" and make "powerful exertions" on her behalf. Surely, then, she hoped that the world would act to help a woman who had lost her whole family while they were yet "still living"; such a woman was afflicted with "all the horrors of wretchedness!"[11]

Sensibility was generally gendered, with women seeming the most naturally sympathetic, but both writers appealed to the sensibility in men too.[12] With men in charge of both the courts and legislatures, and therefore in a position to do something for them, it was necessary to imagine men thus. Dyer illustrated this balance well. The Shakers had proven wholly unresponsive to her "moans and entreaties" for the return of her children. Her readers, she hoped, would prove more responsive. Conjuring up her pain, she asked "what heart could endure" all the "sorrows of an afflicted parent bereft of her children." If readers could not wholly experience her plight, surely they would still be moved to action: "Who can have sensations with me? Oh! can any? I think some mothers can, but they cannot relieve me. I call for the tender feelings of fathers to have pity on the feminine sex."[13]

The scenes that most invoked sensibility in the writings of both Dyer and Chapman were those very moments when children were stolen away from their mothers. In such scenes the Shakers showed their cruelty, violating the dictates of nature. Here too one can see how both mothers and children deprived of love experienced physical distress. Eunice Chapman explained that even before her husband James had carried away their children to the Shakers, his cruelty to her had ravaged her body. After converting to the Shakers, James became increasingly cruel and neglectful. While his "conduct afforded [her] the most bitter and corrosive sorrows," she stood strong and "bore [it] in silence." Still, her body could not help but provide the evidence of a loveless marriage. Once a "blooming maid, the picture of health," she said she was soon "reduced to a depicted skeleton."[14] When her children were torn from her, it wreaked further havoc. When attempting to visit her daughters on one occasion, Chapman was purportedly shoved out of the room where they were being held by Shaker Eldress Hannah Wells, who scolded her that she was a "filthy creature" that was "not fit to be near us!" As Chapman stood in the hall alone, she found herself "trembling and fainting on account of the violent treatment" she had received. Luckily, she was eventually able to regain her composure; other female victims of the Shakers, she noted, were not so lucky: "Here I must pause for a moment, and adore that Allwise and merciful Benefactor, who hath supported me and preserved my reasonable faculties; and not left me to be a wandering idiot, like many other poor women, rendered so by the unkind treatment of the Shakers."[15] Mary Dyer provided similar scenes. She too speaks of wandering "about the village," trying to see her family, her "grief and fatigue" bringing "on a sickness, with fainting, so that [she] thought [she] must fall down, and expire."[16]

The pain was compounded by the distress the women had to watch in their children. Eunice Chapman was pierced to the heart when she heard of her son's trauma. "For a son," she noted, "he was remarkably attached to his mother." When she was ill, he "would stay with me and afford me every relief in his power." She further commented: "I had placed much dependence on him, and flattered myself that he would be a great support to me in my declining years." Thus, when he was told that he *must give up all hopes of seeing me again,*" he fell to the ground and "rolled back and forth over the floor like one in the agonies of death!" Sounding much like sentimental novelist Susannah Rowson, she invited readers to feel the pain she felt as she retold the loss of her son: "What a loss to a mother to be deprived of such a son! But I must drop my pen—and vent my grief in tears!"[17]

Consistent with these pained scenes of separation, both writers dwelled on the harsh treatment children received in the absence of a mother's love. Shakers allegedly whipped, tortured, and drove children to work. In place of a full scriptural education, they frightened children with stories of eternal torment in hell.[18] It is important to note the historical context for these writings. This was a time when middle-class families in America were beginning to turn away from colonial patterns of binding children in apprenticeship and service, instead investing more heavily in education for their young. In addition, the physical punishment of children was increasingly censured, with moral suasion the preferred method for shaping children.[19] The Shakers seemingly resisted both of these trends. Mary Dyer describes the "abuse to children" among the Shakers as "severe"; children were called up by a bell at 4:30 in the morning in winter and at 3:30 in the summer to begin their work-day. She found her son in a closet half clothed on a cold morning in January; he had been denied the comfort of a fire, being put there by a Shaker man who thought the close quarters of a closet might help warm the weeping boy. Another boy, merely seven years old, was pun-ished for his rude tongue by being tied with a rope and hung beside a pond from a tree limb. Contrary to the growing cherishment accorded children in bourgeois circles, the Shakers, Dyer noted, "do not make allowance for children—they think they must be men and women."[20]

Eunice Chapman also detailed the physical and mental abuse of chil-dren. She said she knew of examples where children were "treated with savage cruelty by the Elders, who will torture them and make them go contrary to the word of God." If a child were to "deviate from the paths marked out for them by the said Elders," they would put them "in a lonely place in a very torturing posture" and deny them food. Mean-while, the Elders would "pour their threats and eternal denunciations" on the children."[21] In the process, the children would be "divested of their own will," falling on their knees into complete "obedience to the Elders." To those who wondered why youth seldom escaped the Shak-ers, Chapman depicted the young as victims of brainwashing. Shak-ers could easily "weaken and destroy the little courage and resolution which children possess by telling them frightful and ominous stories." The Shakers taught children that "if they go back to the world, they will either sink immediately to hell, or satan will take them and carry them off alive."[22] If spiritual terror of this sort could have been ascribed to colonial Puritans, their evangelical heirs by the nineteenth century were beginning to embrace a feminized, sentimental piety that was veering away from these described Shaker tactics.[23]

The belief that there was a natural need for mother-child affection reached its rhetorical heights when these writers conjured up the physi-cal intimacy that was being violated by the Shakers. Eunice Chapman spoke of how her husband's conversion to the Shakers led him to sneer at the touches exchanged between mother and child. He would harass her whenever he found her "caressing [her] children," taunting her that she would soon lose them for life.[24] Once her children were with the Shakers, her visits with her children were similarly frustrated. She wrote thus about one visit: "I was even denied the comfort of sleeping with my dear babe, for once, in my wishful arms. I could only look at them, and observe how they delighted to see me, and realize how opposite my situation was to a few weeks ago," a time "when I could enjoy their endearing caresses without control."[25] Mary Dyer provided a petition from the residents of Enfield, New Hampshire, who said the Shakers were so cruel as to take children "away by violence from their mother's arms"; in their view there was "no Society" that was "so destitute of human feelings" as the Shakers.[26]

As historian Nora Doyle has described, the early nineteenth century was a moment when breastfeeding began to be positively lauded as "the highest pleasure of which woman's nature is capable."[27] Eunice Chapman tellingly describes her care for family members, including even her husband, as "nursing." Thus she described the efforts of the Shakers to alienate her son and daughters from her as an attempt to "wean the affections of the children from me."[28] In a deposition provided by Mary Dyer for Eunice Chapman, she described one instance when the Shakers had sought to take an *"infant from the breast of its mother!"* In response, nearby residents were forced *"in dead of night"* to take the child *"from the bed and arms of its mother, and hide it,* where the Shakers could not suspect it was." Chapman similarly likened her situation to "those poor mothers, who have had their children forced from their breasts by the savages."[29] Colonel James Smith asked whether society could tolerate children being "torn from the mother's breast." Of Shaker women, he said they had "rarely been seen to suckle a child." More hauntingly, he said if Shaker women mistakenly "beget children, they put them out of the way."[30] The Shakers denied nature itself by severing mother and child.

Such imagery was politically loaded. Historian Londa Schiebinger has described how the female breast began to gain more attention in the writings of eighteenth-century naturalists at a time when Enlightenment writers were imaging more political and economic rights for women. In her telling, the breast was used as a way to frame women as less than rational creatures, therefore rendering them less able to manage political affairs. By using the label "mammal" to denote the class of animals to which humans belonged (as opposed to other distinguishing characteristics such as hair), naturalists were referring to the mammary gland. Females, with their more pronounced and milk-producing breasts, became the link and buffer between beasts and men. From this perspective, the increasing number of women who were using wet nurses to free themselves for other pursuits were denying the role nature had intended.[31]

Mary Marshall Dyer and Eunice Chapman used their images of the female body to different effect. In their rendering, the female body had more natural sensibility and was built to provide care and sustenance to children. As such, women had a greater claim to children than their husbands. Such rhetoric could be effective, even helping Eunice Chapman receive the first legal divorce before the New York state legislature in 1818. But such a tack did come at a cost. Possessing a more sensitive frame and needing the sustaining love of children, women had to seek the protection of men to advance their claims. Calls for help could be answered, but they also reinforced the notion of female dependency.

Overall, then, the anti-Shaker writings of Eunice Chapman and Mary Marshall Dyer helped clarify and define emerging middle-class religious and family values. Mary Dyer perhaps best summarized how the Shakers denied what nature intended. Simply put, the Shakers were "without natural affection."[32] This natural affection, as described by these two authors, was the intimacy that members of a nuclear family should feel for one another, most especially the mother for her child. An enthusiastic religious group that put communal life over family life had carried their faith too far. In order to claim that the mother-child bond was etched in human nature itself, these writers used the language of sensibility and images of breastfeeding, showing how prying children away from mothers caused emotional and physical distress. The body revealed the natural order: built for caregiving, women were to have precedence over men in parenting. In criticizing the Shakers, these writers helped validate rising bourgeois family values about child-rearing and maternity.

The calls of distress generated action. During the early nineteenth century, mobs repeatedly descended on Shaker settlements to save children held in "captivity."[33] The stakes were high when family members were on the line. Shaker David Darrow reported to Lucy Wright in 1806 that a local man "gave out word that if any of the Shakers came to his house to delude & draw away any of his family, he would shoot them with his rifle." Luckily, the man had converted and joined them.[34] The Union Village Shaker settlement in frontier southern Ohio where Darrow lived proved particularly vulnerable to violence, being invaded on seven different occasions. Most dramatic was the large mob action led by Colonel James Smith. This Kentucky legislator and war hero was tireless in his pursuit of the Shakers. Having lost his adult son and grandchildren to the Shakers at Union Village, he took up the cause of his daughter-in-law Polly to retrieve her children.

Like Dyer and Chapman, Colonel Smith painted a grim picture of childhood among the Shakers. When Polly went to see her children she found her eldest son, a child of only eight years, tasked with chopping wood, with "his hands very sore and all his knuckles bleeding."[35] Education among the Shakers, he said, was "chiefly a pretense," with the young being put to work as soon as they could be used profitably. He insisted that the Shakers whipped children merely for refusing to perform Shaker dances and confessions. He alleged that they devised cruel punishments, once making a little boy stand within a circle only one foot in diameter for an entire day. His offense was taking a piece of cake without permission. Among the Shakers, Smith insisted, parents were taught that "it is a virtue to be without natural affection." Reflecting rising middle-class values, Smith saw affection, not dutiful obedience, as binding together the family. He wondered aloud how Ohioans could tolerate Polly being "robbed of her tender offspring" and seeing her children "consigned to bondage!"[36]

His neighbors answered his call to arms. In August 1810 a crowd numbering at least a thousand, four to five hundred of them armed, invaded the Union Village settlement.[37] Smith was able to take advantage of his local military and political authority to generate such a response. Rumors of other children held in bondage also helped raise the crowd. Reportedly, Smith had been circulating a military subscription in local communities. Meanwhile, news spread about the aims of this unit: they would remove the captive children by force, tar and feather Shaker leader Richard McNemar, and drive the Shakers from the country. The state's attorney and the high sheriff of Warren County both tried to intervene, but to no avail. As described by Shaker Benjamin Seth Youngs, on August 27 the men arrived organized in ranks, accompanied by a committee of twelve men who demanded the Shakers "renounce our faith and practice, our public preaching and mode of worship, or quit the country." Surrounding the organized units was a multitude of "undisciplined persons," displaying a "very mean and mob-like appearance," many of them "armed with guns," with others carrying "poles, or sticks, on which were fixed bayonets," while others carried "staves, hatchets, and knives, and clubs." Against such a menacing backdrop, the committee of twelve demanded to meet with Shaker leaders.[38]

As recounted by Youngs, the leaders of the anti-Shaker crowd presented a series of conditions. They wanted to see the Shakers deliver up several children, including the grandchildren of Colonel Smith, and they wanted the Shakers to give up their creed, which they said was designed to fleece followers of their private property. The Shaker leaders predictably rejected the demands of the committee. They insisted that legal means of redress were available, if they thought the Shakers guilty of any criminal acts. In the midst of this standoff, the leaders of the crowd demanded access to the dwellings of the "younger sisters" so that they might conduct "examinations," asking them "one by one, if they wished to leave the Shakers." They were frustrated with the results. Youngs quotes one young Shaker, Prudence Morrell, as saying "she had much rather lay her head down upon the floor, and have it chopped off, than she should be taken from among the Believers." Rejecting the premise that they were held against their will, "all who were interrogated made firm replies," insisting "they were free, and might go away whenever they chose, but would not." Next visiting the schoolhouse, one anti-Shaker leader asked the children at large whether they were adequately fed, to which all replied, "Yea! yea! yea!" When asked whether they were "whipped more than they deserve," they replied, "Nay! nay! nay!" or "not whipped at all." Youngs says the crowd leaders had to report out their "mortifying disappointment," causing the mob to begin to dissipate "as the darkness of night began to creep over the horizon."[39]

It is doubtful that Colonel Smith would agree with this characterization of how events unfolded, but it is nonetheless clear how important notions of Shaker "captivity" were to this entire drama. Were children treated cruelly and brainwashed by the Shakers? Those who believed so were willing to take up arms against the Shakers. The question about the fate of children was also weighted with larger questions about the vulnerabilities of the human will in a society pledged to uphold religious freedom. If some citizens were enthralled with religious enthusiasm, should the state intervene? If individuals could be manipulated and duped by religious imposters, should there be limits placed on religious speech? The Ohio legislature decided there should. In 1811 they passed a law that explicitly put limits on the Shakers, making it illegal for them to "entice or persuade" anyone to join this sect "whose principle and practice inculcate a renunciation of the matrimonial contract" and "the abandonment of wives and children."[40]

Similarly, when a committee of the New York legislature was asked to consider Eunice Chapman's request for a divorce, they said they were "fully sensible of the importance of preserving to everyone the free and undisturbed exercise of their religious principles." "The rights of conscience," they admitted, "are sacred." It was "better to suffer some public inconvenience from granting indulgence to the wild vagaries of fanaticism" than to "in the least degree impair the great principle of religious toleration." Nonetheless, the Shakers did not deserve such protection. In their estimation, it was not "in the smallest degree improper" to protect society against the dangerous consequences of the "religious tenets" of this "particular society." Speaking as if Chapman's husband had been imprisoned for life, they concluded he was forever estranged by the "barrier" of "religious delusion."[41] Therefore, Chapman was deserving of her divorce petition.

Shakers who spoke out in their own defense did take note of the violation of their religious freedom, but they put more effort into rejoining the portrayals of Shaker cruelties to children. In a book titled *The Other Side of the Question*, religious firebrand and Shaker leader Richard McNemar published a compendium of scorching criticisms of those who had helped organize crowd actions against the Shakers at Union Village. In this collected work, which contains a series of testimonies from members of the Shaker community, we can hear the start of a Shaker defense. McNemar and his fellow Shakers rejected the criticisms leveled at them by insisting that children were raised with tender care in this community.

Most remarkable about this text was the final letter included, a missive composed and signed by ninety-five young Shaker women. Finding a "deficiency of testimony relating to our sex," with special attention to rumors "concerning our being held in bondage," these sisters insisted that such reports were "false and groundless." They regretted that such stories had of late "become so clamorous, as to excite the pretended sympathy of many poor mortals, who have come hither with their clubs, to set us at liberty." Such mobs, they sarcastically noted, had offered "their service to burn and destroy our habitations," acting "as if we were shut up in a nunnery" and "wished to be released from our present manner of life." Such characterizations they declared an "insult on our character, and the character of young people in general, belonging to the society." They certified that their freedom of conscience was protected and that each chose to stay in the society. Referencing a passage from the book of Luke, "By their fruits ye shall know them," they insisted they were quite capable of judging their elders and found them "blameless and harmless." Those who would compare the elders to the Catholic hierarchy misunderstood their commitments. While chastity might "have been imposed upon" the young by the "inventions of priestcraft" in monasteries and nunneries, for them it was a free choice. While Catholic youth were "compelled by their parents to live a life of chastity and continence, for which their parents never set an example," they were free as individuals to "follow the light and conviction of their own conscience." For those who wished to rescue young maidens in distress, they insisted they were quite happy in their supposed captivity.[42]

Anticipating and surely informing Shaker works to be published in the following decade, these young women also began the work of reimagining Mother Ann Lee, suggesting their "unhappy sex" had not been fully restored to God by the sacrifice of Christ. They pointed to the awful burden of sin created by Eve: "the first woman was beguiled by the serpent, and received a poisonous nature from him, by which she lost her true freedom." She left "all her unhappy daughters in bondage to that nature which she ministered to the man." While the "virtuous example of the man Christ Jesus" caused many men to "hope for deliverance," "still [their] unhappy sex were lacking for example and protection from their own order." In fact, women's "right of freedom" had not been "gained till the present day." Now finally their "Saviour, revealed in the person of [their] blessed Mother," had allowed them "to become the heirs of that equal redemption which was purchased for all souls by the precious blood of the Son of God." As the female incarnation of Christ, Mother Ann Lee had finally saved women from Eve's original sin. This Shaker brand of femininity was startling in its bravado.[43]

By the 1820s the Shakers had developed longer-lasting and perhaps more modest strategies to defend themselves. Over the first couple decades of the century, under the capable leadership of Lucy Wright, the sect had steadily grown, capitalizing on the burgeoning religious opportunities presented by the Second Great Awakening. As Americans spread to the frontier, so too did the Shakers, establishing their communities across upstate New York, Vermont, Ohio, Kentucky, and Indiana. Simultaneously, the founding generation of Shakers was passing. A wave of early converts, who first were drawn to the church in the heady days of 1780 following a revival in New Lebanon, New York, were reaching the end of their lives. It was in this moment that the Shakers looked to consolidate their gains. One effort in this regard was to codify their oral rules, publishing their *Millennial Laws* in 1821, the year of Lucy Wright's passing. Another was to shore up the memory of their most important founder, Mother Ann Lee, who had brought the sect to America in 1774 before dying one decade later. The product of this effort was a book titled *Testimonies Concerning the Character and Ministry of Mother Ann Lee and the First Witnesses of the Gospel of Christ's Second Appearing.*[44] Published in 1827, it tried to define and defend the sect to wider society. Not surprisingly, it

rejoined some of the major criticisms aired in the writings of Mary
Dyer, Eunice Chapman, and Colonel Smith, insisting that maternal
impulses were at the very heart of the Shaker faith.

While anti-Shaker writers imagined Shakers as dead to natural maternal impulses, the *Testimonies* reimagined Mother Ann Lee as gentle and
nurturing. But this was a difficult balancing act, for Shakers were still at
war with wider society. The aging brothers and sisters could not so easily
let go of their memories of Lee as a zealous prophet and seer, one who was
a quick and severe judge, smiting sinners for their worldly ways. Senti-
mentality had its limits. Thus, Shakers needed to shore up the maternity
of Ann Lee in other ways. Harkening back to early eighteenth-century
notions of motherhood, Shakers imagined Ann Lee as a fertile woman,
one whose fruits were in evidence in the prospering Shaker villages of
the early nineteenth century. If Lee had famously lost eight children to
miscarriage and early death as a younger woman, in her leadership of the
celibate Shaker sect, she would give birth instead to a church.

In contrast to a set of recollections that had been published a decade
earlier for the benefit of the believers alone, the *Testimonies Concerning
the Character and Ministry of Ann Lee* had to speak to both an internal
and external audience.[45] Seth Wells, in his introduction to the volume,
openly acknowledges the religious marketplace within which the Shakers had to find their niche. Here one can see how Shakers were reposi-
tioning themselves, claiming respectability. During this time of tumult
in religion, he noted, "Many are seriously enquiring, 'What shall we do
to be saved?' Some, he said, are looking to one denomination and some
to another." Those who are seeking salvation might naturally "cleave to
those who appear to have the most zeal, and whose religion is displayed
in many words, and abounds with long prayers, flaming sermons and
much noise." Such an emphasis on enthusiasm could certainly have
been imputed to the Shakers. Early leaders such as Ann Lee were known
to fall into trances, and the group was most notorious for its strange
patterns of dance during service (see figure 3.2). But here Wells dis-
tances this image of the Shakers. Those who are taken in by charismatic
preachers, he notes, are "frequently led into dark mazes of fanaticism,
where they get bewildered and lost amidst a confusion of false ideas
and notions, injected into the mind by the spirit of Antichrist."[46] The
Ann Lee that he and his fellow memorialists offered up thereafter was
a model of respectability.

Many of the writers spoke of the nurturing, meek, and charitable
disposition of Mother Ann Lee. Daniel Goodrich, for example, said he

SHAKERS near LEBANON state of N.YORK.
their mode of Worship.

FIGURE 3.2. Engraving, "Shakers near Lebanon, state of N. York, their mode of worship" (ca. 1830). Library of Congress.

never "felt ashamed to call her Mother," for she "verily brought me forth into the family of Christ." He declared of her: "She is truly my heavenly Mother; and I love her with an everlasting love, which can never be taken from me. She was truly a Mother to every faithful soul who was willing to put away all sin, and follow Christ in the regeneration. Her soul abounded in kindness and charity to the needy and afflicted. She often taught us to remember the poor and needy of this world, and supply their wants and relieve their distresses."[47] Another aging Shaker, Comstock Betts, had similar observations of Mother Ann Lee and the other early leaders of the church, noting that "they seemed to spare no pains to make the brethren and sisters comfortable, both in things spiritual and temporal." Reaching beyond the members, they "were ever free and liberal in extending charity to the poor and needy. Their meekness and humility were manifest in all their conversation and deportment." It surely was a falsehood to ascribe to them hard hearts, for he had "often seen them weep, and thank God for the gospel, with the most heart-feeling sensibility."[48]

This sentimental spirit was also displayed in Mother Ann Lee's interaction with children. Several recalled her gentle touch in this regard.

Samuel Johnson, for example, said she displayed a "remarkably kind and tender feeling towards children." Her love was returned in kind, for "the attachment of such little ones to her was wonderful." Many thereafter became committed to her for life, for even now, he observed, "there are numbers now living, whose first impressions of faith and love to the way of God, were inspired into their souls, by the notice of Mother Ann to them, in their infancy."[49] Elizabeth Johnson seems to have been one such child, for she recalled: "I did really love Mother Ann with that heavenly love which my tongue cannot express, nor my pen describe. And truly I had good reason; for I received my love from her. I have received many precious and heavenly gifts of God from her; and they have felt like the bread of life and the waters of life to my soul."[50] As a generous and loving mother, Ann Lee provided for the spiritual needs of her children.

Furthermore, contrary to those who portrayed the Shakers as destroying families, Mother Ann Lee enjoined wives, mothers, and children to do their duties to their husbands and fathers. This claim particularly stretched the image of Lee, for she had called on her followers to abandon their families and join a commune that leveled all believers before God. Daniel Moseley insisted that Mother Lee had been misunderstood. He noted that some visitors to the early Shakers heard her testimony "against the lust of the flesh" and therefore "spread a report that these people forbid to marry." She told Moseley to correct this misunderstanding, for she believed that some are not suited for the Shaker lifestyle: "some cannot, or will not take up their crosses for the Kingdom of Christ's sake." Such individuals, she would not cast aside; rather, she would counsel them "to marry and live after the flesh, in a lawful manner, and be servants to their families." To do such was "natural," their behavior being "less sinful in the sight of God than any other way of gratifying that nature."[51] Job Bishop similarly recalled how Mother Ann Lee encouraged the domestic arts, calling on women, "particularly those who had families, to be neat and clean, and to keep their houses in good order, and not to indulge themselves in filth and nastiness."[52] According to Daniel Moseley, the relationship between Shaker brothers and sisters was akin to those of the middle-class family, because Ann Lee "instructed the sisters in their duty—to manage their family affairs with prudence, neatness and good economy." They were "to bring up their children in the fear of God, and set good examples before them—to dress and prepare their victuals in good order." If they fulfilled their domestic duties, "when their brethren came in from their hard work, they might bless them, and be able to kneel down together and give thanks to God."⁵³ This sounded much like the separate spheres ideology of the day. Thus were Shaker challenges to society tamed in historical memory.

And yet some of the most challenging aspects of the Shaker tradition in fact survived, no matter how they might rhetorically soften their edges. This was no mainstream denomination. Furthermore, those aging brothers and sisters who had lived their lives committed to the faith had good cause to justify their decision to remain removed from the world. Thus, another dominant theme in the *Testimonies* was the awe-inspiring and fear-provoking nature of Ann Lee. This was a mother with Jehovah-like powers. The image most often conjured up in this respect was that of a woman wielding a burning sword. Eliab Harlow said of her opposition to sin that "her testimony was like a flaming sword against it in all its branches." This earned her much opposition, for her revelations were "so opposite to the nature and feelings of fallen man, that she and her testimony were both despised and hated."⁵⁴ Aaron Wood similarly noted that "her severity against sin was like a flaming fire." To him, it was "no wonder" that "the world hated her; for she was not of the world."⁵⁵ Therefore, it is not surprising that Shaker artist Hannah Cohoon, after receiving heavenly visits from Mother Ann Lee in the 1840s, would be inspired to compose her iconic "gift drawing" of the "Blazing Tree" (see figure 3.3). Such botanical imagery suggests Ann Lee's life-giving powers (a subject to which we'll return), but it also gives a clear indication of her fiery prophetic legacy. Considering that the Shakers had come to see Ann Lee as another incarnation of God, it is fitting that she was depicted as a burning bush, the vessel through which God had spoken to Moses.⁵⁶

To help her in her campaign against sin, Ann Lee had various divine powers, including the ability to perform faith healings and read the secret sins and intents of those she met.⁵⁷ Elizabeth Johnson, for example, shared how she felt when Mother Lee grabbed her arm: "Instantly I felt the power of God flow from her and run through my whole body." Asked by Lee to confess her sins, Johnson felt compelled to unburden her soul: "I was fully convinced, by what I saw and felt, that she had the discerning power of God, so that she could discern the state and situation of my mind, as easily as I could behold my face in a glass."⁵⁸ Not surprisingly, Mother Lee's powers of detection were put to the purpose of detecting the arts of seduction practiced by youth. Daniel Moseley highlighted that she was able "to unmask all the base and unclean

FIGURE 3.3. "The Tree of Light or Blazing Tree." Drawing by Hannah Cohoon (1845). Wikimedia Commons.

desires and deceitful wantonness of both male and female," detecting "all those alluring charms of lust by which they entice and deceive each other." Not unlike sentimental novelists like Susanna Rowson or Hannah Foster, Ann Lee "exposed the subtle craftiness of that filthy nature in the males, by which they seek to seduce and debauch the females." But in telling contrast to such popular authors, she had not accepted passionlessness in fallen women, for she also tried to expose "all the enticing arts of the females to ensnare and bewitch the males, and draw them into wanton embraces."[59] No sentimentalist crying over the fallen woman, in Ann Lee's rendering, women could be either predator or prey.

To balance this tension between Ann Lee, the sentimental mother and Ann Lee, the seer who would smite sinners, many of the Shaker writers would tellingly employ a contrasting conjunction in their summaries of her character. She was stern, *but* soft. She was frightening, *yet* forgiving. One example can illustrate this rhetorical tack. Richard Treat recalled this of Ann Lee: "Her testimony was the most mortifying to a carnal and fleshy nature that can possibly be imagined. Never since the world began, was the filthy, fallen nature of lust so powerfully and so effectually exposed. Yet the tenderness and charity of Mother and the Elders towards poor souls who were lost in the flesh, and honestly desired to find a way out, was as boundless as their severity against sin."[60] In conjuring up this image of Ann Lee as a woman in tension with herself, the Shakers were reflecting some of the tensions inherent in this maturing sect, being both in and outside of wider society.

Recognizing this tension, one elder Shaker, Samuel Johnson, tried to creatively resolve this ambivalent image, trying to show how Ann Lee could embody both tendencies. He imagined Mother Ann Lee as someone who was so sensitive (like a good sentimental mother) that she could see into other souls. He reported that "she was truly a Mother in Christ." She had a "discerning spirit" that could recognize the state of others' souls and therefore "administer to their necessities under all circumstances." In fact, she was so sensitive that "no secret thought of the heart could be hid from her." This gave her the power to ferret out "the secret sins of hypocrites and deceivers," producing their "shame and confusion."[61] In other words, her motherly powers of intuition made her an effective seer, an exposer of sin.

But the more common way that Shaker writers dealt with this tension was to displace Mother Ann Lee's maternity into another location entirely. Rather than further building up the image of Ann Lee as sentimental mother, they instead shored up her maternity by speaking of her fertility. Repeatedly, the narrators made reference to the Gospel of Luke, suggesting that a tree (that is, Mother Ann Lee) must be known by its fruits (the prospering community she left behind). Hannah Cogswell provides one typical example of this rhetoric. Working against rumors that Ann Lee had engaged in sinful activity, such as excess drinking, she asked: "Can an evil tree bring forth good fruit? Let any rational person judge. I can testify with confidence that, in obedience to her precepts, I have been kept from sin and from all manner of pollution and wickedness for more than forty years." Rachel Spencer similarly noted: " 'The tree is known by its fruit; and a corrupt tree cannot bring forth good fruit.' But this testimony of the gospel which Mother Ann planted in the midst of so much opposition, has weathered the storms of persecuting malice nearly forty-six years."[62]

Anne Mathewson applied this metaphor most fully to show how Ann Lee had rewritten Christian eschatology, inverting the story of the Fall of humankind back onto itself. Revisiting the thoughts of the young women from Union Village, she began by chastising the modern generation of Christians who were so intent on forming Bible societies and missionizing abroad while neglecting the simple truth that "*a tree is known by its fruit*; that a thorn-bush cannot bring forth grapes, nor figs grow on thistles." These misguided Christians had allowed "blindness and ignorance" to prevail "at home." She asked them, "How is it that ye do not understand?" Mother Ann Lee was their rightful guide to eternity. Most Americans, she said, would grant the "agency of the first woman in leading mankind into sin." Why, she wondered, would it be hard to imagine "the agency of a woman . . . in leading the human race [now] out of sin?" Ann Lee's "fruits" show clearly that she was led by a "spirit totally opposite" to Eve.[63] The metaphor is enriched here by the fact that Eve had led humankind into sin by biting the fruit of the tree of knowledge. Now Ann Lee was bearing fruit for humankind anew.

The image of Ann Lee as a "Tree of Life" would reach its apotheosis in pictorial form as the enthusiastic impulse reasserted itself in Shaker communities in the mid-nineteenth century. Starting in 1837 and extending into the 1850s, Shaker mediums, known as "instruments," received visions from the departed spirit of Ann Lee, as well as from other early Shaker leaders. Particularly revealing are the "gift drawings" from this "Era of Manifestations" (which also came to be known as the time of "Mother Ann's Work").[64] Shaker women composed various renderings of fruit-laden trees, which resonate deeply with the earlier textual representations of Lee's fertility.[65] The inscriptions that accompanied these pictures reinforced this imagery, while other gifts, such as songs and rituals, similarly employed botanical metaphors.[66]

Consider the "Tree of Life" image composed by Hannah Cohoon in 1854 (figure 3.4). Here the dramatically ripe fruit resonates with the buoyant fruit typical of eighteenth-century portraits of women. Her inscription reinforces the message. Cohoon says that the "spirit" showed her a tree "bearing ripe fruit," learning later that it "grows in the Spirit Land." When she "entreated Mother Ann to tell me the name of this tree," she learned by the "moving of the hand of a medium" that it was the "Tree of Life."[67] Similarly, the work of Polly Collins, titled *A Gift from Mother Ann. Tree of Comfort* (1859), shows a fruit-laden tree depicting Mother Ann's bounty (see figure 3.5). Composed at a time when the Era of Manifestations was waning, it carries an inscription that revisits the softer side of Ann Lee. Not only are the fruits of the tree "freely given," but it promises to "sooth our care worn feelings, to cherish and revive us, while on our toilsome journey."[68] Shakers never escaped the tug of Victorian notions of maternity, but their attempt to keep alive

FIGURE 3.4. "Tree of Life." Drawing by Hannah Cohoon (1854). Wikimedia Commons.

the prophetic and the nurturing sides of Mother Ann Lee produced a striking and creative synthesis in these gift drawings.

Thus, in memory Ann Lee earned her motherhood in two keys ways: first, she was endowed with the sentimental nature that was increasingly expected of mothers in the early nineteenth century. Defying the picture of callous parenting attributed to Shakers by critics such as Eunice Chapman and Mary Marshall Dyer, Lee was portrayed by her heirs as a loving and nurturing mother. Perhaps sensing the uneasy tension between this image and the competing memories of Lee as a severe judge of sinners, the Shakers also granted Ann Lee motherhood by conjuring up older ideals of maternity. She was a fertile woman. While Lee had turned back the sins of Eve by rejecting the fruit of sexual knowledge, she did, in planting a prosperous church, metaphorically obey God's command to "be fruitful and multiply." The debate between Shakers and their critics had appeared at an important transition point in the formation of American gender and family ideals. While chastising the Shakers for violating the bonds of mother and child, writers like Dyer, Chapman, and Smith helped elevate the importance of such

FIGURE 3.5. "A Gift from Mother Ann." Drawing by Polly Collins (1859). Courtesy of Shaker Village.

relationships in American conceptualizations of the family. Responding creatively to such criticism, Shakers produced a unique synthesis of the present and past. But they also purchased their own legitimacy by assenting to a growing culture of American sentimentalism and domesticity. Rather than being seen as victims of religious delusion and enthusiasm, in time the Shakers would come to be seen as a quiet and perhaps a curious people, no longer a threat to the wider American culture.

CHAPTER 4

Mixing "the Poison of Lust with the Ardor of Devotion"

*Conjuring Fears of the Reverend Rake and
the Rise of Anti-Enthusiasm Literature*

In 1811 Baptist minister William Parkinson was publicly tried for sexual assault, specifically for twice grabbing the breasts of his devoted supporter, Mrs. Eliza Wintringham. Garnering a packed courtroom, large and elite legal teams, and presided over by New York City mayor DeWitt Clinton, this trial would be the first in a series of about two dozen highly publicized ministerial trials for sexual misdeeds over the next half century.[1] These cases would be remarkable enough to generate a new popular genre of books and pamphlets: tales of the reverend rake. The woman assaulted, Mrs. Wintringham, was not your stereotypical literary female victim. The trial transcripts, in fact, show a rather bold, wry, and religiously empowered woman. As a woman known for organizing a prayer circle, taking a lead role in sectarian conflicts, and even chiding her husband for his sexual performance, she seems unlikely to have been swooning into the arms of William Parkinson. In fact, she was often seen leading him around by the arm. Yet her own defense attorney, undercutting her account of assault, portrayed her as a victim of seduction.

Purportedly, Parkinson used both romantic and scriptural stratagems. According to the attorney, Parkinson flattered her by saying "her beauty" left him "no will to resist" his passion for her. If giving in to passion was a sin, however, "God forgives his children when they backslide." He coupled this notion of forgiveness with an unconventional interpretation of the Song of Solomon, urging her they should embrace true love. These pleas, the lawyer insisted, were a startling mix of the familiar and foreign. Parkinson's invocation of his irresistible love, which "carried him" along "like a torrent, *en masse*," was not surprising, for it was the "language of the commonest seducer." But what was startling were his scriptural defenses of illicit love. This, the lawyer noted presciently, was the language of a different sort of character, "that of one not yet, thank God, so common—a religious imposter."[2] Within a couple of decades, the figure of the religious imposter would become all too familiar, fully conflated with the character of the seducer.

There are a couple curious things about this trial. First, why did it attract so much attention? Other trials involved much more aggressive and sinful conduct on the part of the ministers, ranging from rape to domestic abuse to the murder of a pregnant lover. Yet three hours before Parkinson's trial began, an "immense throng of spectators filled the benches, as well as extensive space in rear of the bar and galleries." People were so tightly packed, in fact, that one day someone collapsed of heat exhaustion. The attention gained was, in part at least, explained by the prominence of the minister himself. Formerly serving as a chaplain to the US Congress, he had "a large congregation" of five hundred souls "who adhere[d] to him."[3] Leading a Baptist congregation in New York, he came from a rapidly growing, but still relatively novel, evangelical faith tradition that was making inroads in a city dominated by mainline denominations like the Episcopalian, Dutch Reformed, and Presbyterian churches. Repeatedly during the trial, the mayor and others displayed genuine curiosity about how Baptists behaved, asking in particular about the practice of "holy kisses."[4] In addition, while the exact nature of the religious dispute remains murky, it was a church undergoing a sectarian split. As Karin Gedge has observed about nineteenth-century church sex trials, sexual wrongdoing grabbed much more attention when there were two parties with clashing stakes in the outcome. As we saw with William Hogan in chapter 2, fights about religion could amplify and inform trials for sexual misconduct.[5]

More perplexing was the tack taken by her attorney. Why would Wintringham's attorney increase her culpability, saying that she was sweet-talked into intimacy, rather than accept her story of sexual liberty taken by force? In part, it was probably a recognition that a tale of seduction would resonate with an all-male jury. In the wake of the American Revolution, fathers and husbands fretted about the greater volition of women in courtship.[6] Perhaps they would sympathize with Mr. Wintringham, whose wife was at risk of being stolen from him. But a more direct and likely reason was the record of the relationship revealed in the trial. There was no denying that Mrs. Wintringham and Mr. Parkinson spent a lot of time together, visiting each other's houses regularly. To be sure, we know that friends and partners often commit sexual assault, a fact that might even have been appreciated by the jury. Nonetheless, in the eyes of the jury, she probably had to bear some responsibility for having allowed him so closely into her company. In fact, the defense would insist it was Parkinson's later rejection of her, both in not joining her in a church secession and spurning a personal connection, that had created the "fury of a woman scorned."[7] While this sexist trope certainly was not a compliment, it nonetheless hints at the power and autonomy she enjoyed within the church. There was something about the power of women within evangelical churches that helped shape fears of the reverend rake.

A sampling of some of the most prominent cases during the first half of the nineteenth century will illustrate the dynamic interplay between fears of charismatic preachers and anxieties about strong evangelical women.[8] By way of illustration, we will look more deeply into the case of Parkinson and Wintringham, because it neatly anticipates the themes of subsequent trials. Despite the variant details of the trials, there are some enduring themes and concerns that emerge, including fears of religious sophistry, hypocrisy, betrayal of trust, evangelical intimacy, and gender inversion. Added to this pattern of continuity, an important pattern of change emerges as the Second Great Awakening took hold in the Protestant mainstream North. By the 1830s the fears and criticisms of writers broadened and deepened. While earlier trials exposed charges of sexual wrongdoing driven by sectarian tensions, by the 1830s religion itself was put on trial. It was no longer individual pastors who betrayed the trust placed in them. Rather, now enthusiastic Christianity writ large was accused of encouraging fanaticism, destroying patterns of gender relations and marriage. As mainline Protestant denominations adopted revivalism and free will theology, women increasingly joined and led social reform campaigns to stamp out sin. In addition, more radical preachers began to question the pragmatic and civil foundations of marriage. In reaction, enthusiastic religion started to be portrayed as unmoored in reason and scripture. To document this transition to anti-enthusiasm literature, we will concentrate on reactions to the trial of Ephraim Avery, a Methodist minister accused of murdering

his adulterous lover, Sarah Cornell, and the case of the Prophet Matthias, who led a small sect of prominent New Yorkers in establishing
an experimental kingdom of heaven on earth. In both instances, the
focus of commentators was not so much on the particular pathology of
these individuals; rather, the writers used these cases to brush religious
enthusiasts with a broad stroke, suggesting they had concocted a "connexion of carnal feeling with spiritual fanaticism."[9]

Compared to that of her evangelical sisters of a couple decades later,
the activity of Eliza Wintringham was relatively modest. Nonetheless,
people around her noticed her strength and autonomy, which comes
through in the trial records. As is still all too familiar today, when a
man is accused of sexual misconduct, it is the character of his accuser
that is put on trial. This regrettable fact leaves us a full view of her behavior among her family, neighbors, and fellow parishioners. Whether
we entertain the prosecution's or defense's rendering of events, we can
appreciate the prominent figure she cut in her community. First, she organized a female prayer society. The leadership she showed in providing
religious instruction to other women was not appreciated. Under examination, she admitted the opposition of the deacons, noting that "the
society was not in the regular orders of the church."[10] The defense team
mockingly compared her prayer group to a Catholic convent: "Of this
nunnery, she had been prioress." But more troubling than her leadership over other women was the incorporation of a man into her group:
"and into its hallowed recesses, no man had ever the honour to be admitted, save Leonard Bleecker." To be granted such access, they said,
he had to lose his manhood: "shortly after his initiation, it seems that
some of his male attributes were found to annoy the sisterhood; he appears to have been accordingly unsexed." Thereafter, he was "admitted
to all the privileges of unrestrained and harmonious fellowship." But
his cost of entry was his being "dubbed with the endearing appellation
of SISTER BLEECKER." Taunting Wintringham, the defense noted:
"whether this metamorphosis was real, or only a monastic device, is a
point about which the prioress of the institution might perhaps have
given us some information." They also claimed that Wintringham had
said of Bleecker that she "could wind him round her finger."[11] Clearly,
Eliza Wintringham was a little too strong for their comfort.

Of course, the prosecution team representing Eliza Wintringham (or
more properly speaking, her husband) did not fully accept the tone of
this portrayal. But they did not deny her leadership of the prayer circle,

nor Bleecker's position within it. On the stand, when asked whether the deacons had voiced their concerns to her, she admitted scornfully, they "did object, but they did not object manfully." When questioned about the name of "Sister Bleecker," Wintringham said that she did not come up with the name herself; furthermore, she insisted, "all our society called him so, for he was the only one of the men that assisted at our evening prayers, and read prayers for us." When called to the stand himself, Bleecker insisted that "he was not ashamed" of the name and attributed it to those who were "jealous" of him. In fact, he suggested he led the prayer circle himself.[12] In the face of other witness testimony, this claim seems doubtful, but whatever his role, it is clear that observers had some discomfort with his participation in a majority-female prayer group. Anticipating later attacks on religious enthusiasm, the defense for Parkinson attributed his participation to his being "a man of dreams, visions, and supernatural communications;—a man noted for the enthusiasm and zigzaggery of his religious course." Perhaps he was "sailing in a bark hopefully bound to the port of immortal happiness," but his ship was unsturdy, "carrying so much canvass and so little ballast that every change of wind or variation of current wafts him from his track."[13] In other words, by endangering his self-mastery, his religious enthusiasm had lost him his manhood.

While Wintringham's social leadership was censured, her sexual comportment was particularly singled out for criticism during the trial. The defense argued that the "uncontrollable wantonness of her own nature" meant that any sexual advance from Parkinson "could not have been done against her consent." For Parkinson, she felt "so much partiality." This, they insisted, left her claims of assault implausible: "she has caressed, followed, flattered and inveigled the very man she has sworn to have assailed her virtue."[14] In so many words, if Parkinson made any advance, she clearly wanted it. They added to the sexism of this line of argument by again showing how she endangered the manhood of other men. They called on the jury to pity her husband. One witness for the defense, a Mrs. Tappan Remsen, said that Wintringham was "always harassing at her husband," saying that "he would not do." Remsen said that Eliza openly claimed "she was too much for him." Her husband "was not half enough for her." Eliza purportedly said he would "never touch her" unless she was "kicking and spurring him all the time."[15] Similarly, another witness said she heard Wintringham say she had "wicked eyes," for she could not look a man directly in the eyes without him seeing the desire burning within. While Victorian notions of female chastity were still coalescing at this time, the defense surely thought they could cash in on such testimony of female lust.[16]

One final way they tried to besmirch her sexual character was with a story of Wintringham exposing her breasts. When called to the stand, witness Catherine Perrine testified that she "saw her last winter expose her bosom to a gentleman"; she "pulled down her gown and asked him if that was not a handsome bosom." But on further inquiry, the witness admitted that Wintringham at the time was "suckling a young child." Nonetheless, the man in the room, Brother Baudoine, "hid his face and blushed" when Wintringham asked her question of him.[17] Eliza Wintringham's responses to this and the other stories about her sexual character were quite revealing. She stood defiant. She was not going hide behind the shield of the modest woman. Rather, she revealed a certain sexual frankness that must have been discomfiting to at least some of her audience. About the breast-baring incident, she said that a number of friends were in the room, including her husband. Yes, she said, she "might have suckled my child and said that it was no shame."[18] If Brother Baudoine stared, she was willing to call him on it. It was his problem, not hers. Similarly, her legal team characterized her jokes about her husband's sexual performance as "harmless sallies"; they reminded the audience that she had borne him children and said she made her jokes while her husband was easily within earshot.[19]

In its concluding remarks the defense would sharpen its characterization of these incidents. "The events of the present trial," they said, "have removed the dissembling guise from the painted Jezebel"; it had "exposed to public abhorrence the hidden abominations of this whitened sepulchre." About the breastfeeding incident, they said, "she stands convicted of shamelessly exposing to the blushing view of another man, that bosom about the pretended violation of which she now pathetically complains." But, they confided to the all-male jury, "these foul stains whiten into purity compared with the blackness of shame" of how she embarrassed her husband. Saying she deserved not the name of woman but instead to be called a "fiend in female attire," she was guilty "of repeatedly complaining, not under the shade of guilt concealing night, but in the open light of day, that her husband was insufficient to extinguish the fever of lust which was raging in her veins." How dare she, they said, have the "sufficient hardihood of visage, and nerve of tongue . . . [to] complain that *force* has been offered to her chastity."[20] Clearly, they did not like to see manhood mocked.

As seemingly over the top as this language is, it is matched by the language used to describe the sexual character of women in later trials (including Mary Connell, as we saw in the trial of William Hogan). Rhoda Davidson was one such woman. In 1844 in Massachusetts she had accused Reverend Joy Hamlet Fairchild of rape and fathering an illicit child. About her body, Fairchild's lawyers said that "so many men had a hand in the pie that it would puzzle a Philadelphia lawyer to tell who the child belonged to."[21] In the case of Issachar Grosscup in Canandaigua, New York, in 1848, the lawyers sketched the slide of Roxana Wheeler into sexual sin, beginning with reading books such as *Aristotle's Masterpiece*, texts "so filthy, so obscene, so as to be unfit for the perusal of even men, much less of women and young girls." After that, her descent was assured: "when a woman's virtue is gone, all is gone; then are deception, and stealing and falsehood, the fruits of her degradation." Having her "strong passions" awoken by "such infamous books," she "lost all control," causing her to "prostitute herself to their unholy influences," having illicit sex with a range of men before putting a child to Grosscup.[22] Just as in the present day, women came forward at serious risk to their reputations.

What had been the relationship between William Parkinson and Eliza Wintringham? They were undoubtedly close. For some, too close. Mr. Brower, brother-in-law to Mrs. Wintringham, said he found her "uncommonly attached to her clergyman," calling her "mad" in her devotion. Yet in this, he thought, she was not alone, for she was "more reserved with him than a great many others." In fact, he said, "flocks and droves" of women had "run over by day and by night" to him.[23] Mrs. Wintringham agreed she had a close relationship with Parkinson. She regularly had him over for dinner, offering particular support when his wife was traveling. But she seemed to possess a more critical detachment than her brother-in-law suggested. In fact, she thought that Parkinson had taken advantage of their friendship. For example, he once extracted a kiss out of sympathy. One day, when Parkinson was feeling sick, he laid his head down on a pillow, which sat on the lap of Sarah Canton. Canton was a servant to the Wintringhams. To comfort Parkinson, Canton leaned over and kissed him. Eliza said she found the behavior "very unbecoming." But Parkinson and Canton both insisted on its innocence, so much so that they badgered Mrs. Wintringham into also giving him a kiss. Finally, after being asked a third time, she "submitted" to the request, noting "ironically" that it was a "*holy kiss*."[24] Her wry personality shines through in such quotations.

Wintringham's relationship with Parkinson had become compli-
cated because she was in a bind: the church was undergoing division
and she and Parkinson were on the same side. The defense grilled Wintringham because she continued to invite Parkinson over to her house
after he had assaulted her. "It is true," she admitted, that she continued
to send for him to come to their house, as well as to visit his, but it was
"not near so frequently as before." Being the team player, she did not
want to draw suspicion to him. Yet once his assault became known, her
husband exclaimed he now saw "the reason why you were not latterly
so willing to go to Mr. Parkinson's as you used to be." As was true in
many of these trials, sectarian loyalties could influence interpersonal
relationships.[25]

The regular round of visiting was a feature of relations between ministers and women revealed in these trials. It caused some consternation.
For example, in the trial of Presbyterian minister Reverend Van Zandt
of Rochester in 1842, the prosecution noted that "clergymen have more
frequent opportunities" to take liberties with women, for "their avo-
cations bring them oftener in contact with the females of their congregations." It is an "important part of their pastoral duty to visit the
members of their churches at their own dwellings." Because "the male
part of the family is generally out of doors," they observed, their "visits are chiefly to the ladies." Van Zandt reportedly thought "pastoral
visits to his flock an incumbent duty," particularly to "the younger female members," addressing them "with particular zeal, frequency, and
fervor."[26] They concluded that he could not stare down the temptation.
Taking the minister's side in these situations, the counsel for John Maffitt groused, "If some females had been a little more reserved in their
attentions to Mr. Maffitt, we doubt not but many of the reproaches
which he has suffered, would have been avoided."[27]

In her study of female-pastoral relations, Karin Gedge has reported
that the manuscript record does not seem to corroborate such a close
relationship between ministers and women.[28] Instead, she suggests they
often strained to reach across separate spheres to work with one another. This is an important reminder. These trials exposed deep cultural
fears, but they were unlikely to be representative of typical lived experience. That said, in certain times and places, the mutual dependence between ministers and women would have been quite real. For example, as
Christine Heyrman has shown, the dependence of ministers on women
was greater when evangelicals were first getting their footing. Methodist circuit riders and other evangelicals holding down multiple seats

had to rely on the kindness of parishioners to provide lodging, food, and cleaning.[29] Still, if proximity between pastors and women was not the norm, why was this mutual devotion a flashpoint in the trials? For male lawyers and jurors, one suspects that their trust of pastors was being sorely tested. Any proximity that ministers had to wives and daughters left their husbands and fathers feeling vulnerable. These cultural anxieties, however much grounded in lived experiences, had the power to shape American culture. The feeling of female endangerment helped breed fears of clerical betrayal and hypocrisy. Eventually, the suspicion of clergymen would become strong enough to endanger religion writ large.

Again, the case of Eliza Wintringham proved an important harbinger. She accused him of violating his clerical vows. When Parkinson admitted to her that "from the time he first set eyes upon" her "he felt more love than for any in the world," she chastised him that "this conversation [is] very unlike a minister of the gospel." While he quickly apologized, she reported that not long after this he "attempted to put his hand in my bosom." Her sense of betrayal was real. She told him that "after such conduct," she could no longer "take bread from his hands." Now, "contrasting his public preaching with his private conduct," she began to doubt Christianity itself: "I began almost to think that there was no truth in religion, and that I must quit the church." Parkinson tried to salvage the church, reminding her that "you do not come for the love of me, but to commemorate Christ that died for you." Pleading further, he warned her not to "make a scandal," for any revelations could hurt the cause of Christ: "if you have any love for the cause of Christ, though you have none for me, you would never expose it." Then, more menacingly, he warned her that people would take his word over hers. Her reputation would only suffer if she made an accusation.[30]

From the prosecution's standpoint, Parkinson's most shocking evidence of hypocrisy was in his twisting of scripture to meet his sexual ends. While on the stand Wintringham described an assault wholly unwelcome. But her husband's lawyers described a twisted courtship dance of seduction. As previously noted, they probably felt the evidence of their close relationship too much a liability to their case. They seemed willing to concede that, in some limited fashion, she had led him on. The defense had argued that point directly. Playing to emerging notions of natural male lust, the defense team wondered how could Parkinson resist: "she pursued the defendant with a course of seduction, which, if lewdness were permitted to enter the region of blessedness, would be sufficient to draw an angel from his throne." She had "awakened by a lascivious kiss, the embers of nature that lay slumbering in his bosom."[31] Parkinson stood strong, but had he "yielded to the strong current of natural propensity, and sunk a victim to the arts of the prosecutrix," he would have deserved forgiveness "not only in the ingenuous heart of every honourable man, but even in the eye of christian charity."[32] In response, Wintringham's lawyers did not deny an affair, but they turned the tables. He, not she, pursued a course of seduction. He used professions of love coupled with artful deployments of scripture. Admitting some culpability to Wintringham, they said, "A woman has some title to compassion, if not to pardon, when she errs from strong seduction," for "she has two compassions to contend with, her own, and that of the seducer." But the deck was stacked when it was her minister: "if that seducer be her pastor, one of affected piety, who surprises her confidence, under the ambush of religion," she had much greater claims on sympathy. A man like Parkinson could create "a mysterious enthusiasm in her mind," by mixing "the poison of lust, with the ardor of devotion," thereby overtaking "her reason with false and dangerous appeals to faith."[33]

Using a common reference point for absolved sexual sin, Parkinson pointed to God's forgiveness of David for adultery.[34] Going yet further, he framed himself as simply a vessel of God's love, so that sleeping with him was no sin at all: "You do not go to me to worship me, but the Deity; the bread and wine is not my body and blood, but his; it is not contaminated by any act of mine; there is no sin in lying with me." He also reportedly called on notions of love within the Song of Solomon to convince Wintringham. After having chosen this scripture as his text for a public sermon, he afterward confided to her he had an alternative interpretation he wished to share with her alone: "I have preached to you from my pulpit the vehemence of my passion; I have proclaimed aloud that I was sick in love, but I will tell you in secret that I am sick *with* love, and love of none but you."[35] He was lovesick for Eliza.

Such a literal interpretation of the Song of Solomon was hardly a stretch. The text is an extended meditation on the sensual longing of two lovers who see each other as their one true love. Parkinson's interpretation seems to hint at the notions of spiritual wifery that we saw stirring around the early Mormons and will see expressed more fully with the Prophet Matthias. But there had been a long tradition of reading this text as an allegory for the relationship between God and Israel and then Christ and his church.[36] So the counsel for

Wintringham highlighted the perverseness of his suit: "Thus he not only cites scripture to dissuade her from virtue but preaches it *at her*, and for fear that he might not quite be understood takes that pious care of her soul to go and expound it to her at her own house, and to tell her what it meant; that all the other sisters were to hear and be deceived; she only, for whom he was sick in love, was to know the true meaning of his text." Framing their two spouses as "Mordecai at the gate," blocking them from true love, he said, "were I free, and you released; did you love me as I love you, how soon should I carry my desires into effect—for 'I am sick with love!'" Stepping back, the prosecution asked the audience sarcastically, "Is this not pretty conversation for a priest?" Parkinson, they insisted, had deeply abused his trust as a clergyman.[37]

The twin themes of clerical hypocrisy and the betrayal of trust would build over time.[38] In introducing the trial of Reverend Van Zandt, the publisher hoped its printing would provide a "useful lesson" to those who "too often place a blind confidence in their religious teachers, foolishly believing that they have not the same inclinations and appetites as other men." Van Zandt too easily captured his audience, for he was "a popular preacher," having a "pleasing address, and a showy kind of eloquence." Young men "continue[d] his fast friends" even after he was accused, because he had such a "free and easy" social demeanor. Speaking from the perch of 1842, the prosecution could point to the "annals of our courts of law for our present year" and find "religious teachers are as liable to the grosser passions of our nature as others." One could witness that "Episcopalian, Presbyterian, and Catholic clergymen" had all been charged with sexual offenses.[39] The reputation of all churches suffered.

Just as disturbing as a clergyman committing sexual offenses was the fact that their fellow clergymen would rally around them so as to protect the reputation of the church. Jacob Kerr, who openly exposed the sexual sins of Reverend David Barclay, lamented how the clergy turned on him. They were intent "on the delivery of their brother *David*" by censuring him, thereby trying to wipe "away the stigma from their brother—one of their fold." But he would use his pamphlet to lay bare this "dark, crooked, and truly mysterious business" of their cover-up.[40] The theme of a corrupt ministry would soon take hold in the world of American fiction; we will see that the case of Ephraim Avery probably had the biggest role to play in that transition. So strong had anticlerical prejudice become that by 1845 the lawyer for Joy Hamlet Fairchild would complain that being an eminent minister made one *more* vulnerable to suspicion: "the crafty accuser, as well as the trembling accused is aware that by reason of one of the most singular and deplorable, but at the same time most common infirmities of our nature, we are prone to believe the accusation just, in proportion to the exalted standing and professed moral purity of the party assailed."[41] As literary scholar David Reynolds has shown, this was probably more a new sentiment borne of democratic suspicions of the elite, even if perhaps grounded in the natural human impulse of jealousy.[42]

The jury for the Parkinson trial were left with competing images: a hypocritical reverend rake who used his clerical position and personal access to exploit Wintringham, and a spiteful shrew who had embarrassed various men by taking charge in church and family matters. Mayor Clinton's charge to the jury left no doubt where he stood. Before launching into a long speech, he told them that he did not want to "add to their fatigue" after "the unprecedented length of this trial," especially since it is "a mere assault and battery." Nonetheless, he hoped they appreciated that it was "of great importance to a considerable portion of the community." This was evidenced by its having attracted "so many eminent counsel" and a "great number of witnesses," as well as the "great anxiety manifested" by the audience. Offering some support to Wintringham, he urged the jury to deliver a guilty verdict if the charges were true. But he then expressed regret that this verdict would have the "unfortunate tendency" to "disparage religion." He also admitted he had wished the entire matter had "been buried in silence." Clinton next provided a highly detailed interpretation of the evidence, highlighting in particular the fact that Eliza Wintringham had maintained her friendship with Parkinson after the assaults occurred. He ended by tilting the scales of justice even more obviously. He expressed concern for Parkinson's congregation, the majority of whom had stayed loyal to him in a previous church trial in which his innocence was upheld. He worried even more for Parkinson personally. If the jury found him guilty, the mayor predicted, "it will be like a death warrant to the defendant." He would have to retreat in shame to some isolated "corner" of society or stay and spend the "miserable remnant of his life in penitence and tears." If, however, they found him "not guilty," the "consequences of this scrutiny will be sufficient to give a useful lesson to him." It could prove "a great blessing," the mayor said, "if it were possible that your verdict could be at once reconciled with justice and the wishes of the virtuous, religious, and truly respectable congregation who take so much interest in his fate." Not surprisingly, then, the jury delivered up the "not guilty" verdict the mayor had pitched.[43]

If Eliza Wintringham lost this particular court battle, the arguments advanced by her lawyers still carried forward in future cases. So too would those of the defense. These lawyers were wrestling dynamics beginning to unfold in American Christianity writ large. As the experience of Eliza Wintringham helps indicate, women did find an important new realm of choice and action in evangelical religion. If she was perhaps a singular character in how she could mock the manhood of the deacons, stare down a man while breastfeeding, and tease her husband about his sexual performance, she was certainly not alone in finding empowerment in church activities. As the Second Great Awakening took hold, there was a wider variety of religious choices available, enabling women to independently join new churches. As we saw in the fight between the Disciples of Christ and Mormons in Ohio and the fight within the Catholic Church in Philadelphia, the competition unleashed by the Second Great Awakening demanded that women and men alike pick churches and pick sides. Even further, as Catherine Brekus has shown, in the second and third decades of the nineteenth century, more upstart sects were giving women access to preaching.[44] While that opportunity would recede as evangelical sects sought respectability, new avenues of social activism opened for women as revivalism and Arminian theology took hold in mainline denominations, most notably among New School Presbyterians.[45] This increased opportunity for female action helped inspire a reaction of fear. Women were warned not to put themselves in the hands of unscrupulous ministers. Fears about the reverend rake could be deployed to control women.

It is not an accident that Eliza Wintringham could find room for religious action in her Baptist congregation. Gaining traction during the era of the American Revolution and then rapidly expanding in the early nineteenth century, the Baptists were at the vanguard of religious enthusiasm in America. As would be true of other enthusiastic sects and denominations, the Baptists blurred the line between the sacred and the secular, with religious activities suffusing everyday life and time. The laity was much more fully conscripted into upholding gospel order, with believers joining as brothers and sisters to tend to one another's spiritual growth.[46] Eliza Wintringham's prayer circle was a good example of this. Harnessing the power of the laity would prove a key to Christianity's progress. The only church that would expand even more rapidly than the Baptist church in the early nineteenth century was the

Methodist church. Not officially organized until 1784, by 1820 Methodists numbered half a million followers.[47] They took great advantage of the energy and piety of women, including giving women the ability to ascend into the pulpit to preach.[48] Thus, when the Methodist minister Ephraim Avery was accused of murdering Sarah Cornell, a single seamstress in his congregation, it sent shock waves through the nation. By 1834, the year following the trial, at least fourteen different texts had been published about the case, and a New York theater had staged a play about it for months to packed houses (see figure 4.1).[49]

One work in particular, Catherine Williams's *Fall River: An Authentic Narrative*, published in 1833, would particularly influence perceptions of the clergy. By moving away from the trial transcript and reassembling the facts of the case into a narrative, she was handmaiden to moving fears of the reverend rake into the world of fiction, with authors like Nathaniel Hawthorne and George Lippard both taking inspiration from the case.[50] What will most command our attention about her text here is the way her book helped inform a growing literature of anti-enthusiasm

FIGURE 4.1. "A Very Bad Man" (1833). Ephraim Avery appears here as a cold-blooded killer strangling Sarah Cornell to cover his own sexual crime. Library of Congress.

in America. Of course, such criticism had appeared earlier, with authors like Charles Chauncy criticizing revivalists during the First Great Awakening. But as historian James Bratt has shown, starting in the late 1820s and running until the end of the Second Great Awakening, a large and variegated literature taking aim at revivalists and revivalism would emerge in America.[51] I would add that this strain of criticism was actually aimed more broadly than just against revivalism, targeting other forms of religious enthusiasm that might fall outside classic definitions of the evangelical tradition. In previous chapters we have seen how new religious movements like the Shakers and Mormons were accused of fanaticism. In the next chapter we will see how John Humphrey Noyes's perfectionist community was also singled out for spreading delusions. What will come through most fully in the publications we will be considering here, works on Ephraim Avery and the Prophet Matthias, is the call to gender order in anti-enthusiasm writings. These writers helped shape a demand for a moderate and orderly expression of female piety. From their perspective, religious enthusiasm could produce gendered extremes with women either overstepping their bounds in social activism or cowering at the feet of charismatic imposters. The repeated sting of sexual scandal would play a key role in the collapse of the Second Great Awakening in the 1840s in the North.[52]

Catherine Williams looked with disdain at the Methodists who had risen rapidly in New England. As a genteel Episcopalian, she did not want her work to call religion itself into disrepute, but she was willing to challenge the Methodists, for their form of enthusiastic religion and their disruption of gender relations were too dangerous.[53] In *Fall River* she highlighted the Reverend Ephraim K. Avery, a man accused (and Williams was convinced guilty) of seducing, impregnating, and then killing the single mill worker Sarah Cornell. Williams used the occasion of this case to work out a general critique of Methodism and revivalism more generally. Even before her book was published, she thought the affair had worked to expose the Methodists. She opined that the public notice the case had gained had "one good tendency which is obvious": it had "generated a suspicion of those noisy, ranting professors, who go about interrogating every one they meet, to know 'if they love the Lord.'" Such pushy people, she insisted, were "none but grossly ignorant or hypocritical people." A decorous Christianity was the proper mode of religious expression. She trusted that the affair had not "lessened the respect felt for those modest, practical, and retiring Christians, who mind their own concerns," those who would not "obtrude themselves or their own religion, except where propriety sanctions, and duty authorize them to do it." Many opportunities for religious influence existed, but it could be exercised without "disgusting people with impertinent interrogations, discovering an impudence and boldness inconsistent with their sex and professions."[54] Religious enthusiasts had been invading the public square with their camp meetings and political causes in ways that discomfited many more orthodox Americans.[55] Williams was one so discomfited.

Williams's book was composed of two sections: first, the history of Cornell and Avery, and then, an appendix in which she shares her reactions to a Methodist camp meeting she had attended out of curiosity about a decade earlier. Apparently, she now felt more emboldened to share her criticisms of what she had witnessed. In both sections she would level serious criticisms at the church. In the first, she decried how Methodism helped cause Cornell to be a "stranger in a strange land," left without sufficient social support to navigate courtship and society.[56] She also sharply criticized Methodist ministers for exploiting ungovernable passions, leaving believers morally unmoored. Finally, she criticized the hypocrisy of the church leadership during the trial, insisting they closed ranks to protect one of their own. The appendix would reprise many of these themes but would particularly highlight the physical embodiment of Methodist passions, showing scenes of swooning, babbling, and seizures. She was particularly disturbed by the unfettered social mixing of people at camp meetings, leaving women open to insult and assault. She took exception to the familiar and popular style of Methodist preaching, insisting that it did particular damage to women whose delicacy was badly harmed in the pulpit.

Williams narrated Sarah Cornell's fall in joining the Methodists. Cornell had grown up in a traditional Calvinist Congregational church. In a letter Cornell wrote to her sister, she described her spiritual alienation from her friends in joining the Methodists: "perhaps my friends may think strange that I chose a people different in their views and opinions from that which any of my friends have embraced." But, for her, this spiritual declaration of independence was what she needed: "let me tell you my dear sister that the Methodists are my people—with them by the grace of God I was spiritually born."[57] But Williams saw tragedy in this choice; there was no real stable community to be had among the Methodists. Further increasing an itinerant tendency already inherent in being a mill worker, being a Methodist caused Cornell to be a "moving planet." In Cornell's own words, she now "belonged to a people who did not believe in staying long in a place." This was true for ministers too, for circuit riders and even settled pastors were regularly rotated by the Methodist leadership. "Poor unfortunate being," Williams concluded, "she did not realize the danger of changing neighborhoods so often." From Williams's perspective this left Cornell without the reliable support of family and friends who could protect her reputation. Williams feared that "a continual round of going to meetings night and day" would serve to damage "the characters of young women." The "appearance of superior devotedness" would invite "rivalship in churches," making such women targets of the "barbarous insinuations" of gossip.[58] We will see that Williams especially saw the spontaneous communities of camp meetings as prone to the dangers of social atomization.

The relationship between ministers and young women was particularly fraught in this fluid social environment. There was no committed stewardship on the part of the pastor for his flock. Instead, Williams said that Methodist ministers used charismatic authority to attract misguided devotion. She opened her book by warning young women against "that idolatrous regard for ministers, for preachers of the gospel, which at the present day is a scandal to the cause of Christianity." It was, she warned, an "absurd custom of crowding round some handsome preacher on every occasion in order to share his smiles and be distinguished by his gracious gallantries." Ministers were, after all, "mortal men" who would find it hard to resist the temptations bestowed by "continual flattery."[59] A decade earlier the Methodist preacher John Maffitt had invited similar commentary in the Boston press. When J. T. Buckingham was indicted for libel for his criticisms of Maffitt in his paper, he said he wanted to prove wrong "all those young ladies of Boston" who were "overflowing with love" and seemed "ready to sink into [Maffitt's] arms." Even "all those silly old women, whether in breeches or in petticoats," seemed smitten with Maffitt.[60]

From this perspective, the ministers encouraged this devotion by playing on the emotions of their audience. Methodism, Williams concluded, was a "religion of feelings and frames." Once accustomed to the enthusiastic style of their preachers, one could only stay engaged by "constant application of the means which created it," that is, "by frequent attendance on those exciting meetings where highly wrought feeling and sometimes hysterical affection is often mistaken for devotion"[61] (see figure 4.2). Able to cultivate such an appetite in their audience, the Methodists thrived on competition, inserting themselves into new communities, grabbing women's attention where the people

FIGURE 4.2. "Camp Meeting" (ca. 1832), oil painting. Attributed to Alexander Rider. Billy Graham Center Museum, Sacred Arts Collection. Notice the man in the foreground capturing the swooning woman beneath the breasts and two men speaking into the ears of women next to the preaching box. Courtesy of Buswell Library Archives & Special Collections, Wheaton College, IL.

already had spiritual guides. Should a minister, Williams wondered, really be relying on the "charity of poor factory girls" to support new churches?[62] Thus, female freedom and reverend rakes were seen to reinforce one another.

Commanding such attention, Williams said the ministers were willing to betray their own devotees. They cared, she insisted, first and foremost about protecting their fellow minister. While the jury (which heard from 196 witnesses over twenty-seven days), ultimately found Ephraim Avery not guilty, Williams insisted that this was because the Methodists had subverted the legal process. Quoting from another publication, *Strictures on the Case of Ephraim K. Avery*, she validated the sentiment that "never was a criminal trial instituted and carried through in this country in which so much baseness was manifest, so much chicanery practised, the public, the government, the court and the jury, so deeply insulted, nor an accused man acquitted with such a chain of circumstances against him." This was attributed to the church hierarchy: "The whole machinery of the methodist church has been brought into operation and its artillery made to bear on the battlements of the hall of justice. Perjury, base and foul has been committed on the stand, under the sanction of a religious garb to protect a wretch from punishment." Reflecting on Methodist conduct, she wondered whether "the proceedings of these reverend gentlemen resembled those of a religious association." Instead, she thought it looked more "like a combination of men for secular and political purpose—a league offensive and defensive." She wondered rhetorically: "Has it appeared their object is to elicit truth, or suppress it?"[63] Thus, clerical hypocrisy came to define an entire organized ministry. No longer was the reverend rake a solitary sinner; now his clerical allies were complicit in his crimes.

In her appendix on camp meetings, Williams would move yet further, not only criticizing the conduct of the Methodist clergy during the trial but also calling into question Methodists' mode of evangelicalism. Much akin to other anti-revivalist writing being published at this time, she provides a formalist critique of religious enthusiasm.[64] Hers was a respectable religion, one that knew its place. In the mind, it didn't allow emotion to overtake reason; in society, it kept religion properly within the sacred realm, not invading secular time and space. She noted that "men's eyes are now partially open to the great evils of fanaticism generally, and of Camp-Meetings in particular," and she published her criticisms because "everything known on that subject ought to come out." At camp meetings, the godly and the sinners formed a "motley assembly." She found their "free intermingling of society" quite "dangerous," the "tumbling and falling about" quite "indecent." Unguarded camp meetings too easily swelled with "drunkards and gamblers, and horse jockies and pickpockets" alongside those seeking religion.[65] The Methodists also mixed the sacred and profane by speaking to God as if he were one of them. In the camp meetings, she said, Methodists showed "such familiarity with [the] Deity" that God would lose his proper dignity and distance. She said they "frequently speak of the Almighty, and speak to him too" as if "he were an equal" or "even an inferior," for they called on him to perform things for them. Such enthusiasts could not "be reasoned with," but she held out hope that "the light of science breaks upon their minds," so that "bigotry, superstition, and fanaticism" will vanish.[66]

Williams contended that womanhood was much endangered when under the influence of enthusiastic religion. For her, there was a deeply visceral element to this risk. One could see the damage enthusiasm did to their bodies. She saw one "young woman of extreme beauty" "staggering through the Camp, with her clothes torn and her locks disheveled." She was "wringing her hands and mourning that people were not more engaged." If her devotion seemed genuine, others simply gawked: "She appeared to excite attention wherever she moved through the crowd. We observed, as she passed along, that the young men exchanged winks and jogged each other's elbows."[67] She later found this same woman collapsed in a tent. She had a few young men gathered around her, and she looked much worse than before: "her bloom was entirely gone, and her haggard look and tangled hair gave her the appearance of something that had recently escaped from a mad house." Williams asked her directly whether she had a "mother to take care of her," a question that was received with "scorn and anger." As Williams intimates with this young woman, women in camp meeting crowds were in danger of unwanted advances, reporting "a great deal of joggling, pinching, and looking under bonnets." A woman she knew was left "pinched black and blue."[68] There simply was insufficient supervision to protect women. In fact, Cornell herself had been taken by Avery at a camp meeting.

These criticisms centered on risks to female members of the crowd, but Williams also worried about the damage done to femininity when women took the pulpit at camp meetings. Williams said she had long been "a great stickler for women's preaching," so it was not as if she were against it in principle. While attending the camp meeting, she heard that one of her favorites was going to ascend the pulpit, so she rushed to go see her. In the past this preacher had been of "very mild and pleasing manners," and "graceful and winning in her manner." Within the context of a home she could talk easily and be heard, and her doctrine was always reliable. But in this camp meeting environment, even though her teachings were much the same, she now had to use "great exertion" to deliver them. This left her countenance ruined: "the blood looked as though it would burst through her face, the veins of her forehead and temples as well as those of the neck, 'swelled up like whip chords,' and her mouth, usually of sweet and placid expression, from her efforts to speak loud was absolutely disfigured." Williams left this experience convinced this was a woman now "out of her place." While her sermon was better than others, "the great effort of retaining such a masculine attitude entirely destroyed the effect."[69] After then witnessing a "very bold and uncouth looking young female" in the pulpit, Williams said her "faith in woman's preaching began to waver," and she left the scene.

Her impression of revivalist preaching was further reinforced when she saw an "African upon a stump" who gathered a "great crowd" that was "listening with open ears and gaping mouths." The sermon was punctuated with "shouts of the mob" who were crying and clapping, seemingly in jest. His performance inspired "a peal of laughter, long and loud from the profane rabble."[70] In this, Williams was echoing other criticism that had helped drive a wedge between white and Black Methodists. The author of the pamphlet Methodist Error, who self-identified as a "Wesleyan Methodist," had warned against "extravagant emotions and bodily exercises." He singled out the "black Bethel church in Philadelphia" for the "immoderate noise" of its services, which he said drew negative attention as people walked by the church. He was "not sorry" that African Methodists "have now parted from us," for it would allow white Methodists to more easily move in a decorous and modest direction.[71] Enthusiastic religion, in short, was both undignified and dangerous to femininity. Race, class, and gender bias helped underwrite anti-enthusiasm writings.

Two years after Williams published her book, another case of sexual scandal would prove further damaging to enthusiastic religion. Robert Matthews, otherwise known as the Prophet Matthias, would seize the attention of New York and the nation when he was put on trial for murder. While his group of followers was small (only about a dozen people would join his "kingdom"), they were from the upper echelons of New York society. In addition, his claims were astonishing: in turns he said he possessed the "Spirit of the Father" (and therefore eclipsed even Jesus in importance) and claimed to be the Prophet Matthias from the Old Testament. One of the key figures in the society, Elijah Pierson, died during the residency in Westchester, New York, which had raised the questions about a potential homicide. Adding sexual scandal to the mix, Matthias questioned the legitimacy of earthly marriages, calling for spiritual unions, sealing couples who were spiritual matches.[72] Two of the most important published reactions to the career of Matthias were William Leete Stone's *Matthias and His Impostures; or the Progress of Fanaticism* and Gilbert Vale's *Fanaticism: Its Sources and Influence*.[73] Vale's book was written as a response to Stone's. The authors sharply disagreed on who was to blame for the events that unfolded in the commune. But as their titles both suggest, they could agree about the dangers of "fanaticism." Both published in 1835, their books deeply resembled the work of Catherine Williams, highlighting the dangers of religious enthusiasm. Both also, like Williams, highlighted gender disruption caused by revivalism.

William Leete Stone was the son of a Presbyterian clergyman and was married to Susannah Wayland, sister of Francis Wayland, president of Brown University and an important national voice for moderation in religion and education. Like his father-in-law, Stone was a moderate in his politics and religion, rejecting "ultraism" in all its forms.[74] In writing his book about Matthias, he saved his greatest criticism not for Matthias himself but for Frances Folger, an ultraist evangelical woman who played leading roles in the Female Missionary Society and in the Retrenchment Society. The "delusion—gross, palpable, and lamentable" of Matthias, he believed, had "its origin in the fanaticism" of Folger. He called her "the original author of the whole chain of fanatical measures which had prepared the way for Matthews."[75] But Folger had never even joined Matthews. In fact, he received her as a "rival," so why did Stone put such responsibility on her?[76] Part of it was undoubtedly personal. Frances Folger had publicly shamed his wife for her ostentatious dress at church.[77] But he also had serious problems with Folger's brand of religious enthusiasm, which she spread among upper New York society.

To Stone, both the Female Missionary Society and the Retrenchment Society represented an unwarranted arrogation of female religious authority, which was aided by misguided clergy. The Retrenchment Society targeted "the gayety and extravagance of female dress" and other luxuries. Folger called on those who joined to forego "all costly articles of dress or furniture" and "to wear no ornaments or jewels." In addition, they were to give up luxurious foods, being called on "to eat no cake, pastry, sweetmeats, or butter" and "to drink neither tea nor coffee." A clergyman ally agreed to preach on the society's behalf. Emboldened by his support, Stone said Folger and her followers took on a "spirit of severity and bitterness—of censure and denunciation" against anyone "who did not walk agreeably to their standards." Using the same anti-Catholic swipe as William Parkinson's lawyer in criticizing Eliza Wintringham, Stone said this feeling of "spiritual pride" was adopted "not only by the lady superior, but by her disciples."[78]

The Female Missionary Society too, Stone said, was aided by the "religious knight-errantry" of a clergyman. This minister had validated the idea of Folger and her followers that they could accomplish a "speedy conversion of the whole city by a system of female visitation." They were to "enter houses indiscriminately" in groups of two praying for the inhabitants' conversion. If perhaps "well-intentioned," they were "misguided" in their zeal, visiting hotels and even the home of the clergyman who had earlier preached their dress reform sermon, trying to "convert him within his own house." Folger converted the wife of her husband's cousin Benjamin Folger, allegedly taking over his house for prayer sessions. According to Stone, she had "obtained complete and entire ascendency in spiritual matters in his family," making the home "for a long time the centre of her operations" with "female prayer-meetings" being held "on any, and sometimes every, day and evening of the week."[79] She allegedly attacked her own father, a clergyman himself, as unconverted. Witnessing this all, her husband was "rendered miserable by her course" of "fanaticism."[80] As with Eliza Wintringham's husband, Stone delivers a depiction of a man embarrassed by a wife overstepping her bounds.

But it wasn't Folger or her particular clergymen allies who deserved all the blame. According to Stone, evangelicalism itself had gotten out of control. Stone framed his book as an attempt to protect evangelical Christianity by providing a warning against the "indulgence of a self-righteous and fanatical spirit" and the "dangers of enthusiasm."[81] Frances Folger and Matthias both had drawn inspiration from revivalists who had abandoned the customary controls of reason and the revealed word of the Bible. Sounding much like Alexander Campbell in his critique of Joseph Smith, Stone cited favorably the "wisdom" of an eminent minister who said he saw trouble whenever "people become better than the Bible." Stone concluded that the "ultraism of the day," especially among "new measure men," was undercutting the stability of Christianity. Drawing a direct connection between revivalists like

Presbyterian Charles Finney and the Prophet Matthias, he concluded that "nothing can be more dangerous in spiritual matters than tampering with the sacred Scriptures, either by adding to, or taking from, the simple letter of the written word, or wresting its plain and obvious meaning."[82] In fact, Stone connected Finney and Matthias even more directly. He said the religious enthusiasm of Matthias began when he started to attend the services of Edward Norris Kirk, an ally of Finney's, with his wife observing to their daughter, "If your father goes to hear this man preach any more, he will go wild or crazy." "Still," Stone observed, "he behaved rationally enough until one evening when he went to hear Mr. Finney. The services were continued until a late hour, and Matthews came home in a state bordering upon phrensy." Following Finney's lead, Matthias began to be "ultra in his notions," swearing off "meats" and all "strong drinks." It was then not long before he began to receive direct revelations, carrying himself yet further beyond the received wisdom of the Bible.[83]

What made this wave of religious enthusiasm seem so unsettling was that it had now invaded the middle and upper classes. For religious moderates in mainline denominations, it was bad enough that the Methodists were gaining market share. At least Methodists had begun to tamp down some of their more disruptive tendencies.[84] But Methodist methods and beliefs had now seemingly infected the well-to-do. Speaking of an interdenominational prayer group that grew out of Frances Folger's efforts, Stone complained that the members were not "drawn from the lowest and most ignorant walks of life like the followers of Joanna Southcote and the miserable Mormons" but were rather "for the most part well-informed and highly respectable persons, of both sexes."[85] At the end of his book, Stone insisted it was not "the low, the ignorant, and the vulgar who have been the subjects of the delusions we have been unfolding"; rather at "every stage" these errors occurred "among highly respectable and intelligent citizens, men of wealth, of information, and of great public and private worth."[86] In western New York, where Finney and his allies gained their greatest victories, the scenes were especially frightening. Comparing the infamous Kentucky Revival of 1800 to the Burned-Over District, he said Kentucky's scenes of jerking and falling converts were "scarcely more extravagant or revolting than have been witnessed in our own day, and in some of the most enlightened regions of our own state. Look at the present condition of the churches of western New-York, which have become in truth, 'a people scattered and peeled.'" Suggesting again the danger of gender disruption, Stone told of how the Presbyterian revivalist Jedediah Burchard had taken to arranging "a company of persons of both sexes upon their knees to pray." Placing them in lines across from each other, he would walk between them, calling on them with "great violence" to "agonize" for their sins.[87]

From Stone's perspective, believing that one could become "wise above what is written" could lead to spiritual pride and dangerous gender innovations.[88] The religious adherents first gathered by Frances Folger in the Retrenchment Society had joined a wider interdenominational circle led by James Latourette, derisively known as the "Holy Club."[89] This group had "claimed extraordinary gifts," including "working miracles through the prayer of faith" and the power of "prophecy," believing in "dreams and visions," which they then shared for "comment and interpretation." Both men and women delivered prophecies at their meetings. They soon convinced each other that everything had to be sanctified. They denied any special designation to the Sabbath, insisting all days deserved holy observance. They questioned "the institution of marriage," maintaining that "a single life was essential to purity and holiness." Anticipating the teachings of Matthias, some among them insisted that "all marriage bonds were dissolved." From their perspective, the End Times were at hand: "they did not believe in a final Day of Judgment, but maintained that mankind were judged for their deeds every day." This teaching led one "lady orator" to become "almost frantic." Screaming "wildly," she "danced back and forth across the room, declaring, 'This is the judgment-seat of Christ—the Judge is now on the throne, and he is judging every one of you now.'" Once the door to prophesying was open, Stone concluded, it was inevitable that Matthias would walk in. He would deliver "wild, disjointed, and incoherent" sermons to his audience.[90] While some received him with skepticism, others who had been adequately prepared would "drink in every word of it, with as much eagerness as though the imposter's lips had really been touched with live coal from the altar."[91] Stone provided a demand-side analysis of religious enthusiasm. It was the crowd as much as the preachers who were to blame.[92]

The prophecies of Matthias about gender tacked hard away from Frances Folger and her circle. He looked to restore an Old Testament patriarchy. But rather than winning the approval of Stone, whom we have witnessed questioning the assertiveness of women like Frances Folger, Stone condemned the hardline patriarchy of Matthias. In other words, in his reaction to Matthias, we see the other side of his vision of gender moderation. Stone downplayed the ideas of free love associated with Matthias that had circulated in the wider press. As an ally of Benjamin and Ann Folger, he knew the damage these stories could do to them. To him, Matthias demanded too much subjection from women. Matthias provided his hearers a list of abominations, including preaching to women without their husbands. He further "would denounce bitterly all women who did not keep at home. Like Sarah of old, he insisted that it was the duty of women to remain in the tent." He said all who did not "follow her example would be damned," a teaching Stone deemed "nonsense." The misogyny of Matthias showed through even more clearly when he preached that "everything that has the smell of woman will be destroyed," because "woman is the capsheaf of the abomination of desolation—full of all depravity." Women needed to seek deliverance by becoming "obedient," for "in a short time the world will take fire and dissolve." The Folgers told Stone that before they joined Matthias, Mrs. Folger had led a "female school" along with several other women in their home. Matthias told her she now was to "listen to no teacher but her husband" and most certainly was "in no case to preach or teach herself," because "all female preaching was now to be considered unlawful."[93] From Stone's perspective, Matthias had failed to "pay that respectful deference to the female character which is exacted in respectable society," instead imitating the "Mohammedans" and viewing them as "inferior beings."[94] He could only shake his head in disapproval.

According to Stone, Matthias's vision of manhood came to be symbolized by his beard, which he had determined never to trim or shave. Elijah Pierson, who had copied the example of Matthias in growing his beard long, explained the choice, saying, "The beard is the grand visible distinction between the male and female." It signified "age, wisdom, strength, and gives dignity to the being God had made lord of his creation." When Matthias was in danger of a mob attack, a leader of the gathered crowd offered to help Matthias escape on the condition that he shave it off. Some had come to believe that "the secret of the prophet's power over his infatuated followers, like the strength of Samson, lay in his hair." When the leader entered the house and shared that "there were a party of fellows in ambush by the way, determined to seize him and cut off his beard," he grudgingly decided that "discretion was the better part of valour" and allowed the leader to "perform the operation of divesting him at once of his glory and his strength."[95] Akin to the attempted castration of Joseph Smith, we can see how notions of spiritual power and charismatic manhood could be linked.

Stepping back from the immediate events he had observed and taking a longer view of Christian history, Stone saw gender and sexual disruption as endemic to religious fanaticism. He surveyed a wide range of groups, including ancient Gnostics, Fifth Monarchy Men, the Cochranites, and in the present day the "lascivious Mormons" and "sensual Perfectionists."[96] A careful "examination of the history of heresies and impostures" revealed "that whether arising from enthusiasm, or phrensy, or from deliberate imposture," each group had one common feature, that being "licentiousness and criminal intercourse between the sexes." While Stone rejected theories of "animal magnetism" posited by some, he did think that the "principles of sympathy, imitation, nervous sensibility, and imagination" helped explain these events. Only by showing a sufficient Christian modesty and moderation, subjugating one's religious feelings to reason and the Bible, could such errors be avoided.[97]

Gilbert Vale would write his history of the Prophet Matthias to correct the representations of Stone. And yet they agreed that gender disruption was a product of religious enthusiasm. Their work, together with that of Catherine Williams, helped add a popular dimension to the antienthusiasm tracts being written by theologians. Vale based his book on the testimony of Isabella, known to us today as Sojourner Truth.[98] Since she was an African American enthusiast, he worked hard to corroborate her testimony and validate her character. Her testimony was vital. She had been an eyewitness and participant in many of the events tied to the career of the Prophet Matthias. While Stone had strongly suggested that Isabella was involved in a plot to poison Elijah Pierson, Vale cleared her of any such charges. He also took a much more critical view of Benjamin and Ann Folger, the chief informants for Stone. Because the Folgers became intimately involved in the project of spiritual unions, his book provides much more information about how this religious commune began to question the foundations of marriage. In his book, one can see how a theology of spiritual wifery was being formulated just when Joseph Smith and John Humphrey Noyes were also beginning to reimagine marriage.[99] In other words, we are moving beyond mere sexual scandal to an avowed religious defense of unorthodox sexual relations.

Like Stone, Vale warned strongly against the dangers of religious enthusiasm. As an avowed deist, he seemed to have an even more grim assessment of the susceptibility of the people to religious delusion.[100] Vale worried that whenever passions were given precedence, it was nearly impossible to discern human and spiritual sensations. It was, he concluded, the "great source of fanaticism" when people "mistook [their] feelings for divine impressions."[101] He found it troubling that "sincere piety" proved "not a protection against the grossest errors in principles, and the grossest abuse of established morals." This would happen whenever people were willing "to ascribe their feelings to divine influence." If feelings are *natural*, but mistaken for Divine," they are readying themselves to be "dupes of fervent fools or designing knaves."[102] Thus, the followers of Matthias were ready to receive his highly unorthodox teachings on sex and gender. Vale found that only "great fanaticism" could have produced "this strange mixture of spiritual credence and carnal impulses" that came to define the kingdom.[103] In taking stock of Benjamin and Ann Folger, he concluded that he was willing to grant them religious sincerity, but this then convinced him that "conversion is no protection against crimes." In fact, the lesson to be derived was that "any degree of grossness is compatible with sincere religious profession, and the most pious practices and appearances." If some might find that his "language is perhaps strong," he nevertheless insisted it was justified.[104]

While Stone concentrated on the twin, but countervailing, forces of female assertiveness and exaggerated patriarchy in enthusiastic religion, Vale focused on exposing thought about spiritual unions.[105] Matthias from the start had struck at conventional marriage, insisting "that God had never authorized wicked people to multiply, and that preachers who, in the marriage ceremony, said that God had joined them together, were sent of the devil."[106] Thereby calling most all marriages into question (for none but his followers were holy), Matthias freed people to find their true spiritual match. According to Vale, both Matthias and Ann Folger encouraged these views in one another, as they inched ever closer to Ann abandoning Benjamin for Matthias. Vale speculated that they had both believed they had "arrived at a greater degree of perfection than other members of the kingdom." Before consummating their union, they purified themselves in bathing ceremonies, feeling they "had no occasion for masks of shame" and could "subdue their passion in the greatest temptations."[107] Believing in the righteousness of her course, Ann Folger shared with her husband the revelation that Matthias was her match spirit. Vale found it extraordinary that a "virtuous, respected, and amiable married female" would "deliberately undertake to induce her husband to give her up" to another man.[108]

Spiritual unions (otherwise known as spiritual wifery) were to be based on finding a soul mate who matched you in holiness. While a married mother, Ann Folger could yet believe herself a "virgin," for her sex with Benjamin did not represent a union of spiritual equals. Vale could not claim to understand the "mystical" dimensions of her thinking, but he deemed it a "hallucination, or the doctrine of visions or dreams, supposed to be emanations from God." She and Matthias could propose that Ann abandon Benjamin for Matthias, but "if a revelation, then no shame." They even further proposed that she was to give birth to a "holy son." To make up for Benjamin's loss, they then encouraged Benjamin to take the daughter of Matthias, herself a married woman, as his spiritual wife. Thus, Vale insisted, had the "lust of the flesh" been "ascribed to God."[109]

While we can see glimmers of the theological innovations about marriage and sex developing here, ideas that reverberated with that of contemporary perfectionists, Vale maintained his skepticism.[110] He concluded that the "doctrine of Matthias on the subject of marriage" was "extremely artful," seemingly based on "lofty morals and high pretentions to superior power and divine wisdom." But he saw them more as "calculated to overcome the barriers to female purity." While he believed Matthias remained true to Mrs. Folger in their union, he thought his ideas might easily be extended to unions with a "community of females," following the "manner of Mahomet." From Vale's perspective, this was all an act of rationalization. Matthias first decided he wanted Ann Folger as a wife. Once he gained her, he was "obliged to enforce and enlarge upon his former doctrines, of the marriage of devils, match spirits, &c." He had also previously encouraged people to take advantage of God's bounty. This, "in the weak and perverted minds of some of the establishment," led them to embrace "voluptuousness, as yielding the greatest enjoyment." By these means "a gross sensuality pervaded the whole establishment."[111] By mistaking earthly feelings for divine, the followers of Matthias had been seduced into immorality.

For Williams, Stone, and Vale there was a consistent message, a message first sounded in the trial of William Parkinson: there was great danger in mixing "the poison of lust with the ardor of devotion." Witnessing repeated trials, Americans would come to fear reverend rakes. Because ministers were granted greater access and intimacy with women, it was feared they could easily take advantage of the trust they were granted. As the Second Great Awakening unfolded in the North, these fears took on an additional urgency. Passions first kindled by rogue ministers were seemingly being fanned by revivalists like the Methodists and then

New School revivalists. Upstart enthusiastic groups, like the Kingdom of Matthias, were seen as the inevitable next step. Once evangelicals opened the door to revelation, dangerous new groups could emerge. From this perspective, once people began to trust their hearts over their heads, they were susceptible to religious fraud and sexual exploitation. Under the weight of controversies caused by sexual scandal, social activism, revivalism, and the theological innovations that had enabled them, the Presbyterian Church would suffer a schism in 1837. Increasingly it and other mainline denominations would abandon revivalism, looking instead to Sunday schools as a safer way to grow their churches.[112] Education would be preferred over conversions, for there were too many liabilities in heart religion. In the end, moderation in sex, gender, and religion seemed the only safe way to uphold a respectable, and religiously restrained, Christian order.

CHAPTER 5

The Sexual Containment of Perfectionism

John Humphrey Noyes and His Critics

The Reverend Hubbard Eastman had hindsight perspective on the dangers of religious fanaticism. Writing his book *Noyesism Unveiled* in 1849, he believed some of its dangerous potential had been successfully contained within the previous couple of decades. Yet the need to remain vigilant was manifest in the perfectionist threat presented by John Humphrey Noyes. Propagating what Eastman saw as one of the most dangerous heresies to come from the Second Great Awakening, Noyes taught that once men and women were reborn in Christ, they were incapable of sin. The law, whether religious or secular, was no longer needed as a guide for their behavior. Instead, the spirit would lead people to do what was right. With regard to sexual relations, this antinomian perspective meant that the convention of marriage was null and void.

Eastman approvingly quoted Reverend S. B. Yarrington's summary of the recent history of religion in nineteenth-century America. Around 1830, Yarrington noted, an "effervescence of certain minds" had been produced by revivalism: "heresy was begotten in the fumes of fanaticism." While "the heresy spread rapidly for a time," it luckily was "composed of heterogeneous materials, having little affinity" and therefore "soon gave signs of disintegration, and the fire that burnt strong at first, presently smouldered away for want of sustenance." And yet the fire still presented dangers: "the dying embers remain in society, scattered in every direction, and wherever they have fallen, to a certain extent burn and sterilize the moral soil, destroying the seed of truth that is sown therein."[1]

While Yarrington emphasized that the fire had burnt itself out, Eastman also gave credit to the "intelligent and observing" members of society who were able to immediately recognize the "sad consequences" that would flow from a belief in human perfection. The "virtuous part of [the] community" had "anticipated and deeply deplored" the "promulgation" of perfectionist ideas. Despite the opposition he faced, John Humphrey Noyes was still able to garner a following. Eastman granted Noyes a certain savvy self-preservation instinct: "from time to time [he] resorted to various expedients to screen himself and his followers from merited reprobation, and by repeated shufflings succeeded in keeping, to some extent, from public view the practical tendency and results of his pernicious principles." But these tactics would no longer work, for now the practical implications of his teachings had "at length fully come to light, and doubt no longer hangs over the subject."[2] By the time Eastman had written his book, free love had been openly practiced in Putney, Vermont, and then carried away to safety, in Oneida, New York.

Eastman believed the press had grown lax or negligent in its treatment of Noyes. Up until the revelation of wife swapping and adultery in the fall of 1847, newspapers, whether "secular or religious," had treated Noyes's Putney religious community "as an insignificant and harmless affair, unworthy of notice and even undeserving of the notoriety which a public attack would give it."[3] Eastman aimed to correct this error. He wanted to shine a bright light on "Noyesism" and rid the country of this heresy. And yet Noyes managed to keep his experiment in sexual communism going for decades after Eastman published his book. This was because Noyes and his followers resorted to further "expedients" to protect their community. In particular, soon after Eastman printed his book, Noyes publicly forswore any attempts to convert people to his creed. In the end, Eastman and his fellow religious moderates managed to contain, if not fully extinguish, the fire of perfectionism.

Part of the containment of sexual radicalism in the wake of the Second Great Awakening was accomplished by clearing the ground of fuel. As we saw in the previous chapter, anti-enthusiasm critics condemned the emotional and sexual excesses of revivalism and upstart religious movements, thereby mobilizing popular opinion and their fellow ministers in favor of religious and sexual moderation. With the schism of the Presbyterian Church in 1837, the collapse of Millerism after the Great Disappointment of 1844, and the push for respectability among the Methodists and Baptists, the Second Great Awakening had lost much of its tinder. But the "embers" of perfectionism had been scattered through much of the North. While composed of, as Yarrington noted, an unorganized mixture of "heterogeneous materials," perfectionism did eventually cohere under the leadership of John Humphrey Noyes. To achieve this position, however, Noyes had to repeatedly distance himself from sexual scandal and modify his theology, so as to disarm his critics. Once his leadership was secure, he would embrace the more radical "practical" applications of this theology, beginning to practice what he preached. But his security was only guaranteed in retreat. While the Mormons had gained temporary asylum by escaping to Utah, the perfectionists of Oneida had to gain peace by forsaking proselytism.

Over the years, there have been a series of important studies of John Humphrey Noyes and his free love community at Oneida, New York.[4] The effort to narrate the story of the Oneida Community actually began with Noyes and his descendants; those early efforts at documentation seem to have imbued many later scholarly works with a certain sympathy for Noyes and his creative efforts at reimagining sexual and gender relations. Scholarly interest really gained traction in the wake of the 1960s, because that era had witnessed various experiments in utopian community building. Most modern works have shared an interest in the lived experience at Oneida, most especially its various unique social and sexual practices, such as complex marriage, mutual criticism, and male continence. The intellectual and cultural contest between Noyes and his critics, however, has received less notice. While scholars like Lawrence Foster and Louis Kern certainly analyzed quite carefully the thought of Noyes, it was mostly in service of understanding how and why the community adopted its social and sexual practices. More recently, Ellen Wayland-Smith and Anthony Wonderly have tried to move us somewhat beyond Noyes himself. While Wayland-Smith gives special attention to the transition to, and experience of, the Oneida flatware company, Wonderly emphasizes how much of community life at Oneida was shaped in Noyes's absence as he spent long stretches of time living in Brooklyn.

This chapter will take a different approach. It will look at the cultural contest over perfectionism within the larger debate over religious enthusiasm, observing how its threat was reduced together by both Noyes and his critics. Instead of focusing on community life at Oneida,

I will instead give priority to the years leading up to the establishment of the community, showing how a safe shelter was constructed for it. Eventually, the shelter would collapse, caused both by internal community tensions and external pressures. As Michael Doyle has recently demonstrated, the Oneida Community would regain notice during the late nineteenth century, driven by a fresh wave of purity campaigns and renewed attention to Mormon polygamy, as Utah petitioned for statehood. By that time the Oneida Community existed in a very new context, one in which its practices began again to look more ominous. But considering all the attention received by "reverend rakes" in the early nineteenth century, the existence of Oneida as a free love community up until 1880 is quite surprising. The foundation for that survival had been laid in the years leading up to the settlement of Oneida.

The sexual containment of perfectionism happened in a series of episodes. As perfectionism first unfolded in the early 1830s, it promoted the belief in "spiritual wifery," encouraging people to find their soul mates, even if it meant forsaking their lawful marriages. Noyes did his best to tamp down the scandal of spiritual unions, but he ultimately gained safety by dissociating himself from the idea altogether. He incurred more notoriety, however, with the publication of his Battle-Axe letter in 1837. After the letter was purportedly published against his will, Noyes would spend significant time and energy distancing himself from the publisher of his letter, Theophilus Gates. Over the next decade, as Noyes fine-tuned his theology and built a community at Putney, he would mostly fall out of notice until his neighbors in Vermont learned that his theoretical nullification of marriage had become actual practice in their midst. Eastman and the editors of the *Vermont Phoenix* would help raise the alarm against Noyes again. When Noyes established a new community in a remote location in upstate New York, he and his followers continued to exercise a self-preservation instinct. Only by winning peace with their neighbors in their first few years was the religious experiment able to take root at Oneida.

In the previous chapter we began to see some "reverend rakes" use theology to validate expressions of sexual freedom. In the hands of perfectionists, a broader and more systematic theology of free love would develop. Perfectionism originated variously and was never a unified whole, but over time John Humphrey Noyes would emerge as the key leader of one of its two major branches (see figure 5.1). In chapter 4 we saw that in New York City in the late 1820s Frances Folger and her

FIGURE 5.1.   Daguerreotype of John Humphrey Noyes (ca. 1850s). Courtesy of the Oneida Community Mansion House, Oneida Community Collection, Oneida Community Photos #192. Syracuse University Library.

Retrenchment Society, as well as James Latourette and his Holy Club, pushed followers to strive for purity. Their goal was to fulfill God's law to its very letter. This variant of perfectionism would feed various reform movements, inspiring, for example, the Female Moral Reform Society, which fought against prostitution and adultery. Perfectionists of this sort also believed that man's laws sometimes stood at odds with God's laws. Thus, those who saw slavery as a sin vowed to break laws supporting slavery. Eventually the purity variant of perfectionism would coalesce under Charles Finney as he led from Oberlin in Ohio. Noyes would take perfectionism in a very different direction by calling on followers to transcend the law altogether. Or rather, he would substitute the law of ongoing revelation for the law of the Bible.[5] Purity of heart, rather than dead compliance to the law, was their standard. The different versions of perfectionism could lead to dramatically variant sexual practices. Radical purity perfectionists called for complete chastity for all believers, pointing to the recommendations of St. Paul, who uplifted chastity as the most admirable form of devotion to God.[6] In contrast, the antinomian perfectionists under Noyes would come to call on all followers to be in sexual union with their community.

These independent strains of perfectionism only cohered over time. Initially, there actually was a significant congruence in attitudes toward marriage. Perfectionists broadly questioned the legitimacy of earthly marriages. Such unions were seen to be based on worldly and pragmatic concerns, such as economic negotiations between families, rather than spiritual considerations. Spiritual wifery emerged as the godly substitute to earthly contracted marriages. St. Paul again served as an example. He had a traveling female companion who was said to have shared in his spiritual labors in spreading the Good Word.[7] The biggest impetus for spiritual unions came in 1834 when the minister Erasmus Stone had a vivid dream he shared with others. He had imagined people waking up from their graves, madly rushing away from their burial partners to find their soul mates, for they had been wrongly matched during life.[8] Wanting to live in the resurrection state, perfectionists sought out their spiritual partners in this world, rather than waiting for the world to come.

John Humphrey Noyes emerged as a religious leader just as these perfectionist ideas about marriage were emerging. For a time, he too was taken with the idea of spiritual wifery. But seeing the potential for danger, Noyes would perform his first strategic retreat in response to scandals surrounding spiritual wifery. This part of Noyes's experience is not as well documented as later episodes. The best sources we have available are Noyes's own spiritual autobiography and a book written by William Hepworth Dixon in 1868. Almost anthropological in his approach, Dixon was able to sympathetically interview principal actors from the events of the 1830s. The rumors of sexual scandal connected to spiritual wifery were strong enough to have lived on in local memory. The writings of Noyes and Dixon help show the nexus from which Noyes's thought on marriage emerged.

Consistent with the wider perfectionist community, Noyes would consistently preach the "nullity of wives," citing Matthew 22:30, "in the resurrection they neither marry, nor are given in marriage."[9] It was this core belief that would allow Noyes to later express a surprising level of admiration for the Shakers, a group with radically different sexual practices but a shared commitment to abolishing marriage. Noyes would also speak sympathetically of Lucina Umphreville, who gained a following in 1830s New York by preaching that "carnal union was not to be tolerated even in marriage." Consistent with the vision of Erasmus Stone, she taught that "spiritual union whether in or out of marriage represented a high state of attainment."[10] Umphreville was one of a number of outspoken women who would later proceed to find themselves a spiritual partner, in her instance Jarvis Rider, vowing to work with them as chaste companions in furthering the Gospel. Repudiating legal marriage was scandalous enough, but real notoriety was realized when perfectionists Mary Lincoln and Maria Brown decided to prove their commitment to chastity by sleeping in bed with their minister, aiming to prove their ability to stare down temptation. Not long thereafter, the perfectionists gained even more infamy as some spiritual unions began to turn carnal, with couples rejecting the chastity component of spiritual wifery.[11] Noyes played a critical role in that transition.

Noyes would later reflect on how these events unfolded. He explained to William Hepworth Dixon that religious revivals are prone to "revolutionize the relations of man and woman" because they opened society to divine reorganization. He believed that the Shakers, Lucina Umphreville, the Mormons, and his own community were all produced from the same "theocratic" impulse. For him, the critical difference was whether men or women assumed leadership. He observed that "love between the two sexes" had "two stages; the courting stage and the wedding stage." He believed that "women like to talk about love; but men want the love itself." When spiritual unions moved from chaste to sexual companionships, as they did among perfectionists in upstate New York in 1836, Noyes believed it was because male leadership had eclipsed that of women: "Among the Perfectionists women led the way in the bundling with purposes as chaste as those of the Shakers. For a time, they had their way; but in time the men had their way."[12] By naturalizing sexual difference, he seems to be trying to explain his own journey from spiritual wifery toward his later system of socialized sex.

Noyes's relationship to spiritual wifery in these years is best witnessed through the famous episode of the "Brimfield bundling." Noyes had gained notice in perfectionist circles starting in 1834 with his publication, jointly edited with James Boyle, titled *The Perfectionist*. While his unorthodox perfectionist views had cost him his license to preach in New Haven, his writings naturally recommended themselves to the cause of spiritual wifery. Writing in 1834, he had offered a novel interpretation of the Second Coming of Christ, saying it had occurred at the destruction of the temple of Jerusalem, around AD 70. It was at this time, he wrote, that the New Covenant was delivered, which gained "to believers perfect and eternal salvation from sin, full freedom from written law, and human instruction."[13] While humanity had yet to reap the rewards of this gift, it was there for the taking to those reborn in Christ. To perfectionists who believed they had been reborn in the resurrection state, they now had fuller theological support to abandon earthly unions and seek their spiritual partners. Wedding vows had promised "until death shall part us," so those living in the New Birth could now seek their true spiritual mates.[14] The New York minister Simon Lovett, who had formerly served a group of women now settled in Brimfield, Massachusetts, had persuaded Noyes in February 1835 to join him on a proselytizing mission to Brimfield. Lovett had been persuaded to Noyes's viewpoints and wished to carry these teachings back to his former congregants. Noyes's views were at odds with theirs, but his writings nonetheless had garnered interest in Brimfield. These perfectionists leaned toward the purity variant of perfectionism. This, ironically, afforded them greater liberty in relations between the sexes. When there, Noyes found that they addressed each with familiarity and exchanged holy kisses, believing all were simply signs of holy love, not carnal attraction.[15] The heady brew of Noyes's antinomianism, coupled with their warm expressions of spiritual love, was bound to produce trouble.

It did not take long. Through his preaching, he quickly won them to his views, and they placed their trust in his guidance. One night Noyes consoled a disheartened Hannah Tarbell. She was worried he did not have confidence in her. He put his arm around her to reassure her of his support. As he headed to bed, she in turn planted a kiss on his cheek. Noyes must have been stirred in some fashion, because his self-preservation instinct kicked in. Saying he had deduced a "clear view of the situation," he left without word early the next morning, taking a "beeline on foot though snow and cold—below zero—to Putney, sixty miles distant," which he "reached within twenty-four hours."[16] A couple of days after he left, the infamous bundling incident occurred. Mary Lincoln and Maria Brown, seeking to defy the law, while also prove their purity, decided to crawl in bed with Simon Lovett. It does not seem that any sort of sexual exchange occurred, but Lincoln was "abused" enough by wagging tongues that she had a vision that God's wrath was soon to be visited on their town. Convincing Flavilla Howard to join her, they rushed for a nearby hill in supplication, hoping to stay God's avenging hand. In their mad dash, they tattered their clothing, an event that would in subsequent retellings be characterized as "streaking."[17] Believing that the women had successfully stayed God's hands, the pastors Lovett and

Dutton took this as a sign, upholding these young women as a model and concluding that "spiritual pairing was a necessary adjunct of the New York doctrine of spiritual love." Lovett would take Abby Fowler as a match, while Lincoln would pair with Dutton. Spiritual unions that were initially chaste took less than a year to become sexual. William Hepworth Dixon postulated this was the natural workings of human nature, as these perfectionists "fell into love like common mortals."[18] However, we must recognize the inner logic of adopting Noyes's teachings. If "full freedom from written law" had been achieved, why only reject the law of marriage? Why would restrictions on sex not also fall to the wayside under the new dispensation?

In later years, Noyes would admit his own sympathy at the time for the principals during the Brimfield bundling incident. He said that he "sought to shelter rather than to condemn the young women who appealed to me against the storm of scandal which they had brought upon themselves." But when spiritual unions turned to "actual licentiousness and finally into propagandism," he "renounced all sympathy" for those promoting spiritual unions, trying to "stamp them out by word and deed." This renunciation took time, because Noyes first attempted a spiritual union of his own. His initial affinity for spiritual wifery owed something to his personal circumstances. He was particularly close to his first convert in New Haven, Abigail Merwin. Too shy to say it directly, he nonetheless was in love with Merwin. He was stunned in the fall of 1835 when he discovered she had become engaged to another man, Merit Platt. He wrote her a letter, saying he did not wish to interfere with her "earthly engagement." And yet he did. Quoting St. Paul, he said he now existed where "the fashion of this world has passed away." Seeing Merwin as still spiritually asleep, he would wait until she awoke. In time she would "return to your first love and dwell with me in the bosom of God."[19] It was bold enough to ask her to quit her husband and join him in a spiritual union, but Noyes would also move to Ithaca, where the couple had just moved, so as to facilitate her transfer to him. But she proved cold to his entreaties. He would, in turn, reject the notion of spiritual wifery, substituting in its place a theory of sexual union where no man could claim a wife as solely his own. If he could not pry Merwin away from Platt, he would insist that she, as all other women, be shared.[20]

Noyes's new theory of sexual communism would first be announced to the world in his famous Battle-Axe letter of 1837. If Noyes had pre-emptively escaped from the scandal of the Brimfield bundling, he was ready to expose himself to risk again by writing this letter. It is unclear how much exposure he intended, but he did allow for it to be shared. He told his correspondent, David Harrison, that he could judge "whether it is expedient to show this letter to others." In the Pauline lexicon, the notion of expediency was a key concept, for Paul had allowed for Christians to temporarily follow the fashion of the world if others were not quite ready for the truth. That is, the greater cause should be sustained by only gradually sharing revelation. After the letter exchanged a few hands, it landed in those of Theophilus Gates in Philadelphia. Despite Noyes's insistence to the contrary, Gates and Noyes shared essentially the same theology. They differed much more in style than in substance.[21] Gates was much more confrontational. He titled his magazine the *Battle-Axe and Weapons of War*, a reference to Jeremiah 51:20, which warns of "breaking in pieces the nations" and "destroying kingdoms" for the cause of the Lord. Gates delivered the first issue of his incendiary publication directly to the mayor of Philadelphia.[22] When Gates received Noyes's letter, he was thrilled to publish it. He did hide Noyes's identity but wanted to corroborate his own views by showing they were shared by a New England divine. The letter did just that, as we will see by comparing the writings of Noyes and Gates. Noyes and Gates in fact knew each other. While Noyes would later narrate his first meeting with Gates in a way meant to embarrass Gates, both were admired figures in perfectionist circles. In fact, after Noyes left his post at *The Perfectionist*, James Boyle, who was enamored with Gates, handed Noyes's writing duties over to him.[23] Noyes and Gates were essentially rivals for leadership of the movement.

The letter began by Noyes describing how many in the perfectionist community felt spiritually unmoored. He felt the time for bold action had arrived, and he was willing to serve as their pilot. Foretelling of the coming "establishment of God's kingdom over the earth," he warned there would be "a chaos of confusion, tribulation, woe &c. such as must attend the destruction of the *fashion of this world*." He now was ready to describe what heaven on earth would mean: "When the will of God is done on earth, as it is in heaven, *there will be no marriage*. The marriage supper of the Lamb, is a *feast at which every dish is free to every guest*." Extending the metaphor, he said it would be silly "at a thanksgiving dinner" for the gathered to "claim each his separate dish." This did not mean one could not "have each his favourite dish, each a dish of his own procuring," but such claims could be made "without the jealousy of exclusiveness." He might "call a certain woman my wife," but all the same, "she is yours, she is Christ's, and in him she is the bride of all saints." He would "according to [his] promise to her rejoice," not feel violated, if in "the hand of a stranger." This vision of sexual communism was grounded firmly in his antinomian perspective: "in a holy community, there is no more reason why sexual intercourse should be restrained by law, than why eating and drinking should be." The laws regulating sex in the Bible had been established "during the apostasy" and "for good reasons," but these would now be "broken down in the resurrection, for equally good reasons." Those reborn, those who stood "in the holiness of the resurrection," should be prepared to join this new sexual order.[24]

It was a stunning letter and drew quick notice. The most notable response was from the *Advocate of Moral Reform*. Organ of the Female Moral Reform Society, it was a major national evangelical publication with 16,500 subscribers. Led by New York female reformers, it was a major voice for purity campaigns, focusing on God's prohibition of adultery in the seventh commandment. The editors provided sharp criticism, but also astute analysis, of Noyes's writings. This should be no surprise, for they too were wrapped up in perfectionism. They wished to call attention to religious error: "Sentiments have of late been openly advanced by those who call themselves Perfectionists of such an immoral and destructive tendency, that it becomes our duty as humble conservators of the public morals to bear a decided testimony against them." This was particularly necessary, for they had to protect their own good name, because "the names of some among us have been coupled with this dangerous and seductive heresy." They worried about stirring the "stagnant pool of corruption," causing it to be more widely noticed, but they felt it was needed "for the sake of warning the unwary from its brink." Already, "some whom we loved and honored" had "fallen into this snare of the devil."[25] This would have included George Cragin, the sole male employee and literary agent for *The Advocate*, as well as Mrs. H. C. Green, former "Directress of the Moral Reform Society." Both supported Noyes, with Cragin, led by his wife Mary, notably later joining Noyes's perfectionist community at Putney.[26]

The editors then focused on the danger to marriage and the theological challenge against it provided by Noyes. Some perfectionists had advanced the view that "the institution of marriage is set aside as a part of the system of bondage from which Christ is to make us free." They pointed to the scriptural justification offered up for this view: "from the words of our Savior concerning the inhabitants of heaven, 'they neither marry nor are given in marriage,' they argue the abolition of the institution here in a resurrection state which, it seems, some of them have already attained." Such a view, the editors believed, was "a master-stroke of satanic policy" that would "open the floodgate to every species of licentiousness." In such a world, one would see "the marriage covenant annulled, parental and filial obligations trampled in the dust." For "those who are familiar with Ecclesiastical History," they would recognize the root of this disintegrating heresy in the "Antinomianism" of these perfectionists. They believed *that believers under the Gospel dispensation are delivered from the obligation of personal obedience to the moral law.* Rather than forsaking the law, the editors instead believed that the faithful must strive harder: "the church must come up to a higher standard of personal consecration and holiness, before the world can be converted." Such an ultraist goal did risk the danger that one might "run into an extreme more dangerous than the one she seeks to avoid." They needed therefore to disown any who had fallen to this antinomian heresy, insisting they had to "refuse all fellowship or countenance" to them, "though the act of excision, be as painful as the amputation of a limb, or the plucking of an eye."[27] They knew their mark and hit it. The antinomian underpinnings of the Battle-Axe letter represented the views of both Noyes and Gates. Noyes would nonetheless try to pin the scandal on Gates alone.

After admitting to his authorship of the Battle-Axe letter, Noyes would turn to responding to *The Advocate.* While their article had actually focused on Noyes's scriptural justification for abandoning marriage, they had nonetheless noted the practical similarity of his social prescriptions to the views of Robert Owen and Frances Wright, radical social reformers of the day. Noyes would seize on this as a way to clear himself and attack Gates. He was adamant in his disavowal: "I feel that in coupling me with Owen or Gates, you have greatly wronged the truth, inasmuch as my dissent from them, and my abhorrence of their doctrines, is plainly expressed in the *Witness.*" Owen and Wright, he noted, had recommended "onanism," in this instance meaning the withdrawal method of birth control. Gates had also expressed sympathy for onanism in the same issue that held the Battle-Axe letter. Noyes thus used his own writings against onanism in the *Witness* to dissociate himself from Gates.[28] The disagreement on the matter was real, but in this Gates was actually following the logic of antinomian perfectionism more faithfully than Noyes.

Gates wanted women to avoid the pain of childbirth meted out to Eve in the Fall. He said it was no sin to prevent unwanted pregnancy by practicing coitus interruptus. It was "just as easy" for any man to avoid pregnancy "as it was for Onan to do it." Those who fail to "prevent it now, when the woman desires not to conceive," are guilty of an odious and selfish crime. In Gates's view, the reborn were now living under a new dispensation, one that transcended the New Testament, as the New had eclipsed the Old: "the dawning light of a better state of things, indeed, is now enabling them as plainly to see, that conceiving is a curse, as the Apostles saw the outward rites of the Mosaic law were a curse on the coming of the Gospel."[29] Noyes would only later fully wrestle with how to avoid the risk of unwanted pregnancy in a state of sexual communism. One wonders whether his later prescription of male continence (coitus reservatus, that is, intercourse with no ejaculation, rather than coitus interruptus) was an innovation meant to prevent a belated endorsement of his rival's views. Certainly, it did not seem logically consistent for Noyes to point to the condemnation of Onan in the Bible, for Onan's sin was a violation of the law under the state of apostasy. It is unclear why it would still be a violation under the new dispensation.[30]

Noyes also distanced himself from Gates by saying that Gates "never professed to be a Perfectionist." This was disingenuous indeed. Not only had Gates taken over responsibility for writing duties at *The Perfectionist* in 1835, he was much admired as a leader by other perfectionists. Charles Weld, for example, called Gates "pure gold." Most importantly, Gates's views clearly squared with Noyes on the matter of man's relations to the Bible and God.[31] Noyes resisted the label of antinomianism put on him by *The Advocate*. While he was ready to set aside the external laws of the Bible, he insisted they would be replaced by internal guidance, the Holy Spirit: "I believe that in the heavenly state, which is the hope of our calling, the Holy Spirit takes the place of written laws and arbitrary ceremonies in the relation of the sexes and all other matters." Those who were "trusting in written laws instead of the Holy Spirit" would "ere long be found fighting against God." Noyes would provide himself some protection, however, by now emphasizing that he did "*not* believe that any have attained" the heavenly state "who are now on earth."[32] He had left the question of timing vague in the Battle-Axe letter, but here it made sense to emphasize the need for a "transition period." This was in contrast to his opening pronouncements in the opening issue of *The Perfectionist* where he had already claimed "full freedom from written law and human instruction," secured when the New Covenant was delivered by Christ at the time of the Second Coming. In that publication he had insisted that those reborn in Christ could claim the prize: "The battle is fought—the victory is won—their holiness is perfect as obedience, perfect in security, and perfect by victory over suffering." Perfectionists, he had said, were "saved from sin—eternally saved," and merely waiting for the "redemption of their bodies" to heaven.[33]

To illustrate how living by the Holy Spirit, rather than the Bible, worked, Noyes employed the metaphor of a map to explain his views to *The Advocate*: "a child proposing to travel the city of New-York, may take a map, or a person familiar with the city." The latter he saw as superior: "if you should advise him to take a map," he would instead "commend rather the living Guide." So it was with religion. Experience taught that the Bible had proved "ineffectual" in securing the claim of "righteousness" for believers. In contrast, God was a "living Guide" who was "all-sufficient" in guiding behavior.[34] It was with this perspective in mind that Noyes had looked at organized religion with real suspicion. Why accept the written guidance of credos and confessions? In his opening issue of *The Witness* he stated boldly, "We believe that by far the greatest portion of the religion in the world named Christianity is the work of the anti-Christ."[35] And yet in later years he would try to pin the tag of being "anti-organization" on Gates.[36] The shoe of antinomianism, living by the spirit, not the law, certainly seems to fit Noyes well, most certainly during these formative years.

These writings of Noyes resonated with those of Gates. In the opening issue of Gates's *Battle-Axe and Weapons of War*, he also spoke of living beyond the law: "Men must look to and obey Him who alone is right, or they can never become right. They are therefore to obey no wrong law any more, but do what God requires." He squared with Noyes on marriage too. Emphasizing the need for men and women to find their true matches, Gates found blindly obeying the law of marriage to violate the spirit of God's will: "to compel two persons to live together as man and wife, when they can only live in contention and strife" was "highly criminal in the sight of God." Like Noyes, Gates called on Paul for support. He reminded readers that Paul had said that when the *"fashion of this world shall pass away,"* those with "wives [would] be as though they had none." While Paul's emphasis was on believers living for God alone, Gates, like Noyes, emphasized the freedom that could come with the Kingdom of God: "the man and woman will have no claim on each other, whatever, to stay with each other, live together, or be in any way bound to each other, otherwise, than is their free choice, will, or disposition in these respects."[37] Gates continued these antinomian themes in his second issue, the one that carried the Battle-Axe letter. He questioned again the wisdom of following the law: "no outward written law can produce a state of righteousness." Such empty obedience did not allow one to "discover what is the will of God under all circumstances." Like Noyes, he highlighted the "need for a superior guide." Equipped with faith in Christ and led by the spirit, one could "know at all times, and under different circumstances, what is the good, acceptable, and perfect will of God." For him, like Noyes, he had been led by this guide to believe that "there is no jealousy, no exclusiveness, no selfishness" once one had achieved the righteousness of the resurrection state. In this condition "all things are common in the fullest sense of the word, wives and everything else."[38] In their metaphors, their theology, and their views on marriage, the two clearly shared many sentiments.

Thus it is not a surprise that when Gates published Noyes's letter, he held it up for praise. While he did not mention Noyes by name, he touted his credentials, saying he was "a person of a liberal education, who was a preacher in the Presbyterian or Congregational church, and who stood foremost among the Perfectionists, at New Haven, when they first came forth in the light and power of a better state of things." He admired "the open and undisguised manner in which he has expressed himself." He trusted in "the uprightness and purity of his intentions" and gave him credit for "the sacrifices I know he has made, from principle."[39] After Noyes swiped at Gates in *The Advocate*, however, the admiration clearly dissipated. Likely because of the attention it garnered, Gates chose to republish the issue containing the letter, this time sharing an abbreviated version. Noting that "some sentiments contained in it are not very well expressed," he chose just to reproduce the paragraph on the marriage supper. Instead of praising Noyes's courage, he now regretted Noyes's timidity: "the writer seems to have been frightened at the truths he had declared, and regretted that they were not kept more private." While Gates would remain a warrior in the cause, he would "excuse [Noyes] from again appearing as a witness for truth in this publication."[40] As we have seen, Noyes returned the scorn in full.

Feeling burned by the Battle-Axe episode, as well as by his rejection from Abigail Merwin, Noyes would tack back toward expediency. He moved home to Vermont, then he took a seemingly most conventional step in making a marriage proposal. The recipient was Harriet Holton. Holton was a convert of his who had proven her loyalty by helping Noyes pay off his debts incurred in Ithaca.[41] Yet Noyes had not fully retreated in his views. He proposed a most unconventional marriage to her, and he was willing to show the world his letter in an issue of *The Witness* in 1839. It was a proposal of "a partnership" that he would "not call marriage" until he "defined it" for her. As believers, they already were in union in a community of saints: "This primary and universal union, is more radical, and of course more important than any partial and external partnership." He made it clear that he was still aiming to enact the world he described in the Battle-Axe letter: "the object of my connexion with her will be, not to monopolize and enslave her heart or my own, but to enlarge and establish both, in the free fellowship of God's universal family."[42] He would then list a series of practical benefits to their union. It was, by no means, a romantic proposal. But as a true believer, she took it.

In the safety of his hometown of Putney, Vermont, he began to secure a loyal following, preaching to his perfectionist followers who came to join him, including George and Mary Cragin. About two dozen followers were settled in three different residences. They listened to Noyes's sermons and helped him publish and distribute his paper. Using the dowry brought by Holton to their marriage, Noyes had secured a printing press of his own. By 1841 his followers erected a chapel in which he could preach.[43] Their neighbors proved remarkably tolerant of Noyes and his unorthodox views. Undoubtedly, this was because he came from a well-established family, his father having represented the community in Congress. By 1845 the group, which had christened itself "the Putney Community," knit itself together more closely by adopting a communism of property.[44] Edged forward by the amorous connections forming between community members, by 1846 a select circle of Noyes and his followers began to practice a communism of sex too. It was not long before rumors began to spread in the local community. It was one thing to talk about free love in the abstract but another to practice it. For consistency's sake, if nothing else, Noyes needed to explain the shift. In July 1847 he would announce in the *Spiritual Magazine* that the Kingdom of God had begun, thereby explaining the move from theory to practice.[45]

The town of Putney proved tolerant no more. The *Vermont Phoenix*, published in nearby Brattleboro, would do some serious investigative journalism. They had initially been reluctant to get involved, not feeling the paper should get pulled into a local community conflict. But once they did their homework, reading Noyes's previous publications closely, they offered thorough, and highly critical, coverage. In two issues in December 1847 and January 1848 they reviewed the periodicals of Noyes, as well as his recently published book, *The Berean*. In reading his theology, next to his Battle-Axe letter, their overall conclusion was that there was not "the least difference between the doctrines of his letter and those embraced in his 'religious belief,' except that the former develops more fully the practical results of those doctrines." Denying Noyes both the pause he had taken after the scandal of the Battle-Axe letter and the cover of expediency, they insisted his theology and the Battle-Axe Letter "both declare the 'second coming' is *past*; that all believers are perfect, and *cannot* sin; that they are in a state of spiritual resurrection, and at liberty to act as the *spirit* dictates, without any regard to civil or moral law." They backed up this perspective by quoting Noyes's own words about his religious history: "In February 1834, I had a full consciousness that Christ, risen and triumphant, had identified himself with the centre of my being." In that moment, Noyes concluded that he "was *born of God* in the primitive sense of that expression—in that sense which answers to the description of John: 'He that is born of God doth not commit *sin*, for his seed remaineth in him; and he *cannot sin*, because he is born of God." Armed with these quotes, they concluded that Noyes believed that he had "been in a state of holiness and freedom from all *legal* restraint since 1834."[46] In other words, they believed he had embarked on a course of antinomianism from the time of his conversion experience.

But his beliefs nonetheless went unnoticed until the Battle-Axe letter offered "a practical illustration of the *working* of his system, as to shock the moral feeling of [the] community." After the scandal broke, the paper concluded that Noyes "found it necessary to qualify and disavow" his sentiments. Quoting Noyes's response to the *Advocate of Moral Reform*, they concluded the letter "remodels his religious belief" so as to be more palatable. But they did not buy the retreat. They added further corroboration of his enduring belief in his freedom from sin in articles of his from *The Witness*. Noyes's later insistence that he hadn't reached the resurrection state, they said, was "flatly contradicted by himself."[47] They had pinned Noyes down and would give him no quarter. They also held him responsible for the conduct of perfectionists outside his community. In 1842, they noted, perfectionist communities that had "sprung up in other sections of the country" had started to practice "the doctrines of the 'Battle-Axe' letter so openly as to bring down upon them the indignation of community, and the penalties of law." They highlighted how he distanced himself: "Mr Noyes disowned and denounced them, as Perfectionists only in *name*," saying they had fallen victim to religious enthusiasm. But by 1843, they noted, he "had learned to look upon their excesses with a more indulgent eye." Quoting *The Perfectionist* from this year, they found he admitted, "it was impossible to hold forth the general doctrine of anti-legality, without extending its scope specifically to *amativeness*" (sexual desire). Noyes, they noted, was now willing to own this. They quoted him, showing he said of perfectionists that "we must boldly assert, that in *Heaven* as on *Earth*, so far as the Gospel of resurrection takes effect, *amativeness*, as well as the *other passions*, is *emancipated from the law*, and placed under the government of grace." Passions, they found Noyes said, were like "wild beasts" who needed to be released: "*Legality* puts them in cages. Even amativeness, lion as it is, must be *let out* of its *law cage*, and pass into the freedom of righteousness."[48] Their close reading of his writings revealed his open embrace of free love.

In places, their suspicion probably went too far. Historians have concluded that the residents at Putney probably did not begin to have sex outside of wedlock until 1846.[49] The editors of the *Phoenix* suspected it was happening sooner. They did allow that at Putney, "under the immediate eye of Mr. Noyes," the community probably acted "more prudently," but this did not mean nothing was happening. They believed "he kept their practices secret for a time," doubting his assertion in 1842 that in Putney there was "*no practical departure from ordinary sexual morality.*" But they said there was no mistaking what was going on after 1847. In the spring of that year, all the followers, who now numbered about thirty-five, set themselves up to live in a single household. This was, they surmised, "in order to facilitate the promiscuous intercourse enjoined upon believers." Having been encouraged by the "impunity of his previous conduct," they said, he decided to "throw aside the thin cloak of pretended decency he had heretofore maintained, and to *practice openly*, what he had constantly *preached* openly, and doubtless secretly practiced." By June, in the *Spiritual Magazine*, they reported, he announced that the "KINGDOM OF GOD HAS COME." Now well versed in Noyes's theology, the editors correctly interpreted the import of this pronouncement: "this was nothing more than the *public* transfer of themselves, by resolution, to that state of 'perfect holiness' which sanctifies vice and profligacy as a religious duty." Clearly, the editors evince religious and social intolerance toward Noyes and his followers in the language they use. We might disagree with their judgmental tone, but this was more than a hit piece. Their overall conclusion was overly axiomatic but sound: "the recent demonstration at Putney is no casual outbreak or effervescence of excitement, nor the wild excesses of a few *pretended* and *hypocritical* Perfectionists, but the genuine, necessary, and *inevitable* result of their *published* doctrines and creed."[50] They had studied his theology carefully and understood how it could overturn marriage and produce unorthodox sexual practices.

Why not extend religious tolerance? The editors of the *Phoenix*, as well as others soon to join in the chorus against Noyes, expressed the same fears we have seen voiced about other enthusiastic religions. If his community kept to itself, it was one thing, but they feared others were being seduced into this heresy. Noyes had been gaining followers. The community had been engaging in "systematic attempts to entice the young and unsuspecting," threatening to disrupt "the sacred family and domestic institutions." Such a group deserved "neither toleration, nor compromise."[51] The editors noted the complicity of the press. The publications of the Putney Community had "been treated in general, by the religious and political press, with silent contempt," but this was a mistake because their work had "obtained a wide circulation, made converts, and secured for the sect a foothold in many parts of the country."[52] There were known perfectionist communities in locales as far flung as Brimfield and Cape Cod, Massachusetts; Salina, New York; and Newark, New Jersey.[53]

The editors of the *Phoenix* believed Noyes lured people in with false appearances. He only revealed his social intentions in stages. The idea of *"perfect holiness"* was "no doubt alluring and sweet." It was no surprise that "many persons, credulous and unreflecting, or tempest-tost and shipwrecked upon the waves of controverted points of religious doctrine," might "fly for refuge to this infallible soul-preserver, in which every fear and anxiety is banished forever." They said the community hid its designs: "the utter licentiousness and wickedness to which this doctrine of Perfection leads, is glossed over and buried, by specious denials, and a multitude of words, which mean nothing." New converts were initially "unconscious" of the "practical results of their religious belief." Instead, they were led "step by step," until they were "gradually prepared to swallow Perfectionism, with all its revolting abominations."[54] The result was broken families: "Husband and wife, parent and child, brother and sister, must banish every feeling of affection, and regard each other as not of kin." Ordinary family relations were "annihilated," for "among the 'perfect'—they are all brothers and sisters, and husbands and wives together."[55] Like those who feared losing spouses and children to the Shakers and Mormons, the editors of the *Phoenix* saw danger in proselytism.

SMITTEN   141

These expressed fears about disrupted families would become more pronounced in the writings of Hubbard Eastman. A pastor in Brattleboro, he had helped lead the charge against Noyes and his community. He had first urged the *Phoenix* to investigate the perfectionists and sent letters to the paper to supplement their reporting. In 1849 he published his book *Noyesism Unveiled*. By the time it was printed, Noyes had already fled for Oneida. Suit had been brought against him in Putney for adultery, he had suffered embarrassment at a failed faith healing, and word of a mob action was circulating.[56] But some of the community remained, and it was unclear whether Noyes might attempt a return. And while they had promised they would no longer practice group marriage, Eastman was unconvinced. He wrote his book with the intention of bringing an end to perfectionism. That aim wasn't fully realized, but Eastman played a part in isolating the group.

Eastman contextualized Noyes's religion as part of a wider trend of religious enthusiasm. It was, in his estimation, "the worst form and most dangerous species of, the Come-outism of the present age." That is, Noyes, like other enthusiasts, had been so bold as to eschew the guidance of established religious organizations and follow his own inspiration. What made him particularly dangerous was that he had a strong pedigree, having been trained at Andover and Yale. It was easier to fight "infidelity and irreligion" if they "would appear in their native dress, and sail under their own black colors," but they were much more threatening when they came "in a borrowed garb of superior goodness," thereby fooling the "unwary and unsuspecting." Noyes used religious sophistry to win his converts: "Error, in all its diversified forms, is ever dangerous and destructive, but never more so than when it assumes an apparently sanctimonious garb, and is so interwoven with truth, that to trace it through all its devious and intricate windings, and detect and expose it, would be an arduous work—an almost hopeless task."[57] But Eastman was up to it. His 432-page tome left no rock unturned. Like the *Vermont Phoenix*, Eastman did his homework. He provided a thorough review of Noyes's writings and arrived at largely the same conclusions of the *Phoenix*, emphasizing the inherent dangers of antinomian teachings.[58]

Similar to the criticisms we have seen of Joseph Smith and the Prophet Matthias, Eastman particularly emphasized the hazards that ensued when one went beyond the writings of the Bible through revelations. Noyes's 1843 book, *The Berean*, he said was regarded by the "Noyesites" as "an inspired book!" It could be put "upon the shelf by the Golden Bible got up by Joe Smith"; both were probably "coined at the same mint!"[59] Extending the comparison, he pointed to how Noyes had employed miracles, such as faith healings, to extend his influence. Such knavery, he said, had "been seized upon by all the petty impostors, from the days of Mahomet down to the times of *Joe Smith* and *John H. Noyes*." Noyes was a "magician," no less a pretender than "the wonderful seer of Palmyra" and the "far-famed Arabian Prophet!"[60] Like Alexander Campbell on Mormonism or William Leete Stone on the Kingdom of Matthias, Eastman rejected contemporary revelations, believing the age of miracles past.

The door to all this trouble, Eastman believed, was opened by the spirit of "latitudinarianism." In the name of religious tolerance, the ministry had allowed religious confusion: "a great diversity of views and conflicting sentiments, and the consequent multiplication of erroneous systems, is a prolific source of evil." In his estimation, "Noyesism" was "but one of the offspring of a parent evil whose numerous progeny are coming up, like the plagues of Egypt." Quoting the Reverend E. T. Taylor, he said that "religious croakers" are simply "religious overmuch." Such enthusiasts "eat religiously, and breathe religiously, and walk religiously, and comb down every hair religiously." Adopting this self-righteous pose, they "soon begin to fall out with the world; fall out with their brethren; fall out with the church," soon enough have a "quarrel with Almighty God himself," and become "rank infidels." Following inspiration, "the lightnings in all their zig-zags through the sky," they ignored the tempering effect of other sources of knowledge. "True religion," Eastman said, could "by no possibility be hostile to science and intellectual improvement."[61] Here were ministers of the gospel, once again, arguing to keep religion reined in.

Whether Noyes was a wild-eyed enthusiast or a deliberate impostor, he was equally dangerous. The most vulnerable to his preaching were the young. Eastman highlighted for a wider audience what citizens of Putney believed. Noyes and his followers, he said, had been pursuing for some time a plan to "deceive, seduce, and ruin the young and unsuspecting." They had held out "allurements" with the intent of "enticing the young, drawing them in, and sealing their ruin." Luckily, in Putney, word of the community's licentiousness got out, so that even though "most flattering invitations were extended to several young ladies of this village and vicinity," the number of "victims" was small. They had been delivered "like the bird from the snare of the fowler, or the fascination of the wily serpent." Eastman wished to send out warning to Oneida, where Noyes had now carried his operations. He said that Noyes was busy trying to ingratiate himself with the people in the Oneida area. They needed to "protect their own firesides" so that they could "preserve the sanctity of 'sweet home.' " They would "do well to keep a vigilant eye upon the Noyesite Community there." If they allowed "their sons and daughters to be enticed from under the parental roof, and by the soft hand of persuasion drawn within the 'charmed circle,' " he warned, "their ruin would be sealed."[62] Fears of seduction of the young continued to haunt anti-enthusiasm writings.

To further illustrate this danger Eastman served up detailed examples of youth who had been lost to the perfectionists in Putney in his appendix. He gave special attention to the case of fifteen-year-old Lucinda Lamb, a case that had also had drawn the attention of Putney residents. Along with twenty-year-old Helen Campbell, Lamb had converted to perfectionism. Lucinda's father, Russell Lamb, would end up suing Noyes for "enticing away" his daughter, producing "serious injury and expense."[63] The family and the Putney Community did a tug-of-war over Lucinda. After she converted, her parents tried to break the connection by moving her ten miles away. George Noyes, younger brother of John, paid her a visit there, purportedly proposing marriage as a seductive ploy. According to Eastman, his real intent was to add her to the "great supper which was fast being prepared." Her family, in turn, moved her seventy-five miles away to live with relatives in Massachusetts, believing she was suffering under "mesmeric influences." To illustrate the theft of Lucinda, Eastman provided a copy of a letter that Noyes penned to Lamb's father. In it, Noyes insisted that Lucinda now belonged to his community: "I think the present project of sending Lucinda away from her religious friends is as unnatural and as cruel to her soul, as it would be to take a newborn infant away from its mother. I do not believe that you will succeed in alienating her from her present faith or from us." But the move did, in fact, create enough distance. While the family managed to get Lucinda away, for Eastman the lesson was clear: "in the case of Miss Lamb we can clearly see the course pursued by the Noyesites for the purpose of drawing young and virtuous females into the vortex of ruin." They employed "secret and subtle influences" to "lead the victim along, step by step, till the nefarious scheme is accomplished."[64] From the perspective of Hubbard Eastman, as well as the *Vermont Phoenix*, Noyes could be ignored no longer.

And their neighbors agreed. After Noyes fled, the village extracted a promise from the remaining community members. They demanded that the perfectionists' pledge to give up their group marriage. And in the name of expediency, the perfectionists did. For some Putney residents, this was enough. Others wished for an admission of guilt, something that would represent a renunciation of their perfectionism.[65] Noyes convinced his Putney brethren it was time to join him. They would find safety in central New York, on a remote farm where Jonathan Burt, a Noyes convert, had established a new perfectionist community. Others would follow. By 1848 there were already eighty-four people living in union on this Oneida farm.[66]

Once ensconced at Oneida, Noyes and his fellow perfectionists, adopting the name the Oneida Association, would fully establish the community life they had begun at Putney (see figure 5.2). Noyes would turn bold again, providing a systematic public statement of his vision in the *First Annual Report of the Oneida Association* with an appendix titled "Bible Argument Defining the Relations of the Sexes in the Kingdom of Heaven." As summarized by Lawrence Foster, this document was not only a "recapitulation" of the "ideals which underlay the initial efforts at Putney," it was forward-looking, holding "every important idea for the revision of relations between the sexes that Noyes would implement during the subsequent thirty years at Oneida."[67] If in his early years

FIGURE 5.2. "Early Mansion House Complex." Drawing by Charlotte Miller (ca. 1851). The image seems to evoke Oneida as a rural retreat from the world. Courtesy of the Oneida Community Mansion House.

Noyes had railed against organization as much as Theophilus Gates, he now was ready to establish order. This document has a much more secular and frank tone when discussing sex. But it definitely remained rooted in revelation. Noyes believed that to "usher in the kingdom of God," one needed "bona fide communication with the heavens," even if some might see this as a "fanatical principle." He rejected those who believed that "the age of miracles is past."[68] Noyes remained committed to transcending the law, while also consolidating his position as a privileged recipient of the new dispensation.

In summing up his past views on marriage, Noyes affirmed that "in the kingdom of heaven, the institution of marriage, which assigns the exclusive possession of one woman to one man, does not exist," citing again Matthew 22:23–30, "in the resurrection they neither marry nor are given in marriage." As a side note, so as to clearly put purity perfectionism behind, he adds that "Christ, in the passage referred to, does not exclude the sexual distinction, or sexual intercourse, from the heavenly state, but only the world's method of assigning the sexes to each other." In this community, there would not simply be a nullity of marriages. Noyes describes his emerging vision of complex marriage. Overall, he believed that a religious community had to find a unity of spirit in Christ. Sex, as one of the strongest urges toward fellowship, had to be harnessed so as to promote community feeling. Noyes believed that religious feelings naturally yielded sexual feelings: "the tendency of religious unity to flow into the channel of amativeness, manifests itself in revivals and in all the higher forms of spiritualism—Marriages or illegitimate amours usually follow religious excitements." These "amative tendencies," which had visited "almost every spiritual sect," were "not to be treated as unaccountable irregularities." Instead they were "expressions of a law of human nature." "Amativeness," he concluded, was "the first and most natural channel of religious love." Rather than trying to fight this fact, it ought to "be investigated and provided for."[69] Here Noyes was in perfect agreement with anti-enthusiasm writers saying that religious enthusiasm yielded sexual impulses. But while they wished to suppress them at the source, he was ready to embrace them.

Monogamy, in his view, was unnatural. Despite the romanticism one could find in novels, he said, experience had taught that "sexual love is not naturally restricted to pairs." Instead, men and women had both discovered that "love is not burnt out by one honey-moon, or satisfied by one lover." Those who were willing to look into the "secret history of the human heart" found that it was "capable of loving any number of times and any number of persons." The "one-love theory" was simply the product of the " 'green-eyed monster,' jealousy." Hearkening back to the Battle-Axe letter, he emphasized the importance of "variety," which was as welcome in food and drink as in sex. This did not mean that one might not have particular "affinity" for another and engage in "special pairing," but "the fact that a man loves peaches best, is no reason why he should not, on suitable occasions, eat apples, or cherries."[70] In time, Noyes would come to fear special unions more, fighting to break apart instances of "sticky love," which could interfere with devotion to the wider community.[71] Thus, the Bible Argument retains a vestige of spiritual wifery while moving toward complex marriage.

The Oneida Association would channel and organize sexual feelings by various means, refining and building on practices initiated at Putney. As mentioned previously, Noyes would catch up with Gates by devising a means by which to prevent the difficulties of childbirth, calling on men to practice coitus reservatus. The young had particular trouble gaining mastery over sexual expression. Therefore, the association adopted the principles of "ascending and descending fellowship," pairing young men with postmenopausal women and young women with older men, often Noyes himself. "Mutual criticism" sessions were also used to help keep a commitment to the wider community, approving and regulating sexual pairings with an eye to improving believers and preventing the growth of exclusive attachments.[72] It is telling too that Noyes now used the term "complex *marriage*." While he dismissed the exclusiveness of conventional marriage, there was a commitment bond, with rules and processes for his system of uniting the group.

One might wonder why community-based sexual love might then not flow within same-sex unions. Noyes's explanation on the limits to same-sex pairings proved strained. But he did entertain the question, saying one might wonder what "the difference between the love of man towards man, and that of man towards woman" is. He allowed that "attraction" was the "essence of love in both cases" but said heterosexual unions differed in that "man and woman are so adapted to each other by the differences of their natures, that attraction can attain a more perfect union between them than between man and man, or between woman and woman." He was not just thinking about temperamental differences. Using the metaphor of a magnet and steel, he said two flat surfaces did not lock together as well as a "ball and socket." Thus, "love between man and man can only advance to something like plain contact," but men and women could "advance to interlocked contact."[73] If he could not transcend heteronormativity in intercourse, he was at least willing to allow for same-sex attraction.

For all its bold expressions, the Bible Argument did try to antici-pate the troubles that had visited Putney. Noyes realized the biggest fear would be that of neighbors frightened of losing family members to the perfectionists. Thus, he addressed the topic head-on and forsook proselytism, declaring, "The Association abstains from all proselyting" and "aggressive operations." To the extent it engaged in "publishing its sexual theory," it was done "only in self-defense, and at the command of public sentiment." The association would "limit itself to its own fam-ily circle, not invading society around it." Theirs would be a separatist group, no longer interested in bringing wider society to the Kingdom of God. In this, the group came to adopt the stance of the Shakers, erecting clearer boundaries to find safety.[74] Noyes sought "toleration," reminding his audience "that liberty of conscience is guaranteed by the Constitution of the United States, and of the several states." He also suggested that "Quakers, Shakers, and other religionists are tolerated in conscientious deviations from the general order of society."[75] Such toleration came at a cost. They would limit their aims to keep the peace.

But this preemptive retreat did not prove sufficient. Whether they ac-tively recruited or not, new followers continued to join the perfection-ists at Oneida over its first few years. By 1851 they had grown to a com-munity of 205.[76] Perhaps the Oneida Community itself had more fervor to grow their ranks than their founder. He had removed to Brooklyn in 1849, soon after establishing the community, saying he wanted a "more quiet place for reflection, and a better opportunity to act upon the As-sociation than a residence directly in it."[77] Joined by about a dozen fol-lowers, he concentrated on publishing and penning letters of instruc-tion back to Oneida. But before he left he had also been responsible for the conversion of twenty-one-year-old Tryphena Hubbard. It was not long after her conversion that Tryphena's father, Noahdiah, con-fronted Noyes about her alienation from her family, likely playing a role in Noyes's departure for Brooklyn. The community did admit that Noy-es's leaving did have the effect of "quelling the excitement against the Association."[78] They actually had been cautious in how they brought Tryphena into the group, having her marry a member, Henry Seymour. But when her father discovered their marital practices, he became furi-ous. The scandal grew when Henry Seymour was indicted for abusing his new wife, who was apparently suffering mental illness. The family wanted her removed to an asylum with the association covering the costs. At one point Noyes even offered up the possibility of shutting down the Oneida Community. Several attempts to settle out of court were initiated and abandoned, until eventually a lasting settlement was reached in 1852.[79]

This case also likely inspired the coverage of the *New York Observer*, the last major Noyes critic we will consider. Unlike the *Advocate of Moral Reform*, the *Vermont Phoenix*, or Eastman Hubbard, the *Observer* seemed to have a more tenuous hold on their subject, emphasizing sensationalism over substance. But their article nonetheless proved consequential in the history of the Oneida Community. They wanted to shine a bright light on their new neighbors, saying that "it is hardly known, but it is true, that there is a weekly newspaper published in this immediate neighborhood" that propagated "the doctrines of the Oneida Perfectionists." This group, they explained, rejected "all the laws, both human and divine, that are designed to regulate the marriage relation." In their place, "the unrestrained indulgence of the human passions is practiced." Aggravating the crime, such practices, they said, were advocated by a purported man of God, a former student of two prominent seminaries who taught that free love was a "MEANS OF GRACE OR HELPS TO HOLINESS." At least the Mormons in Utah, they said, "rigidly maintained" the "distinction of husband and wife." But in Oneida such distinctions were "utterly abolished" with the "freest licentiousness practiced as the highest developments of holiness."[80] Apparently strictly enforced polygamy was preferable to complete sexual freedom. The nuances of complex marriage were lost on them, but they did achieve their aim of drawing negative attention to Noyes.

They also bemoaned the respectability of some converts, noting that "persons thus living in this beastly manner, were but recently members of orthodox, evangelical churches, some of them well educated and most of them respectably connected." Echoing earlier anti-enthusiasm critics, they thought the Oneida Community revealed "the danger of error, and the infinite necessity of holding fast to the truth." If they were to allow "loose teaching from the pulpit and the press," this would be the result: "the only safety is in steadfast adherence to the good old-fashioned morality of our fathers and mothers, on whose principles the first half of the 19th century has made no improvement." Give them that old-time religion, indeed.

A couple of months later the *Observer* was happy to report that the perfectionists were "retracting." Their reporting, they believed, "had called the attention of our Legislature to the fact that these people are defying the laws of the land, and living in a state of social corruption." The "exposure" of this group produced a fear in the association that "the laws should be brought to bear upon them." They reprinted the association's public retreat statement: "It may be understood henceforth that the Oneida Association, and all associations connected with it, have receded from the practical assertion of their views, and formally resumed the marriage morality of the world, submitting themselves to all the ordinances and restrictions of society and law on this subject. This definite concession to public opinion, made in good faith, we trust will be satisfactory, and give peace."[81] The *Observer* may have claimed too much credit, for threats of prosecution by the district attorney on behalf of Hubbard were still in the offing at this time. But Noyes himself, in a letter dated the following month, said to his correspondent that they were "dealing with the enemy on the field of public opinion." He wished to settle with Hubbard as soon as possible, for a public trial would be "reported to the newspapers," thereby turning "a local difficulty into a general scandal."[82] Recalling the Lucinda Lamb case, with the accompanying coverage in the *Phoenix*, he was willing to settle at most any cost.

According to Anthony Wonderly, however, it was the Oneida Community, more than Noyes himself, who proved the real peacemakers. They held a strawberry festival for their upstate New York neighbors in the summer of 1852, with about three hundred attending, even Noahdiah Hubbard. It proved a successful public relations strategy. Afterward, their neighbors circulated a petition, calling on the district attorney to drop the case. He proved willing to respect the wishes of the local community.[83] This public relations campaign was coupled with renewed avowals of separatism. In 1850 the association had announced that they were not actively seeking new members; by 1856 they would not even accept any applications for admission. Though the suspension of complex marriage probably lasted only six months, enough concessions had been gained to earn quiet solitude for the Oneida Association for the next couple of decades.[84]

The "dying embers" of perfectionism had reignited, but ultimately the fire was contained. In the next few decades, John Humphrey Noyes did manage to build a commune at Oneida that would house a steady population of about 250 people. But his influence outside this community remained limited. This retreat to separatism was due both to Noyes's critics and his own willingness to withdraw to safety. Public pressure was applied by various writers, such as Hubbard Eastman, the *Advocate of Moral Reform*, the *Vermont Phoenix*, and the *New York Observer*. Noyes's self-preservation instinct had typified his career from the start. He had renounced those who embarrassed his cause. In so doing, he would also renounce his own earlier self.

Following the Brimfield bundling, he rejected spiritual wifery, even though his antinomian teachings had helped catalyze the spread of such unions. As he distanced himself from the embarrassment, he also eclipsed the incipient leadership of women like Lucina Umphreville and Mary Lincoln. He would reclaim scandal as his own, albeit reluctantly, with the publication of the Battle-Axe letter. The *Advocate of Moral Reform* connected the dots between Noyes's theology and his views on free love. The editors renounced the antinomian wing of perfectionism to protect their cause of purity. In reaction, Noyes would displace blame onto Theophilus Gates and insist, contrary to his own earlier writings, that the resurrection state, which allowed sexual freedom, was not yet achieved by anyone on earth.

He then sought safety in his hometown of Putney. There he gathered his followers and further developed his sexual and social thought. When the Putney Community launched into sexual communism, the town took notice. The exposé published by the *Vermont Phoenix* laid bare everything Noyes had been saying, largely unnoticed, in his publications for over a decade. They made a convincing case that sexual disorder was inherent in antinomian perfectionism. Their investigative work was followed up by that of Hubbard Eastman, who concentrated on the danger that Noyesism presented to families. This was a familiar strategy. We have seen how fears of the loss of children had also been deployed against revivalists, the Mormons, and the Shakers.

Noyes would find a new haven for perfectionists in rural upstate New York. Here antinomian impulses were put under his inspired authority. Finishing work started at Putney, he would develop an orderly system of complex marriage in place of the "marriage Supper of the Lamb" where every dish was free to every guest. But the specter of proselytism, conjured by Eastman, still haunted his efforts. The case of Tryphena Hubbard, coupled with the unwelcome attention of the *New York Observer*, highlighted the risks faced by the cause of perfectionism. Noyes offered to disband his community at Oneida, but the association's neighborly relations and renewed promises to stop conversions proved sufficient. Having once hoped to bring the fullness of the Second Coming to the world, Noyes and his community would settle for a private utopia.

Conclusion

When famed backwoods Methodist itinerant preacher Peter Cartwright composed his memoirs in 1856, he lamented the end of the contest for souls. Criticizing his own church for taking on airs, now valuing college education over religious enthusiasm, he reminisced about the glory days of the Second Great Awakening. In his years as a preacher, he was not satisfied preaching to the converted. Rather, he relished the battle for souls. He was suspicious of those who had become cozy with the status quo.[1]

He began his career in Kentucky but grew upset with the way the church there became "entangled" with slavery, with ministers marrying into elite southern families. In 1824 he moved to the frontier circuit of Sangamon, Illinois, where he extended his missionary endeavors.[2] Throughout his career he battled a series of rivals as he rode his circuits and preached at camp meetings. His memoirs recount spars with the Shakers, Mormons, Universalists, Campbellites, Presbyterians, and Baptists, among others. He was willing to break apart families if it meant gaining more followers to his Methodist cause. His retrospective account of past skirmishes and his regret about the end of revivalism suggest the larger arc of the Second Great Awakening. In his telling, enthusiastic religion had been rife with gender disruption and sexual tensions. To him, it was a point of pride.

Cartwright bragged about how he could make women and men swoon under his preaching. For example, at one camp meeting he said he was able to conquer a "fashionable, wealthy family" raised as Calvinists who held a "diabolical hatred" against the Methodists. Cartwright first made inroads by converting the wife and two daughters. These women "felt greatly attached" to him as "the instrument" of "their salvation." Not surprisingly, this "enraged the husband and father of these interesting females very much." He threatened Cartwright with a whipping and murder. The father considered him a "very bad man," for, Cartwright noted, "all the women in the country were falling in love with me." The father criticized him for playing on "their passions," suggesting Cartwright had converted them with "bad intentions." It was the father's goal to expose him to "put a stop to the women all running mad" after him.[3]

However, Cartwright would prove the victor. First disarming him with kindness, he approached the father and invited him to the preacher's tent. After the "trumpet sounded for preaching," Cartwright mounted the pulpit. Under the preaching of Cartwright, the father soon began to experience a "hard struggle" in his mind. Thrown into doubt about his soul, as the camp meeting progressed, the father's "convictions increased till he could neither eat nor sleep." Cartwright soon swept him up in a larger round of conversions. One night, a "tremendous power fell on the congregation." A "gang of rowdies" that had hassled Cartwright soon "fell by the dozens on the right and left." At the same time, the father "fell suddenly, as if a rifle ball had been shot through his heart." Laying powerless all night, he came to consciousness the next morning, giving up "shouts of glory." The converted father's daughter "came leaping and skipping" to Cartwright.[4] The family had all been won to the Methodists.

Cartwright also admitted defeats. Sometimes denominational devotion was too strong to overcome. During one revival season, he found that "a great many professors of religion in other Churches professed to wish their children converted," yet "they could not trust them at a Methodist meeting, especially a camp meeting." At one such camp meeting, he had converted "many young ladies whose parents were members of a sister Church." The mother of two young women decided to put a stop it. When she heard "her daughters were kneeling at the altar of God, praying for mercy," she sent an elder from her own church to bring them out. Cartwright chased the man out, but the mother then came in to retrieve them. When she entered, all were down on their knees, including Cartwright, who was "stooping down" while "encouraging the mourners." Blocked direct access to her daughters, the mother actually stepped on Cartwright's shoulders to reach them. She tried to drag them out of the meeting, but Cartwright forced her out instead. Nonetheless, the mother ultimately had her way. While Cartwright had converted the daughters, their mother still prevented them from becoming Methodists. She "compelled them to join her Church, sorely against their will." Later they married men in their mother's church, leaving Cartwright to worry that their souls had been lost forever.[5]

In time, the impulse to tend to one's own, rather than seek fresh converts, would also overtake the Methodists. Cartwright regretted the shift, noting he was "sorry to say that the Methodist Episcopal Church of late years, since they have become numerous and wealthy, have almost let camp-meetings die out." It was in such meetings where he had enjoyed his greatest successes, where "the word of God" had found "the hearts of thousands" who would have otherwise been lost. He called on his brethren to return to the heroic standard of the early years, using all Methodist means available to rouse the people. He hoped that "the day be eternally distant, when camp-meetings, prayer-meetings and love-feasts shall be laid aside."[6] In addition to producing conversions, such meetings had empowered ordinary believers, including women.

As Cartwright's boasts about his conquests seem to play to the stereotype of the reverend rake, he also mourned the way the church was now encouraging decorum and modesty in women. Discussing prayer meetings, in particular, he noted how their "disuse" effectively silenced women. Such meetings had allowed all, "men and women, young and old," to speak. While in recent years "fashionable objections" had been raised against "females praying in public," he disagreed with the changing sentiment. He had witnessed the transformative power of female prayer. He had seen some "dull and stupid prayer-meetings suddenly changed from a dead clog to a heavenly enjoyment, when a sister [had] been called on to pray." Such a woman could "pray with words that burned." She could bring "many tall and stout-hearted sinners" to "quake and tremble before God."[7] Now striving for respectability, the Methodists had left such scenes of female public prayer behind. In this, they were like other mainline denominations who had frowned on the religious assertiveness of women like Eliza Wintringham, let alone someone so bold as Frances Folger.

Even before they turned toward female reserve, the Methodists had not been the most disruptive church with respect to sex and gender.

While Methodist women had prayed publicly, and even preached, they certainly did not wield the social authority enjoyed by Shaker women. There was no Methodist equivalent to Lucy Wright and certainly not Mother Ann Lee. Nor had Methodists defied marital monogamy in the ways that the Shakers, Mormons, Catholic clergy, and Oneida Community did.[8] They embraced nothing as unusual as spiritual wifery, nor celestial or complex marriage. In narrating his competition with religious rivals, Cartwright described a middle path for Methodists. While they believed in experiential religion, especially the moving of the spirit during rebirth, they stopped short of believing in enthusiastic practices such as speaking in tongues and faith healings. To his mind, opening the door wide to inspiration could lead to unreliable and dangerous revelations. In his estimate, while the Campbellites were too cold, adhering to mere logic and debate, the Mormons were too hot, led away by delusions.[9] As the Second Great Awakening drew to a close in the North, with Methodists and other mainline denominations encouraging more modesty in women, the religious outliers who had more radically broken sex and gender conventions were marginalized to contain their threat.

Whether externally imposed or internally erected Mormons, Shakers, Catholics, and the Oneida Community all had religious boundaries built between them and wider American society. By mid-century even enthusiastic religion itself (branded as fanaticism) had been sequestered from the evangelical mainstream. Each of these religious expressions had presented tests to the religious, gender, and sexual order. They had invited, perhaps lured, women and men to convert to religious groups that were actively reimagining patterns of sex and gender. Challenges like charismatic masculinity, clerical or universal celibacy, plural marriage, and sexual communism represented real threats. Religious rivals and skeptics exposed and criticized these dangers, forcing these religious groups into retreat.

Shakers would follow the isolationist route by living in closed communities and adopting unique sexual and social arrangements. They also kept the peace by emphasizing their adherence to domesticity, highlighting the maternity of Mother Ann Lee. Mormons failed to achieve such a détente, forced by mob and print attacks to seek safety by migrating to the Utah desert. This would buy them time to assimilate by eventually rejecting polygamy. Following the Hogan Schism, the Catholic Church would reject the egalitarian impulse of trusteeism that had opened a voice for women and the laity more generally. Their critics, in turn, would accuse priests of imprisoning women, casting Catholics as un-American. The religious opponents of John Humphrey Noyes and the Oneida Community had exposed the dangers of the antinomian impulse, which threatened monogamy and the gospel order. Under duress, Noyes and his community abandoned proselytism. Like the Shakers and Mormons, they achieved safety in separatism.

To be sure, prophetic impulses endured in American life. Some of the social challenges first incubated in revival religion would take on a life of their own. Reform movements like abolitionism, health reform, and women's rights would survive the larger collapse of the Second Great Awakening, moving into orbits of their own.[10] And enthusiastic movements still thrived in some marginalized communities. For northern African Americans, for example, the push for a more contained piety made less sense. Generally denied access to the exercise of secular power, they inhabited a "sacred world" of their own.[11] Prophecy and politics were forged together. A telling example is Frederick Douglass. In the years approaching the Civil War, even as Douglass sought political change, he lacked any real prospect of inhabiting political office. The Radical Abolitionist Party that he joined and helped lead was deeply grounded in a prophetic and millennial vision, an expression of "Bible politics." America was to be cleansed of sin through a violent confrontation with slavery, followed by a world of racial equality. But in the years following the Civil War, when Douglass actually was able to take political office, he began to adopt a more secular perspective. Increasingly, he embraced compromise and moderation, while he became a Republican Party loyalist. He lost his religious enthusiasm along the way.[12] If less dramatic a turn, such had been the journey of many evangelicals seeking respectability in America.

The radical reordering of sex and gender relations proposed by some enthusiastic groups was only kept alive by protecting them within isolated religious communities. The act of religious containment not only staved off sex and gender disruption; it also served to shape the values of middle-class northern Americans. Religious boundaries, lines between enthusiastic groups and the evangelical mainstream, defined those both on the inside and outside. Bourgeois ideas about the proper voice and place of women, domesticity, child-rearing, sexual behavior, romance, and companionate marriage were constructed in reaction to religious tests. It proved easier to imagine women as smitten than to imagine they would actively choose to join such unconventional churches. Under this new dispensation, charismatic preachers would no longer make their followers swoon under the spell of religious visions. Instead, ministers would help uphold stable churches and families, consolidating whatever gains they might have made during the seasons of revival.

NOTES

Introduction

1. On the thought of Campbell and the Disciples more generally, see Rose-Ann Benson, "Alexander Campbell: Another Restorationist," *Journal of Mormon History* 41, no. 4 (October 2015): 1–42; Nathan Hatch, "The Christian Movement and the Demand for a Theology of the People," *Journal of American History* 67, no. 3 (December 1980): 545–67.

2. Rigdon joined Campbell's movement after visiting with him in Buffaloe, Virginia (later Bethany, West Virginia) in the summer of 1821. Two years later they solidified their alliance as they traveled on a mission through Ohio and Kentucky. The nominal dispute in Pittsburgh was over Rigdon's refusal to teach infant damnation, but Baptists were dividing more generally over the Campbellite reformist agenda. See Steven L. Shields, "Joseph Smith and Sidney Rigdon: Co-Founders of a Movement," *Dialogue: A Journal of Mormon Thought* 52, no. 3 (Fall 2019): 1–18; Hans Rollman, "The Early Baptist Career of Sidney Rigdon in Warren, Ohio," *Brigham Young University Studies* 21, no. 1 (Winter 1981): 37–50; F. Mark McKiernan, "The Conversion of Sidney Rigdon to Mormonism," *Dialogue: A Journal of Mormon Thought* 5, no. 2 (Summer 1970): 71–78; Richard S. Van Wagoner, *Sidney Rigdon: A Portrait of Religious Excess* (Salt Lake City: Signature Books, 1994), 26–38.

3. Shields, "Joseph Smith and Sidney Rigdon," 1–18; McKiernan, "Conversion of Sidney Rigdon," 71–78; Van Wagoner, *Sidney Rigdon*, 39–67; Benson, "Alexander Campbell," 1–42; Richard Lyman Bushman, "The Restoration of All Things," chap. 6 in *Joseph Smith and the Beginnings of Mormonism* (Chicago: University of Illinois Press, 1987); 179–88; Bushman, *Joseph Smith: Rough Stone Rolling* (New York: Vintage Books, 2005), 123–25, 148–50.

4. Karl Keller and John Wickliffe Rigdon, "I Never Knew a Time When I Did Not Know Joseph Smith: A Son's Record of the Life and Testimony of Sidney Rigdon," *Dialogue: A Journal of Mormon Thought* 1, no. 4 (Winter 1966): 14–42; Van Wagoner, *Sidney Rigdon*, 58–64; Bushman, *Rough Stone Rolling*, 148–50.

5. Lawrence R. Flake, "A Shaker View of a Mormon Mission," *BYU Studies Quarterly* 20, no. 1 (Fall 1979): 94–99.

6. For a copy of the original revelation and a fuller contextualization of this document, see the historical introduction and annotations in Revelation, 7 May 1831 (*Doctrine and Covenants* 49), Joseph Smith Papers, accessed January 13, 2021, https://www.josephsmithpapers.org/paper-summary/revelation-7-may-1831-dc-49/1; on emerging Shaker beliefs regarding the divinity of Ann Lee and vegetarianism, see Stephen J. Stein, *The Shaker Experience in America:*

A History of the United Society of Believers (New Haven, CT: Yale University Press, 1994), 68–72, 156–58.

7. For the full revelation on plural marriage, see Revelation, 12 July 1843 (*Doctrine and Covenants* 132), Joseph Smith Papers, accessed January 13, 2021, https://www.josephsmithpapers.org/paper-summary/revelation-12-july-1843-dc-132/1; on the likely possibility that Smith was already formulating plural marriage at this time, see Daniel W. Bachman, "New Light on an Old Hypothesis: The Ohio Origins of the Revelation on Eternal Marriage," *Journal of Mormon History* 5 (1978): 19–32.

8. For a fuller view of this particular usage, see Glendyne R. Wergland, *One Shaker Life: Isaac Newton Youngs, 1793–1865* (Amherst: University of Massachusetts Press, 2006), 33–48.

9. Flake, "Shaker View of a Mormon Mission," 96–97.

10. Flake, "Shaker View of a Mormon Mission," 97.

11. Flake, "Shaker View of a Mormon Mission," 97–98.

12. Flake, "Shaker View of a Mormon Mission," 98.

13. Flake, "Shaker View of a Mormon Mission," 98–99.

14. Some of the classic treatments of the Second Great Awakening that reveal its radicalism compared to other episodes of revivalism include Whitney Cross, *The Burned-Over District: The Social and Intellectual History of Enthusiastic Religion in Western New-York, 1800–1850* (Ithaca, NY: Cornell University Press, 1950); Nathan Hatch, *Democratization of American Christianity* (New Haven, CT: Yale University Press, 1989); Robert H. Abzug, *Cosmos Crumbling: American Reform and the Religious Imagination* (New York: Oxford University Press, 1994).

15. On the American commitment to monogamy, see Nancy F. Cott, *Public Vows: A History of Marriage and the Nation* (Cambridge, MA: Harvard University Press, 2002).

16. On the community benefits of high demands made by outsider religious groups, see Stephen Taysom, *Shakers, Mormons, and Religious Worlds: Conflicting Visions, Contested Boundaries* (Bloomington: Indiana University Press, 2011), esp. 100–151; Laurence R. Iannaccone, "Why Strict Churches Are Strong," *American Journal of Sociology* 99, no. 5 (March 1994): 1180–1211.

17. Francis Roloff, *The True Sentiments of the Writer of the Last Appeal to the Congregation of St. Mary's Church* (Philadelphia: Bernard Dornin, 1821), 6.

18. A number of previous studies have looked at particular aspects of sexual scandal and religion in the early republic. See esp. William McLoughlin, "Untangling the Tiverton Tragedy: The Social Meaning of the Terrible Haystack Murder of 1833," *Journal of American Culture* 7, no. 4 (1984): 75–84; Daniel A. Cohen, "The Respectability of Rebecca Reed: Genteel Womanhood and Sectarian Conflict in Antebellum America," *Journal of the Early Republic* 16, no. 3 (Autumn 1996): 419–61; Patricia Cline Cohen, "Ministerial Misdeeds: The Onderdonk Trial and Sexual Harassment in the 1840s," *Journal of Women's History* 7, no. 3 (1995): 34–57; Kathleen Kennedy, "A Charge Never Easily Made: The Meaning of Respectability and Women's Work in the Trial of the Reverend William Hogan, 1822," *American Nineteenth Century History* 7, no. 1 (March 2006): 29–62; Bruce Dorsey, "'Making Men What They Should Be': Male Same-Sex Intimacy and Evangelical Religion in Early Nineteenth-Century New England," *Journal of*

the History of Sexuality 24, no. 3 (2015): 345–77; Karin E. Gedge, *Without Benefit of Clergy: Women and the Pastoral Relationship in Nineteenth-Century American Culture* (New York: Oxford University Press, 2003); Paul E. Johnson and Sean Wilentz, *The Kingdom of Matthias: A Story of Sex and Salvation in 19th-Century America* (New York: Oxford University Press, 1994); Christine Leigh Heyrman, *Doomed Romance: Broken Hearts, Lost Souls, and Sexual Tumult in Nineteenth-Century America* (New York: Knopf, 2021); Kara French, *Against Sex: Identities of Sexual Restraint in Early America* (Chapel Hill: University of North Carolina Press, 2021). I have benefited from their insights, while also using an array of new research findings to investigate the relationship between religious enthusiasm and sexual disorder, showing how sexual disruption was broadly implicated in the rise and fall of the Second Great Awakening.

19. See Gary Nash, *Forging Freedom: The Formation of Philadelphia's Black Community* (Cambridge, MA: Harvard University Press, 1988), 190–202, 213–23.

20. See subsequent chapters for a fuller accounting of the scholarship on the religious groups covered in this study. Some essential ones will be listed here. On the religious and social experience of the Mormons in this era, see Bushman, *Rough Stone Rolling*; Laurel Thatcher Ulrich, *A House Full of Females: Plural Marriage and Women's Rights in Early Mormonism, 1835–1870* (New York: Knopf, 2017). On the Shakers, see Stein, *Shaker Experience in America*; Glendyne Wergland, *Sisters in the Faith: Shaker Women and Equality of the Sexes* (Amherst: University of Massachusetts Press, 2011). On the Catholic experience, see Dale Light, *Rome and the New Republic: Conflict and Community in Philadelphia Catholicism between the Revolution and the Civil War* (Notre Dame, IN: University of Notre Dame Press, 1996); Jay P. Dolan, *The American Catholic Experience: A History from Colonial Times to the Present* (Garden City, NJ: Doubleday, 1985). On perfectionists and the Oneida Community, see Anthony Wonderly, *Oneida Utopia: A Community Searching for Human Happiness and Prosperity* (Ithaca, NY: Cornell University Press, 2017); Ellen Wayland-Smith, *Oneida: From Free-Love Utopia to the Well-Set Table* (New York: Picador, 2016). Two classic texts that looked at the sexual and religious experience of Shakers, Mormons, and the Oneida Community together are Lawrence Foster, *Religion and Sexuality: The Shakers, the Mormons, and the Oneida Community* (Urbana: University of Illinois Press, 1984); Louis J. Kern, *An Ordered Love: Sex Roles and Sexuality in Victorian Utopias—the Shakers, the Mormons, and the Oneida Community* (Chapel Hill: University of North Carolina Press, 1981). Two important more recent attempts to look at groups together are French, *Against Sex*; Taysom, *Shakers, Mormons, and Religious Worlds*.

21. On the vexed history of defining Mormons, see Terryl L. Givens, *The Viper on the Hearth: Mormons, Myths, and the Construction of Heresy* (New York: Oxford University Press, 1997), 76–93.

22. Cross, *Burned-Over District*.

23. Bruce Lincoln, *Holy Terrors: Thinking about Religion after September 11* (Chicago: University of Chicago Press, 2006).

24. Variations on this Mormon phrase appear in numerous places; see, for example, Vision, 16 February 1832 (*Doctrine and Covenants* 76), Joseph Smith Papers, accessed February 19, 2022, https://www.josephsmithpapers.org/paper-summary/vision-16-february-1832-dc-76/2; Campbell's fullest criticism of

Mormons is developed in Alexander Campbell, *Delusions: An Analysis of the Book of Mormon; with an Examination of Its Internal and External Evidences, and a Refutation of Its Pretenses to Divine Authority* (Boston: Benjamin H. Green, 1832).

25. Joseph A. Dowling, *The Trial of the Rev. William Hogan, Pastor of St. Mary's Church, for an Assault and Battery on Mary Connell. Tried before the Mayor's Court in and for the City of Philadelphia* (Philadelphia: R. Desilver, 1822), Appendix: The Charge, 2.

26. On the accommodations of evangelicals to southern society, see Christine Leigh Heyrman, *Southern Cross: The Beginnings of the Bible Belt* (Chapel Hill: University of North Carolina Press, 1997); Monica Najar, *Evangelizing the South: A Social History of Church and State in Early America* (New York: Oxford University Press, 2008); John E. Boles, *The Great Revival: The Beginnings of the Bible Belt* (Lexington: University Press of Kentucky, 1972).

27. Foundational studies of the Burned-Over District include Cross, *Burned-Over District*; Paul E. Johnson, *A Shopkeeper's Millennium: Society and Revivals in Rochester, New York, 1815–1837* (New York: Hill & Wang, 1978); Mary Ryan, *Cradle of the Middle Class: The Family in Oneida County, New York, 1790–1865* (New York: Cambridge University Press, 1981). On the urban religious experience, see Richard Carwardine, "The Second Great Awakening in the Urban Centers: An Examination of Methodism and the 'New Measures,'" *Journal of American History* 59, no. 2 (September 1972): 327–40; Carroll Smith-Rosenberg, *Religion and the Rise of the American City: The New York City Mission Movement, 1812–1870* (Ithaca, NY: Cornell University Press, 1971); Bruce Dorsey, *Reforming Men and Women: Gender in the Antebellum City* (Ithaca, NY: Cornell University Press, 2002); Terry Bilhartz, *Urban Religion and the Second Great Awakening: Church and Society in Early National Baltimore* (Rutherford, NJ: Fairleigh Dickinson University Press, 1986). For views of frontier revivalism, see John Wigger, *Taking Heaven by Storm: Methodism and the Rise of Popular Christianity in America* (New York: Oxford University Press, 1998), chaps. 2–3; Paul K. Conkin, *Cane Ridge: America's Pentecost* (Madison: University of Wisconsin Press, 1990); Ellen Eslinger, *Citizens of Zion: The Social Origins of the Camp Meeting Revival* (Knoxville: University of Tennessee Press, 1999). As suggested by Bilhartz's book on Baltimore, and even more so by treatments of frontier religion, it is clear there was no clean boundary between northern and southern evangelical experiences. Nonetheless, the religious and egalitarian ethos expressed at Cane Ridge took on a more socially radical turn in the North over the first half of the nineteenth century, producing greater sexual and gender challenges and a resulting rejection of religious enthusiasm.

1. "Fanaticism Can Wield Such a Mighty Influence over the Female Heart"

1. Luke Johnson, "History of Luke Johnson," *Deseret News*, May 19, 1858; Richard S. Van Wagoner, *Sidney Rigdon: A Portrait of Religious Excess* (Salt Lake City: Signature Press, 1994), 108–22.

2. Joseph Smith Jr., *History of the Church of Jesus Christ of Latter-day Saints*, vol. 1 (Salt Lake City: Deseret Book Company, 1951), 259–67.

3. Chris Beneke, *Beyond Toleration: The Religious Origins of American Pluralism* (New York: Oxford University Press, 2006).

4. The literature on both anti-Mormonism and anti-Catholicism is immense; one of the most important early explorations of them in tandem was David Brion Davis, "Some Themes of Counter-Subversion: An Analysis of Anti-Masonic, Anti-Catholic, and Anti-Mormon Literature," *Mississippi Valley Historical Review* 47, no. 2 (September 1960): 205–24.

5. Givens, *Viper on the Hearth*, 21; see also Beneke, *Beyond Toleration*, 208–16.

6. Givens, *Viper on the Hearth*, 7.

7. J. Spencer Fluhman, *"A Peculiar People": Anti-Mormonism and the Making of Religion in Nineteenth-Century America* (Chapel Hill: University of North Carolina Press, 2012).

8. As such, Givens provides only brief mention of the Hiram episode; see *Viper on the Hearth*, 43.

9. *Public Discussion of the Issues between the Reorganized Church of Jesus Christ of Latter-day Saints and the Church of Christ [Disciples], Held in Kirtland, Ohio, Beginning February 12th, and Closing March 8th, 1884, between E. L. Kelley, of the R.C. of J.C. of Latter-day Saints, and Clark Braden, of the Church of Christ* (St. Louis: Christian Publishing, ca. 1884), 202.

10. Van Wagoner, *Sidney Rigdon*, 114–15, 120n28.

11. "Historical Discourse Delivered by Elder George A. Smith, in the Tabernacle, Ogden City, on Tuesday, November 15, 1864," *Journal of Discourses* 11, no. 1, accessed February 20, 2022, https://jod.mrm.org/11/1; Luke Johnson, "History of Luke Johnson."

12. Fawn M. Brodie, *No Man Knows My History: The Life of Joseph Smith* (1945; New York: Vintage Books, 1995), 118–20. The story is then also retold in Van Wagoner, *Sidney Rigdon*, 116, and resurfaces with skepticism in Bushman, *Rough Stone Rolling*, 179.

13. *Public Discussion*, 202.

14. Bushman, *Rough Stone Rolling*, 177–78; see also Van Wagoner, *Sidney Rigdon*, 108–18; Brodie, *No Man Knows My History*, 118–19; Linda King Newell and Valeen Tippets Avery, *Mormon Enigma: Emma Hale Smith* (New York: Doubleday, 1984), 41.

15. This portrait of the intolerance of the Disciples cuts against the grain of Nathan Hatch's definitive treatment, because Hatch emphasizes their fight for religious freedom. While the Disciples most certainly railed against religious restrictions within their own former churches, they nonetheless sought to contain rival groups like the Mormons; see Hatch, "Christian Movement," 545–67; for a closer view of Disciples and Mormon relations on the Western Reserve, especially with respect to Sidney Rigdon and Alexander Campbell, see Van Wagoner, *Sidney Rigdon*, 39–122; on the religious competition and conflict in the neighboring Burned-Over District, see Cross, *Burned-Over District*, 43–51, 126–37.

16. In contrast to J. Spencer Fluhman, I am emphasizing more the continuity in the opposition to Mormonism. Fears of both religious imposture and sexual power had long reinforced one another in the minds of Mormon critics; for a succinct statement of Fluhman's stages of anti-Mormonism, see his *"Peculiar People,"* 9.

17. "Mormonism," *Ohio Star* (Ravenna), October 20, 1831, 3.

18. David S. Reynolds, *Beneath the American Renaissance: The Subversive Imagination in the Age of Emerson and Melville* (Cambridge, Mass.: Harvard University Press, 1988); Karen Halttunen, "Humanitarianism and the Pornography of Pain in Anglo-American Culture," *American Historical Review* 100, no. 2 (April 1995): 303–34; R. Laurence Moore, *Selling God: American Religion in the Marketplace of Culture* (New York: Oxford University Press, 1994).

19. "Mormonism," *Ohio Star*, 3.

20. Ezra Booth, "Mormonism—No. VII," *Ohio Star* (Ravenna), November 24, 1831, 1; Thomas Campbell, "The Mormon Challenge," *Telegraph* (Painesville, OH), February 15, 1831; Alexander Campbell, "Delusions," *Telegraph* (Painesville, OH), March 8, 1831; "Internal Evidences," March 15, 1831.

21. Ezra Booth, "For the Ohio Star," *Ohio Star* (Ravenna), October 13, 1831, 3. Alexander Campbell would publish his critique of Mormonism, which first appeared in the *Millennial Harbinger* and soon thereafter in the *Telegraph*, under the title *Delusions: An Analysis of the Book of Mormon*.

22. Booth, "For the Ohio Star," 3.

23. On the clash between the Disciples and Mormons over the possibility of divine revelations in their own age, see Bushman, *Joseph Smith and the Beginnings of Mormonism*, 179–88.

24. Ezra Booth, "Mormonism—No. IV," *Ohio Star* (Ravenna), November 3, 1831, 3.

25. Ezra Booth, "Mormonism—No. III," *Ohio Star* (Ravenna), October 27, 1831, 3. E. D. Howe offered similar descriptions; see Bushman, *Rough Stone Rolling*, 150.

26. Ezra Booth, "Mormonism—No. V," *Ohio Star* (Ravenna), November 10, 1831, 3.

27. Ezra Booth, "Mormonism—Nos. VIII–IX," *Ohio Star* (Ravenna), December 8, 1831, 1.

28. Ezra Booth, "Mormonism—No. VI," *Ohio Star* (Ravenna), November 17, 1831, 3.

29. Booth, "Mormonism—No. VII," 1.

30. Van Wagoner, *Sidney Rigdon*, 115.

31. Booth, "For the Ohio Star," 3.

32. Booth, "Mormonism—Nos. VIII–IX," 1.

33. Booth, "Mormonism—Nos. VIII–IX," 1. Tyler Parsons similarly anticipated this potential in Mormonism in Tyler Parsons, *Mormon Fanaticism Exposed: A Compendium of the Book of Mormon, or Joseph Smith's Golden Bible* (Boston: Printed for the Author, 1841).

34. Booth, "Mormonism—Nos. VIII–IX," 1; "Mormonism—No. V," *Ohio Star* (Ravenna), November 10, 1831, 3.

35. Bushman, *Rough Stone Rolling*, 169.

36. Booth, "For the Ohio Star," 3.

37. Brodie, *No Man Knows My History*, 94–95; Van Wagoner, *Sidney Rigdon*, 109.

38. Bushman, *Rough Stone Rolling*, 170.

39. Van Wagoner, *Sidney Rigdon*, 53–55.

40. "To the Public," *Ohio Star* (Ravenna), December 15, 1831, 3.

41. Symonds Ryder, "For the Ohio Star," *Ohio Star* (Ravenna), December 29, 1831, 3.

42. Revelation, 1 December 1831 (*Doctrine and Covenants* 71), Joseph Smith Papers, accessed January 13, 2021, https://www.josephsmithpapers.org/paper-summary/revelation-1-december-1831-dc-71/1. The historical introduction provided to this revelation more fully details the linkage between this revelation and the *Ohio Star* letters.

43. Ryder, "For the Ohio Star," 3.

44. Charles H. Ryder, "History of Hiram," 1864, Hiram History Narratives, box 2/A/1/a, Hiram College Archives, Hiram, Ohio.

45. Luke Johnson, "History of Luke Johnson."

46. On the fears surrounding property, particularly the Johnson farm, see Van Wagoner, *Sidney Rigdon*, 114; Agnes M. Smith, "Folklore and History in the Mormon Encounter with the Disciples of Christ at Hiram, OH, March 1832," August 1966, Hiram Archives, 3/C Mormons, Hiram Library Archives, Hiram, Ohio.

47. Booth, "For the Ohio Star," 3. On the problems of embarrassment for manhood in the early republic, see Bertram Wyatt-Brown, *Southern Honor: Ethics and Behavior in the Old South* (New York: Oxford University Press, 1982); Joanne B. Freeman, *Affairs of Honor: National Politics in the New Republic* (New Haven, CT: Yale University Press, 2002); Toby L. Ditz, "Shipwrecked; or, Masculinity Imperiled: Mercantile Representations of Failure and the Gendered Self in Eighteenth-Century Philadelphia," *Journal of American History* 81, no. 1 (January 1994): 51–80.

48. Nor should it be imagined that religious rivalry disappeared as an important dynamic in explaining religious conflict. Sarah Barringer Gordon and Jan Shipps have revealed how conflict between the Methodists and Mormons was a key ingredient in the Mountain Meadows Massacre of 1857; see Sarah Barringer Gordon and Jan Shipps, "Fatal Convergence in the Kingdom of God: The Mountain Meadows Massacre in American History," *Journal of the Early Republic* 37, no. 2 (2017): 307–47.

49. John C. Bennett, *The History of the Saints, or, An Exposé of Joe Smith and Mormonism*, 3rd ed. (Urbana: University of Illinois Press, 2000), 223–29; Lawrence Foster, *Religion and Sexuality*, 170–74; Andrew F. Smith, *The Saintly Scoundrel: The Life and Times of Dr. John Cook Bennett* (Urbana: University of Illinois Press, 1997), 98–128.

50. Bushman, *Rough Stone Rolling*, 538–50.

51. Alfreda Eva Bell, *Boadicea, The Mormon Wife: Life Scenes in Utah*, ed. Kent Bean, Book Verve E-Books (Baltimore: A. R. Orton, 2014), Kindle edition; Orvilla Belisle, *The Prophets or Mormonism Unveiled* (Philadelphia: William White Smith, 1855); Maria Ward, *Female Life among the Mormons: A Narrative of Many Years' Personal Experience; by the Wife of a Mormon Elder, Recently from Utah* (1855; New York: Derby & Jackson, 1860); Metta Victoria Fuller, *Mormon Wives: A Narrative of Facts Stranger than Fiction* (New York: Derby & Jackson, 1856); John Hyde Jr., *Mormonism: Its Leaders and Designs* (New York: W. P. Fetridge, 1857).

52. On the popularity of these texts and Ward's sales in particular, see Leonard J. Arrington and Jon Harupt, "Intolerable Zion: The Image of Mormonism in Nineteenth-Century American Literature," *Western Humanities Review* 22 (Summer 1968): 243–60.

53. Sarah Barringer Gordon, " 'Our National Hearthstone': Anti-Polygamy Fiction and the Sentimental Campaign against Moral Diversity in Antebellum America," *Yale Journal of Law and the Humanities* 8, no. 2 (1996): 295–350; Sarah Barringer Gordon, "The Liberty of Self-Degradation: Polygamy, Woman Suffrage, and Consent in Nineteenth-Century America," *Journal of American History* 83, no. 3 (1996): 815–47; Sarah Barringer Gordon, *The Mormon Question: Polygamy and Constitutional Conflict in Nineteenth-Century America* (Chapel Hill: University of North Carolina Press, 2002).

54. Rosemarie Zagarri, *Revolutionary Backlash: Women and Politics in the Early American Republic* (Philadelphia: University of Pennsylvania Press, 2007); Lucia McMahon, *Mere Equals: The Paradox of Educated Women in the Early American Republic* (Ithaca, NY: Cornell University Press, 2012); Mary Kelley, *Learning to Stand and Speak: Women, Education and Public Life in America's Republic* (Chapel Hill: OIEAHC/University of North Carolina Press, 2006); Jan Lewis, "The Republican Wife: Virtue and Seduction in the Early Republic," *William and Mary Quarterly* 44, no. 4 (October 1987): 689–721; Anya Jabour, *Marriage in the Early Republic: Elizabeth and William Wirt and the Companionate Ideal* (Baltimore: Johns Hopkins University Press, 1998).

55. See B. Carmon Hardy, "Lords of Creation: Polygamy, the Abrahamic Household, and Mormon Patriarchy," *Journal of Mormon History* 20, no. 1 (1994): 119–52; Charles Sellers, *The Market Revolution: Jacksonian America, 1815–1846* (New York: Oxford University Press), 222–25; Johnson and Wilentz, *Kingdom of Matthias*, 6–11; Bushman, *Rough Stone Rolling*, 260–64; Kern, *Ordered Love*, 144–57.

56. Ulrich, *House Full of Females*; Laurel Thatcher Ulrich, "Runaway Wives, 1830–60," *Journal of Mormon History* 42, no. 2 (April 2016): 1–26. Prior to Ulrich, others have considered the benefits of Mormon plural marriage to women. See Kern, *Ordered Love*, 170–89; Lawrence Foster, *Religion and Sexuality*, 211–20; Maxine Hanks, ed., *Women and Authority: Re-Emerging Mormon Feminism* (Salt Lake City: Signature Books, 1992). A recent survey of the forms of agency available to women in Mormonism is Kate Holbrook, *Women and Mormonism: Historical and Contemporary Perspectives* (Salt Lake City: University of Utah Press, 2016).

57. Ulrich, *House Full of Females*, xiii.

58. In this way, these anti-Mormon texts resembled the seduction fiction of previous decades; see Lewis, "Republican Wife"; Carroll Smith-Rosenberg and Wai Chee Dimock, "Domesticating Virtue: Coquettes and Revolutionaries in Young America," in *American Literary Studies: A Methodological Reader*, ed. Michael A. Elliott and Claudia Stokes (New York: New York University Press, 2003), 19–40; on the difficulty of imagining female consent when enmeshed in patriarchal power relations, see Sharon Block, *Rape and Sexual Power in Early America* (Chapel Hill: University of North Carolina Press, 2006), 16–52.

59. John L. Brooke, *The Refiner's Fire: The Making of Mormon Cosmology, 1644–1844* (New York: Cambridge University Press, 1996), 56–57, 216–17, 264.

60. Bennett, *History of the Saints*, 223–57.

61. Ward, *Female Life among the Mormons*, 68; see also Hyde, *Mormonism*, 84–85; Bell, *Boadicea*, loc. 462–66 of 1561.

62. Belisle, *Prophets*, 152–53. Mrs. Brandish also gives testimony to the benefits of polygamy to women; see Ward, *Female Life among the Mormons*, 300–302.

63. Fuller, *Mormon Wives*, 139, 313–14. Equally surprising is the character of Mrs. Brandish in Maria Ward's novel. She supported polygamy, while often physically besting men in her encounters with them; she was held as "a sort of priestess" among the elders of the church. See Ward, *Female Life among the Mormons*, quotation on 38.

64. Fuller, *Mormon Wives*, 179; see also Bell, *Boadicea*, loc. 195–98 of 1561.

65. Fuller, *Mormon Wives*, 312.

66. Ulrich, *House Full of Females*, 13–14.

67. Ward, *Female Life among the Mormons*, 199.

68. Gordon, "Liberty of Self-Degradation," 834–37. On the perceived importance of monogamy to the stability of America in the nineteenth century, see Cott, *Public Vows*.

69. Laurel Thatcher Ulrich shows that Mormons, in fact, did maintain an insistence that women freely choose to join a marriage. See Ulrich, *House Full of Females*, 131–32.

70. On the rise of youth-directed marriages, see Ellen K. Rothman, *Hands and Hearts: A History of Courtship in America* (New York: Basic Books, 1984), 17–55; Lisa Wilson, *Ye Heart of a Man: The Domestic Life of Men in Colonial New England* (New Haven, CT: Yale University Press, 1999), 37–74; McMahon, *Mere Equals*, 90–115. On the rejection of parental control of marriage, see Jay Fliegelman, *Prodigals and Pilgrims: The American Revolution against Patriarchal Authority, 1750–1800* (New York: Cambridge University Press, 1982); Lewis, "Republican Wife," 689–721.

71. Bell, *Boadicea*, loc. 1253–64 of 1561.

72. Hyde, *Mormonism*, 56.

73. Ward, *Female Life among the Mormons*, 307; see also 357.

74. Howard P. Chudacoff, *How Old Are You? Age Consciousness in American Culture* (Princeton, NJ: Princeton University Press, 1989), 93–98.

75. Hyde, *Mormonism*, 55; on entrapment by shame (a standard seduction trope), see also Belisle, *Prophets*, 228.

76. Ward, *Female Life among the Mormons*, 357–58; see also 302.

77. Bell, *Boadicea*, loc. 691–93 of 1561.

78. Ward, *Female Life among the Mormons*, 103, 313–14.

79. Belisle, *Prophets*, 367–68. To corroborate these claims, Metta Fuller provides a list of "Maxims for Mormon Wives" from the *Deseret News*; see Fuller, *Mormon Wives*, 325–26.

80. Ward, *Female Life among the Mormons*, 103.

81. Belisle, *Prophets*, 137. While the dialogue and dramatic flair is clearly concocted by Belisle, it is true, in fact, that Emma Smith stood opposed to polygamy; see Bushman, *Rough Stone Rolling*, 493–96.

82. Hyde, *Mormonism*, 57.

83. Ward, *Female Life among the Mormons*, 104–5, 152, 300–301, 391–98, 410–12; Hyde, *Mormonism*, 52; Bell, *Boadicea*, loc. 850, 873 of 1561; Belisle, *Prophets*, 113, 139–40, 189–90, 374–77.

84. Ward, *Female Life among the Mormons*, 410–11.

85. See Ward, *Female Life among the Mormons*, 90, 216–20; Hyde, *Mormonism*, 52–53, 62; Bell, *Boadicea*, loc. 157–66 of 1561; Belisle, *Prophets*, 113; Fuller, *Mormon Wives*, 185, 312.

86. Fuller, *Mormon Wives*, 185.

87. Hyde, *Mormonism*, 52; on Hyde's career as a Mormon and popular apostate speaker, see Lynne Watkins Jorgensen, "John Hyde, Jr., Mormon Renegade," *Journal of Mormon History* 17 (1991): 120–44.

88. Fuller, *Mormon Wives*, 199.

89. Bell, *Boadicea*, loc. 157–66 of 1561.

90. On the importance of boundary maintenance to religious outsider groups, see Kristen Tobey, *Plowshares: Protest, Performance, and Religious Identity in the Nuclear Age* (University Park: Pennsylvania State University Press, 2016), 7–15; Taysom, *Shakers, Mormons, and Religious Worlds*. On how Mormons used a sharpened sense of difference to invite persecution, allowing them to feel righteous, see R. Laurence Moore, "How to Become a People: The Mormon Scenario," in *Religious Outsiders and the Making of Americans* (New York: Oxford University Press, 1986), 25–47.

91. On the American commitment to monogamy in the nineteenth century, see Cott, *Public Vows*.

92. See Catherine A. Brekus, *Strangers and Pilgrims: Female Preaching in America, 1740–1845* (Chapel Hill: University of North Carolina Press, 1998), 117–231; Heyrman, *Southern Cross*, 161–206; Christine Leigh Heyrman, *Doomed Romance: Broken Hearts, Lost Souls and Sexual Tumult in Nineteenth-Century America* (New York: Knopf), 9–22, 75–81, 88–95, 100–103, 161–66; Rodney Hessinger, *Seduced, Abandoned, and Reborn: Visions of Youth in Middle-Class America, 1780–1850* (Philadelphia: University of Pennsylvania Press, 2005), 96–124; Ryan, *Cradle of the Middle Class*; Nancy A. Hewitt, *Women's Activism and Social Change: Rochester, New York, 1822–1872* (Ithaca, NY: Cornell University Press, 1984); Cross, *Burned-Over District*, 177–78.

93. Bushman, *Rough Stone Rolling*, 436–46.

94. Ward, *Female Life among the Mormons*, 79, 103; Bell, *Boadicea*, loc. 403–11, 462–66, 787–89; Hyde, *Mormonism*, 70–72; Fuller, *Mormon Wives*, 187.

95. Bell, *Boadicea*, loc. 403–11.

96. Fuller, *Mormon Wives*, 187.

97. Bell, *Boadicea*, loc. 190–92.

98. Terryl Givens highlights how notions of seduction and coercion were used to cover deeper fears of Mormon heresy; my goal here is to show how portrayals of Mormon coercion were used to contain the release proffered to women in both marriage and religion by expanding religious choices. See Givens, *Viper on the Hearth*, 131–64. On how notions of Mormon coercion were used to undermine arguments for female suffrage, see Gordon, "Liberty of Self-Degradation," 815–47.

99. Bell, *Boadicea*, loc. 192–94; Ward, *Female Life among the Mormons*, 12, 24, 40, 65, 76, 93, 100, 142, 416–17; Belisle, *Prophets*, 115, 200, 202–3; Hyde, *Mormonism*, 72, 111.

100. Belisle, *Prophets*, 115.

101. Ward, *Female Life among the Mormons*, 24–26, 65.

102. Ward, *Female Life among the Mormons*, 14, 15, 37–38, 76, 85, 140–42, 416–17; Hyde, *Mormonism*, 69; Belisle, *Prophets*, 107, 152–56, 162–63, 228; Fuller, *Mormon Wives*, 72, 84, 158–63, 198; thus the theme of deception continued to

exist in mutual reinforcement with fears of seduction. On the earlier emphasis on imposture, see Fluhman, *"Peculiar People,"* 21-48.

103. Hyde, *Mormonism*, 111, and see also 66, 69; Belisle, *Prophets*, 107, 173, 179, 229-30; Ward, *Female Life among the Mormons*, 12, 25; Fuller, *Mormon Wives*, 170.

104. Bell, *Boadicea*, loc. 977-80.

105. Ward, *Female Life among the Mormons*, 291-92, 446; for other examples of coercion or captivity, see Belisle, *Prophets*, 277-78, 281, 354, 381; Bell, *Boadicea*, loc. 1308-11, 1341-47.

106. Hessinger, *Seduced, Abandoned, and Reborn*, 23-43.

107. Hyde, *Mormonism*, 59; Bell, *Boadicea*, loc. 853-54, 948-51; Belisle, *Prophets*, 370, 377; Fuller, *Mormon Wives*, 214, 236-46, 269-87.

108. Ward, *Female Life among the Mormons*, 106.

109. Ward, *Female Life among the Mormons*, 76.

110. Hyde, *Mormonism*, 111, 72.

111. Bell, *Boadicea*, loc. 183-86.

112. Fuller, *Mormon Wives*, 252.

2. "A Base and Unmanly Conspiracy"

1. Dowling, *Trial of the Rev. William Hogan*, Appendix: The Charge, 2.

2. Rosemarie Zagarri, "Politics and Civil Society: A Discussion of Mary Kelley's *Learning to Stand and Speak*," *Journal of the Early Republic* 28, no. 1 (Spring 2008): 61-73, quotation on 73. While Zagarri is thinking here of only oratory, I think it is useful to take up this agenda to speech writ large (publications, conversations, court testimony, etc.).

3. See Jeanne Boydston, "The Woman Who Wasn't There: Women's Market Labor and the Transition to Capitalism in the United States," *Journal of the Early Republic* 16, no. 2 (Summer 1996): 183-206; Susan Branson, *These Fiery Frenchified Dames: Women and Political Culture in Early National Philadelphia* (Philadelphia: University of Pennsylvania Press, 2001); Cynthia Kerner, *Beyond the Household: Women's Place in the Early South, 1700-1835* (Ithaca, NY: Cornell University Press, 1998); Elizabeth Varon, *We Mean to Be Counted: White Women and Politics in Antebellum Virginia* (Chapel Hill: University of North Carolina Press, 1998); Heyrman, *Southern Cross*; Dorsey, *Reforming Men and Women*; Mary Ryan, *Women in Public: Between Banners and Ballots, 1825-1880* (Baltimore: Johns Hopkins University Press, 1990); David Waldstreicher, *In the Midst of Perpetual Fetes: The Making of American Nationalism, 1776-1820* (Chapel Hill: OIEAHC/ University of North Carolina Press, 1997).

4. See Zagarri, *Revolutionary Backlash*; Nancy Isenberg, *Sex and Citizenship in Antebellum America* (Chapel Hill: University of North Carolina Press, 1998); Helen Lefkowitz Horowitz, *Rereading Sex: Battles over Sexual Knowledge and Suppression in Nineteenth-Century America* (New York: Knopf, 2002); Lori D. Ginzberg, *Women and the Work of Benevolence: Morality, Politics, and Class in the Nineteenth-Century United States* (New Haven, CT: Yale University Press, 1990); Julie Roy Jeffrey, *The Great Silent Army of Abolitionism: Ordinary Women in the Antislavery Movement* (Chapel Hill: University of North Carolina Press, 1998); Zagarri, "Politics and Civil Society"; Smith-Rosenberg, *Religion and the Rise of the American City*, 97-124.

5. The shame attached to the events would seemingly extend to those women who gave them public notice. Mary Clarke, who would become notorious for her biographies of Ann Carson, chose to anonymously publish a transcript of the trial; see Susan Branson, *Dangerous to Know: Women, Crime, and Notoriety in the Early Republic* (Philadelphia: University of Pennsylvania Press, 2009), 90–91. Jennifer Schaaf has shown that within the community of Catholic women, there was greater appreciation of female involvement in church affairs. See Jennifer Schaaf, "'With a Pure Intention of Pleasing and Honouring God': How the Philadelphia Laity Created American Catholicism, 1785–1850" (PhD diss., University of Pennsylvania, 2013), *Publicly Accessible Penn Dissertations 925*, https://repository.upenn.edu/edissertations/925, 87–100.

6. Some of the most important works that expose these dynamics of evangelical religion in this era include Hatch, *Democratization of American Christianity*; Charles E. Hambrick-Stowe, *Charles G. Finney and the Spirit of American Evangelicalism* (Grand Rapids, MI: Wm B. Eerdmans, 1996); Ryan, *Cradle of the Middle Class*; Bilhartz, *Urban Religion*; Wigger, *Taking Heaven by Storm*; Moore, *Selling God*, 2–65.

7. The closest modern study of the Hogan Schism is Light, *Rome and the New Republic*, 52–244; see also Schaaf, "With a Pure Intention"; Francis E. Tourscher, *The Hogan Schism and Trustee Troubles in St. Mary's Church Philadelphia, 1820–1829* (Philadelphia: Peter Reilly, 1930); Patrick J. Dignan, *A History of the Legal Incorporation of Catholic Church Property in the United States, 1784–1932* (New York: P. J. Kenedy & Sons, 1935), 113–24; Arthur J. Ennis, "Henry Conwell, Second Bishop of Philadelphia," in *The History of the Archdiocese of Philadelphia*, ed. James F. Connelly (Philadelphia: Archdiocese of Philadelphia, 1976), 83–104; Martin I. J. Griffin, "Life of Bishop Conwell of Philadelphia," *Records of the American Catholic Historical Society of Philadelphia*, ed. Lemuel B. Norton, vols. 24–25 (1913–14). The most important general history of trusteeism is Patrick W. Carey, *People, Priests, and Prelates: Ecclesiastical Democracy and the Tensions of Trusteeism* (Notre Dame, IN: University of Notre Dame Press, 1987); see also Patrick W. Carey, "Republicanism within American Catholicism, 1785–1860," *Journal of the Early Republic* 3, no. 4 (Winter 1983), 413–37; James O'Toole, *The Faithful: A History of Catholics in America* (Cambridge, MA: Belknap Press of Harvard University Press, 2008), 50–73; Dolan, *American Catholic Experience*, 110–11, 114–16; John Tracy Ellis, *American Catholicism* (Chicago: University of Chicago Press, 1956), 44–46; Robert F. McNamara, "Trusteeism in the Atlantic States, 1785–1863," *Catholic Historical Review* 30, no. 2 (July 1944): 135–54; Thomas T. McAvoy, *A History of the Catholic Church in the United States* (Notre Dame, IN: University of Notre Dame Press, 1969), 92–122.

8. Light downplays the class dimension, suggesting that the conflicts at St. Mary's in the 1820s "cut across the class divisions that had previously polarized the congregation." His emphasis rests more on an ideological divide between democratic modernists and traditionalists. Light gives serious attention to anti-Irish rhetoric, but as he admits, such could not have served as the major dividing line, for there were Irish clergy and laity on both sides of the dispute; see *Rome and the New Republic*, 52–179, quotation on 106. For a well-balanced assessment of the relative importance of class, as well as inter- and intra-ethnic

divisions in trusteeism nationally, see Patrick Carey, *People, Priests, and Prelates,* 133–53.

9. Kennedy, "Charge Never Easily Made."

10. William Hogan, *An Address to the Congregation of St. Mary's Church, Philadelphia* (Philadelphia, 1820), 33.

11. Many of the pamphlets are now bound in *Carey's Miscellanies* at the Library Company of Philadelphia. On Carey's experiences with political-oriented publishing, see Rosalind Remer, *Printers and Men of Capital: Philadelphia Book Publishers in the New Republic* (Philadelphia: University of Pennsylvania Press, 1996), 34–38; James Green, *Mathew Carey: Publisher and Patriot* (Philadelphia: Library Company of Philadelphia, 1985), 25–29.

12. On the general trust in the public value of published discourse, see Michael Warner, *The Letters of the Republic: Publication and the Public Sphere in Eighteenth-Century America* (Cambridge, MA: Harvard University Press, 1990).

13. On the place of print in evangelical Protestantism, see Hatch, *Democratization of American Christianity,* 73–77, 125–33, 141–46; Moore, *Selling God,* 12–22.

14. A number of participants and observers of the conflicts at St. Mary's identified church property disputes as one key source of the conflict; see St. Mary's Church (Philadelphia, Pa.), *Sundry Documents, Submitted to the Consideration of the Pewholders of St. Mary's Church, by the Trustees of That Church* (Philadelphia: Lydia R. Bailey, 1812), 1–4, 14; Hogan, *Address to the Congregation,* 21, 23, 26; Richard W. Meade, *An Address to the Roman Catholics of the City of Philadelphia, in Reply to Mr. Harold's Address* (Philadelphia, 1823), 5–6; *Address of the Lay Trustees to the Congregation of St. Mary's Church, on the Subject of the Approaching Election* (Philadelphia: Robert Desilver, 1822), 10, 12. For a wider view of this problem across American Catholic churches in this era, see Dignan, *History of the Legal Incorporation,* 67–179.

15. The most thorough synthesis of early American religious developments, Mark Noll's *America's God,* is representative; he declares Catholic theology to have been "a thing apart" from the evangelical Protestant mainstream. While a strict definition of theology might exclude the distribution of spiritual power, the overall emphasis of Noll's book on evangelicals effectively marginalizes Catholics in the early republic. See Mark A. Noll, *America's God: From Jonathan Edwards to Abraham Lincoln* (New York: Oxford University Press, 2002), 228. There are some important exceptions to this general trend. Daniel Walker Howe's synthesis of the early republic called for Catholics to be brought into the Second Great Awakening; see Daniel Walker Howe, *What Hath God Wrought: The Transformation of America, 1815–1848* (New York: Oxford University Press, 2007), 197–202. The fullest effort to link Catholics to nineteenth-century evangelicalism, with an emphasis on missions is Jay P. Dolan, *Catholic Revivalism: The American Experience, 1830–1900* (Notre Dame, IN: University of Notre Dame Press, 1978); see also Dolan, *In Search of American Catholicism: A History of Religion and Culture in Tension* (New York: Oxford University Press), 29–37.

16. On the Presbyterian experience in Philadelphia, see Hessinger, *Seduced, Abandoned, and Reborn,* 96–124; George M. Marsden, *The Evangelical Mind and the New School Presbyterian Experience: A Case Study of Thought and Theology in Nineteenth-Century America* (New Haven, CT: Yale University Press, 1970).

17. Michael S. Carter, "Under the Benign Sun of Toleration: Mathew Carey, the Douai Bible, and Catholic Print Culture, 1789-91," *Journal of the Early Republic* 27, no. 3 (Fall 2007): 437–69; Dolan, *In Search of American Catholicism,* 12–43; Dolan, *American Catholic Experience,* 101–24, 166–67; William W. Warner, *At Peace with All Their Neighbors: Catholics and Catholicism in the National Capital, 1787–1860* (Washington, DC: Georgetown University Press, 1994); Joseph Agonito, *The Building of an American Catholic Church: The Episcopacy of John Carroll* (New York: Garland, 1988), 146–78.

18. On Carroll's early gestures toward American sensibilities, including republicanism, see Dolan, *American Catholic Experience,* 103–9; Agonito, *Building of an American Catholic Church,* 10–54, 124–45, 205–31; on John England, see Patrick Carey, *An Immigrant Bishop: John England's Adaptation of Irish Catholicism to American Republicanism* (Yonkers, NY: U.S. Catholic Historical Society, 1982); Light, *Rome and the New Republic,* 131–38, 176–77, 242–43.

19. Patrick Carey, "William Hogan," in *American National Biography,* ed. John A. Garraty and Mark C. Carnes, vol. 11 (New York: Oxford University Press, 1999), 8–9.

20. Mathew Carey, *Address to the Right Reverend the Bishop of Pennsylvania, the Catholic Clergy of Philadelphia, and the Congregation of St. Mary's in This City* (Philadelphia: H. C. Carey & I. Lea, 1822); Hogan, *Address to the Congregation* 10–11, 19–20; Layman of the Congregation, *An Inquiry into the Causes Which Led to the Dissentions Actually Existing in the Congregation of St. Mary's; and Observations on the Mode Best Calculated to Prevent Its Increase* (Philadelphia, 1821), 8, 10; An Admirer of Fenelon, *A Letter to the Rev. William Vincent Harold, of the Order of Dominican Friars on Reading His Late Reply to a "Catholic Layman"* (Philadelphia: Robert Desilver, 1822), 24, 32; Dowling, *Trial of the Rev. William Hogan,* 73, 156.

21. See Dorsey, *Reforming Men and Women;* Hessinger, *Seduced, Abandoned, and Reborn;* Hewitt, *Women's Activism and Social Change;* Ginzberg, *Women and the Work of Benevolence;* Ryan, *Cradle of the Middle Class;* Anne Boylan, *Sunday School: The Formation of an American Institution, 1790–1880* (New Haven, CT: Yale University Press, 1988).

22. Ennis, "Henry Conwell," 83–91.

23. Mathew Carey, *Address to the Right Rev. Bishop Conwell and the Members of St. Mary's Congregation* (Philadelphia, 1821), 3, 4; Mathew Carey, *Address to the Right Reverend the Bishop of Pennsylvania,* iv–v, 15–16; William Hogan, *Continuation of an Address to the Congregation of St. Mary's Church, Philadelphia* (Philadelphia, 1821), 33; Layman of the Congregation, *Inquiry into the Causes,* 11–12; St. Mary's Church (Philadelphia, Pa.), *Address of the Committee of Saint Mary's Church of Philadelphia to Their Brethren of the Roman Catholic Faith throughout the United States of America on the Subject of a Reform of Sundry Abuses in the Administration of Our Church Discipline* (New York: Kingsland, 1821), 3–4; Meade, *Address to the Roman Catholics,* 8; Mathew Carey, *Brief Address to the Roman Catholic Congregation Worshipping at St. Mary's, on the Approaching Election for a Board of Trustees* (Philadelphia, 1822), 9–10.

24. Mathew Carey, *Address to the Right Reverend the Bishop of Pennsylvania,* iii–v; see also Mathew Carey, *Address to the Right Rev. Bishop Conwell,* 2–4.

25. Hogan, *Address to the Congregation,* 10–12, 33.

26. Francis Roloff, *Last Appeal to the Congregation of St. Mary's Church* (Philadelphia, 1821), 2; Roloff, *True Sentiments*, 3-6. While colloquially today the term "animal magnetism" has taken on sexual overtones, it is unclear whether it had assumed such connotations yet in Hogan's day. For a similar portrait of women whipped into a frenzy during the election riot at St. Mary's, see *The Battle of Saint Mary's, A Seriocomic Ballad, with Desultory Remarks on the Dissension in That Church by an Observer, Wholly Unconnected with the Parties, but Wishing Well to Liberty and Peace* (Philadelphia, 1822).

27. Roloff, *True Sentiments*, 3-4.

28. Quoted in Hogan, *Address to the Congregation*, 22-23.

29. Mathew Carey, *Address to the Right Reverend the Bishop of Pennsylvania*, 12; for similar commentary by an anti-Hogan pamphleteer, see An Irish Catholic, *A Short Address to the Roman Catholic Congregation of St. Mary's Church, on the Approaching Election for Trustees* (Philadelphia: Bernard Dornin, 1822), 6-7.

30. Light, *Rome and the New Republic*, 92.

31. Robert Waln, *The Hermit in America on a Visit to Philadelphia*, 2nd ed. (Philadelphia: M. Thomas, 1819), 101, 128-29, 180-81. For more on the gender implications of such terminology in early American society, see Kate Haulman, "Fashion and the Culture Wars of Revolutionary Philadelphia," *William and Mary Quarterly* 62, no. 4 (October 2005): 625-62; Thomas A. Foster, *Sex and the Eighteenth-Century Man: Massachusetts and the History of Sexuality in America* (Boston: Beacon Press, 2006), 110-27; Patricia Cline Cohen, *The Murder of Helen Jewett: The Life and Death of a Prostitute in Nineteenth-Century New York* (New York: Knopf, 1998), 301-29. Hogan does seem to have prioritized personal appearance and comfort. One of the other charges reportedly tied to his suspension was his refusal to lodge with certain fellow priests from St. Mary's. In one pamphlet he described the arrangements as being forced to be "kenneled together." A supporter similarly justified Hogan's right to live as a "gentleman," rather than "in the midst of filth." During the Connell trial, the audience reportedly gasped when Hogan produced for the jury a fancy cane that held within it a sword, an accoutrement seemingly not befitting a clergyman. See Hogan, *Address to the Congregation*, 27; Layman of the Congregation, *Inquiry into the Causes*, 6; Dowling, *Trial of the Rev. William Hogan*, 184.

32. Catholic Church Diocese of Philadelphia (Pa.), *A Pastoral Charge Delivered by the Right Revd. Henry, Bishop of Philadelphia, February 11th, 1821* (Philadelphia, 1821), 7; for elaborations of such rumors, as expressed in later decades, see Light, *Rome and the New Republic*, 92.

33. Mathew Carey, *Address to the Right Rev. the Bishop of Pennsylvania, and the Members of St. Mary's Congregation* (Philadelphia, 1820), 3; Mathew Carey, *Address to the Right Rev. Bishop Conwell*, 3-4; Mathew Carey, *Address to the Right Reverend the Bishop of Pennsylvania*, iv-v; Hogan, *Address to the Congregation*, 19, 22-23; Hogan, *Continuation of an Address*, 33; St. Mary's Church, *Address of the Committee of Saint Mary's Church*, 3, 6-9; *Last Appeal to the Congregation*, 4; An Irish Catholic, *Short Address*, 6; An Admirer of Fenelon, *Letter to the Rev. William Vincent Harold*, 16; *Battle of St. Mary's*, 2; Meade, *Address to the Roman Catholics*, 18-19; *Address of the Lay Trustees*, 3-4, 18-20, 24.

34. Hogan, *Address to the Congregation*, 19. Concerns about reputation loomed large among congregants at St. Mary's in the early nineteenth century, suggesting a marketplace of opinion. See Mathew Carey, *Address to the Right Rev. the Bishop of Pennsylvania*, 3; Mathew Carey, *To the Congregation of St. Mary's, "On the Banks of the Rubicon"* (Philadelphia, 1821); Mathew Carey, *Brief Address*, 3; Hogan, *Address to the Congregation*, 19–20; Layman of the Congregation, *Inquiry into the Causes*, 3; An Admirer of Fenelon, *Letter to the Rev. William Vincent Harold*, 15, 24.

35. See Mathew Carey, *Address to the Right Reverend the Bishop of Pennsylvania*, 14–16; Hogan, *Address to the Congregation*, 21, 22–23, 26; Catholic Church, Diocese of Philadelphia, *Pastoral Charge*, 9–11; St. Mary's Church, *Address of the Committee*; Layman of the Congregation, *Inquiry into the Causes*, 12; William Hogan, *Strictures on a Pamphlet Written by William Vincent Harold Entitled Reply to a Catholic Layman* (Philadelphia: Robert Desilver, 1822), 7–9; An Admirer of Fenelon, *Letter to the Rev. William Vincent Harold*, 6, 7–10, 16; *Battle of St. Mary's*, 2, 5; Rev. William Vincent Harold, *An Address to the Roman Catholics of Philadelphia* (Philadelphia: Printed for the Trustee of Harriet and Jane Dornin, 1823), 3–5; Meade, *Address to the Roman Catholics*, 5–6; Layman of St. Mary's Congregation, *An Address to the Roman Catholics of the United States* (Philadelphia, 1821), 6.

36. St. Mary's Church, *Address of the Committee*, 3–7.

37. St. Mary's Church, *Address of the Committee*, 9.

38. Harold, *Address to the Roman Catholics*, 3–7; see also Layman of St. Mary's Congregation, *Address to the Roman Catholics*.

39. Hogan, *Strictures on a Pamphlet*, 6–9, 20. In making this appeal to the primitive order of the church, Hogan was much like others advocating for trusteeism in this era. See Patrick Carey, "Republicanism within American Catholicism," 413–37. The desire to restore the primitive church was also echoed by trustee dissenters at St. Mary's. See Light, *Rome and the New Republic*, 183–84.

40. Susan Branson, *Dangerous to Know*, 90–91; Ann Carson and Mary Clarke, *The Memoirs of the Celebrated and Beautiful Mrs. Ann Carson, Revised, Enlarged, and Continued till Her Death, by Mrs. M. Clarke, in Two Volumes*, 2nd ed. (Philadelphia, New York, 1838), 82.

41. *Letter to Henry, Bishop of Philadelphia, by a Lady* (Philadelphia: Printed for the author, 1821), 1–9.

42. *Battle of Saint Mary's*.

43. Light, *Rome and the New Republic*, 112–18, 144–59.

44. McLoughlin, "Untangling the Tiverton Tragedy," 75–84; Heyrman, *Southern Cross*, 182–84; Patricia Cline Cohen, "Ministerial Misdeeds," 34–57; Hessinger, *Seduced, Abandoned, and Reborn*, 113, 217; Reynolds, *Beneath the American Renaissance*, 260–62.

45. See Light, *Rome and the New Republic*, 106, 113–14, 151–52.

46. Dowling, *Trial of the Rev. William Hogan*, 18–19.

47. Dowling, *Trial of the Rev. William Hogan*, 215.

48. Dowling, *Trial of the Rev. William Hogan*, 19, 24–25; see also Mary Clark Carr, *A Compendious Trial of the Rev. William Hogan, Pastor of the Roman Catholic Church of St. Mary's on an Indictment for an Assault and Battery on the Person of Mary Connell* (Philadelphia, 1822), 5–6, 8, 11.

49. Dowling, *Trial of the Rev. William Hogan*, 73–74; Carr, *Compendious Trial*, 11.

50. Dowling, *Trial of the Rev. William Hogan*, 107.

51. Hessinger, *Seduced, Abandoned, and Reborn*, 23–43; Reynolds, *Beneath the American Renaissance*, 260–62. Thomas Foster successfully dates such notions of natural male desire even earlier than this era. See Foster, *Sex and the Eighteenth-Century Man*, 6–12, 24–30.

52. Dowling, *Trial of the Rev. William Hogan*, 182.

53. On the anti-Catholic critique of celibacy, see Marie Anne Pagliarini, "The Pure American Woman and the Wicked Catholic Priest: An Analysis of Anti-Catholic Literature in Antebellum America," *Religion and American Culture* 9, no. 1 (1999): 97–128; French, *Against Sex*, 21–32, 39–42; Kara M. French, "Prejudice for Profit: Escaped Nun Stories and American Catholic Print Culture," *Journal of the Early Republic* 39, no. 3 (Fall 2019): 503–35; On the embrace of male chastity, see Hessinger, *Seduced, Abandoned, and Reborn*, 148–76. For a wider perspective on the sexual debates of this era, see Horowitz, *Rereading Sex*.

54. Dowling, *Trial of the Rev. William Hogan*, 230. For the most influential exploration of the "repressive hypothesis," see Michel Foucault, *The History of Sexuality*, vol. 1: *An Introduction*, trans. Robert Hurley (New York: Vintage Books, 1990).

55. Dowling, *Trial of the Rev. William Hogan*, 182–84, 194, 235.

56. Dowling, *Trial of the Rev. William Hogan*, 244, 195, 229.

57. See entry on Reed's father, "Reed, Joseph," in James Grant Wilson and James Fiske, eds., *Appletons' Cyclopaedia of American Biography* (New York: D. Appleton, 1888), 208–9; John Hill Martin, *Martin's Bench and Bar of Philadelphia* (Philadelphia: R. Welsh), 97. My gratitude goes to Bruce Mann for helping me uncover the recorder's identity.

58. Such allegations would have made her sexually suspect in this time and place too. See Lyons, *Sex among the Rabble*, part 3.

59. See Dowling, *Trial of the Rev. William Hogan*, 102–4, 106, 132, 245; Carr, *Compendious Trial*, 8, 22.

60. See Ryan, *Cradle of the Middle Class*; Ann Douglas, *The Feminization of American Culture* (New York: Knopf, 1977); Cott, *Bonds of Womanhood*.

61. Dowling, *Trial of the Rev. William Hogan*, 43–44, 104, 132; Carr, *Compendious Trial*, 22.

62. Dowling, *Trial of the Rev. William Hogan*, 52–54.

63. See Dowling, *Trial of the Rev. William Hogan*, 77–78, 89–92, 102–3, 213; Carr, *Compendious Trial*, 11–12.

64. Dowling, *Trial of the Rev. William Hogan*, 94–96.

65. David R. Roediger, *Wages of Whiteness: Race and the Making of the American Working Class*, 2nd revised and enlarged ed. (New York: Verso, 1999), esp. chap. 7; Nash, *Forging Freedom*, 213–23.

66. Dowling, *Trial of the Rev. William Hogan*, 94, 213.

67. Dowling, *Trial of the Rev. William Hogan*, 100–101.

68. Dowling, *Trial of the Rev. William Hogan*, 217, 224. Hessinger, *Seduced, Abandoned, and Reborn*, 44–68.

69. Dowling, *Trial of the Rev. William Hogan*, 202, 217–18.

70. See Dowling, *Trial of the Rev. William Hogan*, 9, 25, 36–37, 55, 64–65, 73–74, 77, 80, 83, 110, 111, 128–29, 156, 158, 181–82, 198–99, 215, 217–18, 228–30, 246–49; Carr, *Compendious Trial*, 7, 8, 11–14, 18, 46–47.

71. Dowling, *Trial of the Rev. William Hogan*, 215, 217.

72. Dowling, *Trial of the Rev. William Hogan*, 228–30.

73. Dowling, *Trial of the Rev. William Hogan*, 198.

74. This situational deployment of separate sphere is best displayed by Rosemarie Zagarri in *Revolutionary Backlash*, but she also tries her hand at drawing a trajectory for the ideological construct; see also sources cited in notes 3 and 4 above.

75. Dowling, *Trial of the Rev. William Hogan*, Appendix: The Charge, 1–6.

76. Light, *Rome and the New Republic*, 170–74; Tourscher, *Hogan Schism*, 108–24.

77. Patrick Carey, *People, Priests, and Prelates*, 214–15, 253–65; Light, *Rome and the New Republic*, 238–44; Robert F. Trisco, "Bishops and Their Priests in the United States," in *The Catholic Priest in the United States: Historical Investigations* (Collegeville, MN: Saint John's University Press, 1971), 119–23. Catholic devotional practice soon began to break more clearly from Protestant patterns at this moment too; see John T. McGreevy, *Catholicism and American Freedom: A History* (New York: Norton, 2003), 25–37.

78. Patrick Carey, "Republicanism within American Catholicism," 413–37, esp. 436–37; Light, *Rome and the New Republic*, 34, 109–11, 123, 140.

79. See Jenny Franchot, *Roads to Rome: The Antebellum Protestant Encounter with Catholicism* (Berkeley: University of California Press, 1994), 117–61; Nancy Schultz Lusignan, *Fire and Roses: The Burning of the Charlestown Convent, 1834* (New York: Free Press, 2000); Pagliarini, "Pure American Woman," 97–128; French, *Against Sex*, 21–32, 39–42.

80. Ray Allen Billington, *The Protestant Crusade, 1800–1860: A Study of the Origins of American Nativism* (Chicago: Quadrangle Books, 1964), 38–41; Branson, *Dangerous to Know*, 90–91.

81. Light, *Rome and the New Republic*, 180; Patrick Carey, "William Hogan," 8–9.

82. William Hogan, *Popery! As It Was and Is; also, Auricular Confessions and Popish Nunneries* (Hartford, CT: Silas Andrus & Son, 1845, 1853), 252–57; on the portrait of auricular confession in antebellum anti-Catholic literature, see Gedge, *Without Benefit of Clergy*, 57–58.

83. Hogan, *Popery!*, 258–61.

84. On the intersection of religion and sensationalism, see Reynolds, *Beneath the American Renaissance*, 15–91; Moore, *Selling God*, 12–39.

3. "The Fruits of Shakerism"

1. Mary Marshall Dyer, *The Rise and Progress of the Serpent from the Garden of Eden, to the Present Day: With a Disclosure of Shakerism* (Concord, NH: By the Author, 1847), 128, 187; for the original, see James Smith, "An Attempt to Develop Shakerism" (Chillicothe, OH, July 10, 1810), in Christian Goodwillie, ed., *Writings of Shaker Apostates and Anti-Shakers, 1782–1850*, vol. 1, *1782–1811* (London: Pickering & Chatto, 2013), 183.

2. On Shaker steadfastness on celibacy, see Taysom, *Shakers, Mormons, and Religious Worlds*, 100–128. I am emphasizing how the dynamic between Shakers and their critics helped produce this embrace of motherhood, but internal dynamics had a role to play as well. On the internal draw of this emphasis on motherhood for Shaker women, see Suzanne Thurman, "'Dearly Loved

Mother Eunice': Gender, Motherhood, and Shaker Spirituality," *Church History* 66, no. 4 (1997): 750–61.

3. The fullest biographical treatments of these women and their widely followed campaigns against the Shakers are Ilyon Woo, *The Great Divorce: A Nineteenth-Century Mother's Extraordinary Fight against Her Husband, the Shakers, and Her Times* (New York: Atlantic Monthly, 2010); Elizabeth A. DeWolfe, *Shaking the Faith: Women, Family, and Mary Marshall Dyer's Anti-Shaker Campaign, 1815–1867* (New York: Palgrave, 2002).

4. Susan E. Klepp, "Revolutionary Bodies: Women and the Fertility Transition in the Mid-Atlantic Region, 1760-1820," *Journal of American History* 85, no. 3 (December 1998): 910-45; Susan E. Klepp, *Revolutionary Conceptions: Women, Fertility, and Family Limitation in America, 1760–1820* (Chapel Hill: OIEACH/ University of North Carolina, 2009).

5. See Ruth H. Bloch, "American Feminine Ideals in Transition: The Rise of the Moral Mother, 1785-1815," *Feminist Studies* 4, no. 2 (June 1978): 100–126; Ryan, *Cradle of the Middle Class*; Cott, *Bonds of Womanhood*; Douglas, *Feminization of American Culture*.

6. Taysom himself admits the relatively modest external tension generated by celibacy but shows how Shakers nonetheless used celibacy as a distinguishing boundary. See Taysom, *Shakers, Mormons, and Religious Worlds*, 100–128.

7. French, *Against Sex*, 20-23, 36-39, 172n61; see also Suzanne Thurman, "The Seat of Sin, the Site of Salvation: The Shaker Body and the Nineteenth-Century American Imagination," *Nineteenth Century Studies* 15 (2001): 1–18.

8. On the lived experience of Shaker celibacy, see Wergland, *One Shaker Life*, 33-48; French, *Against Sex*, 50-56. The literature on the ideal of celibacy in antebellum bourgeois culture is extensive. The most influential work with respect to women is Nancy F. Cott, "Passionlessness: An Interpretation of Victorian Sexual Ideology, 1790-1850," *Signs* 4, no. 2 (1978): 219-36; for the growing emphasis on male chastity, see Hessinger, *Seduced, Abandoned, and Reborn*, 148-76.

9. See Markman Ellis, *The Politics of Sensibility: Race, Gender, and Commerce in the Sentimental Novel* (Cambridge: Cambridge University Press, 1996); G. J. Barker-Benfield, *The Culture of Sensibility: Sex and Society in Eighteenth-Century Britain* (Chicago: University of Chicago Press, 1992).

10. Christopher Lawrence, "The Nervous System and Society in the Scottish Enlightenment," in *Natural Order: Historical Studies of Scientific Culture*, ed. Barry Barnes and Steven Shapin (Beverly Hills, CA: Sage, 1979); Raymond Stephanson, "Richardson's 'Nerves': The Physiology of Sensibility in *Clarissa*," *Journal of the History of Ideas* 49, no. 2 (1988): 267-85; Sarah Knott, *Sensibility and the American Revolution* (Chapel Hill: OIEAHC/University of North Carolina Press, 2009).

11. Eunice Chapman, *No. 2, being an Additional Account of the Conduct of the Shakers, in the Case of Eunice Chapman and Her Children* (Albany, NY: I. W. Clark, 1818), iii.

12. On the gendering of sensibility in the early American republic, see Hessinger, *Seduced, Abandoned, and Reborn*, 29-33.

13. Mary Marshall Dyer, *A Brief Statement of the Sufferings of Mary Dyer Occasioned by the Society Called Shakers* (Boston: William S. Spear, 1818), 12-13.

14. Eunice Chapman, *An Account of the Conduct of the Shakers, in the Case of Eunice Chapman & Her Children* (Lebanon, OH: Van Vleet & Camron, 1818), 10.

15. Eunice Chapman, *An Account of the Conduct of the People Called the Shakers* (Albany, 1817), 39.

16. Dyer, *Brief Statement*, 16; see also 34.

17. Chapman, *No. 2, being an Additional Account*, 14; Dyer also describes herself dropping her pen in grief in *Brief Statement*, 10.

18. See Dyer, *Brief Statement*, 12, 17–18, 24–25, 33; Chapman, *Account of the Conduct of the People Called the Shakers*, 32, 54; Chapman, *An Account of the Conduct of the Shakers, in the Case of Eunice Chapman & Her Children*, ii, 9; Chapman, *No. 2, being an Additional Account*, 13, 18, 35, 48, 50, 55.

19. Ryan, *Cradle of the Middle Class*, chap. 4; W. J. Rorabaugh, " 'I Thought I Should Liberate Myself from the Thraldom of Others': Apprentices, Masters, and the Revolution," in *Beyond the American Revolution: Explorations in the History of American Radicalism*, ed. Alfred F. Young (DeKalb: Northern Illinois University Press, 1993), 185–217; Barry Levy, "Girls and Boys: Poor Children and the Labor Market in Colonial Massachusetts," in "Empire, Society and Labor: Essays in Honor of Richard S. Dunn," ed. Nicholas Canny, Joseph E. Illick, Gary B. Nash, and William Pencak, special issue, *Pennsylvania History* 64 (Summer 1997): 287–307; Myra C. Glenn, *Campaigns against Corporal Punishment: Prisoners, Sailors, Women, and Children in Antebellum America* (Albany: State University of New York Press, 1984).

20. Dyer, *Brief Statement*, 17–18.

21. Chapman, *No. 2, being an Additional Account*, 48.

22. Chapman, *Account of the Conduct of the People Called the Shakers*, 54.

23. See Douglas, *Feminization of American Christianity*.

24. Chapman, *Account of the Conduct of the Shakers*, 9.

25. Chapman, *No. 2, being an Additional Account*, 16.

26. Dyer, *Rise and Progress*, 34.

27. Nora Doyle, " 'The Highest Pleasure of Which Woman's Nature Is Capable': Breast-Feeding and the Sentimental Maternal Ideal in America, 1750–1860," *Journal of American History* 97, no. 4 (2011): 958–73; Sarah Knott, *Mother Is a Verb: An Unconventional History* (New York: Sarah Crichton Books, 2019).

28. Chapman, *Account of the Conduct of the People Called the Shakers*, 24, 45, quotation on 18; Chapman, *No. 2, being an Additional Account*, 19.

29. Chapman, *No. 2, being an Additional Account*, 60, 18.

30. James Smith, "Remarkable Occurrences, Lately Discovered among the People Called Shakers," in Goodwillie, *Writings of Shaker Apostates*, 196, 198.

31. Londa Schiebinger, "Why Mammals Are Called Mammals: Gender Politics in Eighteenth-Century Natural History," *American Historical Review* 98, no. 2 (April 1993): 382–411.

32. Dyer, *Rise and Progress*, 18, also 9, 10; Chapman, *Account of the Conduct of the People Called the Shakers*, 21, 41.

33. DeWolfe, *Shaking the Faith*, 5, 86–97, 153; Woo, *Great Divorce*, 323–31; Stein, *Shaker Experience in America*, 97–98; Edward Deming Andrews, *The People Called Shakers: A Search for the Perfect Society* (New York: Oxford University Press, 1953), 40–43; Brian Bixby, "Seeing Shakers: Two Centuries of Visitors to Shaker Villages" (PhD diss., University of Massachusetts Amherst, 2010), 71–73.

34. Cheryl Bauer and Rob Portman, *Wisdom's Paradise: The Forgotten Shakers of Union Village* (Wilmington, OH: Orange Frazer Press, 2004), 40. For other strong parental reactions to losing children to the Shakers, see French, *Against Sex*, 77–79.

35. Smith, "Remarkable Occurrences," 194.

36. Smith, "Attempt to Develop Shakerism," 181–85, quotations on 182, 185.

37. Goodwillie, *Writings of Shaker Apostates*, 207–12; Benjamin Seth Youngs, *Transactions of the Ohio Mob, Called in the Public Papers, "An Expedition against the Shakers"* (Ohio, 1810).

38. Youngs, *Transactions of the Ohio Mob*, 1–3.

39. Youngs, *Transactions of the Ohio Mob*, 4–10.

40. Bauer and Portman, *Wisdom's Paradise*, 86; Joseph R. Swan, ed., *Statutes of the State of Ohio* (Cincinnati: H. W. Derby, 1854), 870–72.

41. Chapman, *Account of the Conduct of the People Called the Shakers*, v–vi.

42. Richard McNemar, *The Other Side of the Question in Three Parts* (Cincinnati: Looker, Reynolds, 1819), 169, Supplement, i–vi.

43. McNemar, *Other Side of the Question*, Supplement, iv; on the status of women in Shaker society, see Wergland, *Sisters in the Faith*.

44. Seth Y. Wells, ed., *Testimonies Concerning the Character and Ministry of Mother Ann Lee and the First Witnesses of the Gospel of Christ's Second Appearing, Given by Some of the Aged Brethren and Sisters of the United Society* (Albany, NY: Packard & Van Benthuysen, 1827).

45. On the testimonials published in 1816, see Jean M. Humez, "'Ye Are My Epistles': The Construction of Ann Lee Imagery in Early Shaker Sacred Literature," *Journal of Feminist Studies in Religion* 8, no. 1 (Spring 1992): 83–103; Ann Kirschner, "At the Gate of Heaven: Early Shaker Dreams and Visions," in *Heavenly Visions: Shaker Gift Drawings and Gift Songs*, curated by France Morin (New York: Drawing Center; Los Angeles: UCLA Hammer Museum; Minneapolis: University of Minnesota Press, 2001), 169–78.

46. Wells, *Testimonies*, 5; on the early attraction to ecstatic experiences in Shaker worship, see Douglas L. Winiarski, "Seized by the Jerks: Shakers, Spirit Possession, and the Great Revival," *William and Mary Quarterly* 76, no. 1 (January 2019): 111–50.

47. Wells, *Testimonies*, 129; see also 16, 19, 25, 26, 28, 29, 36, 37, 41–42, 45, 48, 68, 75, 91, 93, 115, 133. Marjorie Procter-Smith similarly notes a move toward domestication and shows that the shadowy figure of Holy Mother Wisdom, the female counterpart of God the Father, was described as a nurturing mother. See Marjorie Procter-Smith, "'In the Line of the Female': Shakerism and Feminism," in *Women's Leadership in Marginal Religions: Explorations Outside the Mainstream*, ed. Catherine Wessinger (Urbana: University of Chicago Press, 1993), 23–40, esp. 30, 33.

48. Wells, *Testimonies*, 133.

49. Wells, *Testimonies*, 115.

50. Wells, *Testimonies*, 91; see also 70–71 for Mother Lee as a surrogate mother. Ann Lee's capacity for extending love to followers was also indicated in the 1816 narratives, but, as an internal document meant to record and inspire visionary experiences, it also conveyed more openly Lee's visions of the torments that awaited those who rejected God. See Kirschner, "At the Gate of Heaven," 169–78.

51. Wells, *Testimonies*, 73–74; see also 37, 110.

52. Wells, *Testimonies*, 161.

53. Wells, *Testimonies*, 75.

54. Wells, *Testimonies*, 23; see also 29, 48, 122, 128.

55. Wells, *Testimonies*, 119.

56. Edward Deming Andrews and Faith Andrews additionally suggest a linkage to an early vision of a burning bush seen by Father James Whittaker. See Edward Deming Andrews and Faith Andrews, *Visions of the Heavenly Sphere: A Study in Shaker Religious Art* (Charlottesville: Henry Francis du Pont Winterthur Museum / University Press of Virginia, 1969), 16.

57. Wells, *Testimonies*, 12, 13, 30, 51–53, 90, 93, 115, 122.

58. Wells, *Testimonies*, 90.

59. Wells, *Testimonies*, 77; see also 21, 41–42.

60. Wells, *Testimonies*, 42; see also 29, 48, 94, 119, 130, 131.

61. Wells, *Testimonies*, 115.

62. Wells, *Testimonies*, 29, 28; see also 14, 17, 45, 49–50, 60, 64, 71, 78, 83, 86, 95, 147.

63. Wells, *Testimonies*, 49–50.

64. France Morin, "Simple Gifts," in *Heavenly Visions*, 27–53; Andrews and Andrews, *Visions of the Heavenly Sphere*. On the era of manifestations, see Stein, *Shaker Experience in America*, 165–83.

65. Andrews and Andrews, *Visions of the Heavenly Sphere*, 36, 43, 48, 53, 54, 66, 71, 75, 90, 107; Morin, *Heavenly Visions*, 38, 55, 108, 130.

66. Andrews and Andrews, *Visions of the Heavenly Sphere*, 19, 21, 27, 28, 37, 39, 52, 55, 67, 70, 91.

67. Andrews and Andrews, *Visions of the Heavenly Sphere*, 70–71.

68. Andrews and Andrews, *Visions of the Heavenly Sphere*, 66–67.

4. Mixing "the Poison of Lust with the Ardor of Devotion"

1. For a list of those trials popular enough to have generated the publication of books and pamphlets, see Gedge, *Without Benefit of Clergy*, 51–52, 261–69. Gedge's is the most comprehensive list of published trials, but other cases still await in the published and manuscript record; see for example, the case of Augustus Littlejohn in Cross, *Burned-Over District*, 193–94. In 1844 Theodore Weld estimated that no fewer than thirty evangelical ministers had been accused of sexual misdeeds in just the preceding four years; see McLoughlin, *Modern Revivalism: Charles Grandison Finney to Billy Graham* (Eugene, OR: Wipf & Stock, 2004), 132.

2. William Sampson, *Trial of Mr. William Parkinson, Pastor of the First Baptist Church in the City of New-York, on an Indictment for Assault and Battery upon Mrs. Eliza Wintringham* (New York: Largin & Thompson, 1811), 72.

3. Sampson, *Trial of Mr. William Parkinson*, 3, 5.

4. On discussion of "holy kisses" in this trial, see Sampson, *Trial of Mr. William Parkinson*, 20, 23, 46, 53, 69, 83.

5. Gedge, *Without Benefit of Clergy*, 50, 52; see also Dorsey, "Making Men What They Should Be," 345–77; Patricia Cline Cohen, "Ministerial Misdeeds,"

34–57. As Cohen observes, while the Onderdonk case was amplified by church divisions, Onderdonk's offense was harder to comprehend because he stood against the revivalists, the party usually blamed for inflaming passions.

6. Hessinger, *Seduced, Abandoned, and Reborn*, 23–43.

7. Sampson, *Trial of Mr. William Parkinson*, 10.

8. Primary texts used in this chapter will include Sampson, *Trial of Mr. William Parkinson*; Jacob Kerr, *Several Trials of the Reverend David Barclay before the Presbytery of New Brunswick with their Judgment at Oxford* (Elizabeth Town, NJ: R. & P. Canfield, 1814); John Maffitt, *Report of the Trial of Mr. John N. Maffitt: Before a Council of Ministers of the Episcopal Church* (Boston: True & Greene, 1823); John Newland Maffitt and Joseph T. Buckingham, *Trial: Commonwealth vs. J. T. Buckingham, on an Indictment for a Libel, before the Municipal Court of the City of Boston, December Term, 1822* (Boston: New England Galaxy, 1822); Catherine Williams, *Fall River: An Authentic Narrative* (Providence, RI: Marshall, Brown, 1833); William Leete Stone, *Matthias and His Impostures; or the Progress of Fanaticism*, 3rd ed. (New York: Harper & Brothers, 1835); G. Vale, *Fanaticism: Its Source and Influence, Illustrated by the Simple Narrative of Isabella, in the Case of Matthias, Mr. and Mrs. Folger, M. Pierson, Mr. Mills, Catherine, Isabella, &c. &c.; A Reply to W. L. Stone*, in 2 Parts (New York: G. Vale, 1835); Ray Potter, *Admonitions from the Depths of the Earth: or the Fall of Ray Potter; in Twenty-Four Letters: Written by Himself to His Brother, Nicholas G. Potter* (Pawtucket, RI: R. Sherman, 1838); Sophia Murdock and Washington Van Zandt, *The Trial of the Rev. Van Zandt, Rector of Grace Church, Rochester, N.Y., for the Seduction of Miss Sophia Murdock, A Young and Beautiful Member of His Church* (Philadelphia, 1842); W. E. P. Weeks, *Trial of Rev. Joy Hamlet Fairchild on a Charge of Adultery with Miss Rhoda Davidson* (Boston: Published at the "Times" Office, 1845); Harvey Wheeler, *Trial of Rev. Issachar Grosscup for the Seduction of Roxana L. Wheeler, Comprising the Testimony in the Case, and Also a Sketch of the Arguments Addressed to the Jury* (Canandaigua, NY, 1848).

9. Vale, *Fanaticism*, part 1: 70.

10. Sampson, *Trial of Mr. William Parkinson*, 9.

11. Sampson, *Trial of Mr. William Parkinson*, 63–64, 9, 14.

12. Sampson, *Trial of Mr. William Parkinson*, 9, 30.

13. Sampson, *Trial of Mr. William Parkinson*, 63; on other nautical renderings of endangered manhood in early America, see Ditz, "Shipwrecked."

14. Sampson, *Trial of Mr. William Parkinson*, 11.

15. Sampson, *Trial of Mr. William Parkinson*, 19.

16. Sampson, *Trial of Mr. William Parkinson*, 14; on the rise of Victorian female chastity, see Bloch, "American Feminine Ideals in Transition"; Cott, "Passionlessness"; Hessinger, *Seduced, Abandoned, and Reborn*, 23–43.

17. Sampson, *Trial of Mr. William Parkinson*, 17.

18. Sampson, *Trial of Mr. William Parkinson*, 40; see also 8.

19. Sampson, *Trial of Mr. William Parkinson*, 19, 74.

20. Sampson, *Trial of Mr. William Parkinson*, 59.

21. Weeks, *Trial of Rev. Joy Hamlet Fairchild*, 16.

22. Wheeler, *Trial of Rev. Issachar Grosscup*, 49, and also 23, 35, 40; Weeks, *Trial of Rev. Joy Hamlet Fairchild*, 15, 21–22; Williams, *Fall River* (all references to

Williams are to the 1833 edition), 60–61, 62, 64–65; McLoughlin, "Untangling the Tiverton Tragedy," 79, 81.

23. Sampson, *Trial of Mr. William Parkinson*, 45.

24. Sampson, *Trial of Mr. William Parkinson*, 11–12, 43.

25. Sampson, *Trial of Mr. William Parkinson*, 41; for additional evidence of sectarian dimensions to these cases, see Sampson, *Trial of Mr. William Parkinson*, 18–19, 23, 30, 36, 47, 56; Kerr, *Several Trials*, 153–58; Maffitt, *Report of the Trial*, 27–28; Wheeler, *Trial of Rev. Issachar Grosscup*, 39, 48; Potter, *Admonitions from the Depths*, iii–iv, 25, 33, 66–68, 90, 148–58; Williams, *Fall*, 107–9, 113, 162; Stone, *Matthias and His Impostures*, 321; Vale, *Fanaticism*, part 1: 50–51.

26. Murdock and Van Zandt, *Trial of the Rev. Mr. Van Zandt*, 4.

27. Maffitt, *Report of the Trial*, 13–14, 16, quotation on 24; see also Wheeler, *Trial of Issachar Grosscup*, 2–3; Williams, *Fall River*, 90–91; Stone, *Matthias and His Impostures*, 36; Vale, *Fanaticism*, part 1: 63–64.

28. Gedge, *Without Benefit of Clergy*, 163–95.

29. Heyrman, *Southern Cross*, 131–35, 161–63, 169–71. Bruce Dorsey has shown that the dependency of itinerants also encouraged intimacy among men, encouraging homoerotic encounters; see Dorsey, "Making Men What They Should Be," 361–63, 366. For the classic statement on a mutual dependence between women and ministers in the nineteenth century, see Douglas, *Feminization of American Culture*, 80–120.

30. Sampson, *Trial of Mr. William Parkinson*, 6–7.

31. On the naturalization of male lust in the early republic, see Hessinger, *Seduced, Abandoned, and Reborn*, 23–43.

32. Sampson, *Trial of Mr. William Parkinson*, 60.

33. Sampson, *Trial of Mr. William Parkinson*, 76; for additional depictions of the preacher as seducer, see Weeks, *Trial of Rev. Joy Hamlet Fairchild*, 4, 7; Maffitt, *Report of the Trial*, 13–14; Maffitt and Buckingham, *Trial*, 25; Wheeler, *Trial of Rev. Issachar Grosscup*, 56; Potter, *Admonitions from the Depths*, 81; Williams, *Fall River*, 25; Stone, *Matthias and His Impostures*, 297; Vale, *Fanaticism*, part 2: 41.

34. Sampson, *Trial of Mr. William Parkinson*, 8, 60–61, 74.

35. Sampson, *Trial of Mr. William Parkinson*, 72–73.

36. Richard Norris Jr., *The Song of Songs: Interpreted by Early Christian and Medieval Commentators* (Grand Rapids, MI: Eerdmans, 2003).

37. Sampson, *Trial of Mr. William Parkinson*, 73.

38. See Wheeler, *Trial of Rev. Issachar Grosscup*, 56; Murdock and Van Zandt, *Trial of Rev. Mr. Van Zandt*, 3–4; "Article 2—for the Inquirer," *Religious Inquirer, Published by an Association of Gentlemen*, January 11, 1823, 36; Kerr, *Several Trials*, iii–iv; Williams, *Fall River*, 22, 25, 43–47, 74, 89, 144–45; Vale, *Fanaticism*, part 1: 63, 68–96, 74; McLaughlin, "Untangling the Tiverton Tragedy," 80.

39. Murdock and Van Zandt, *Trial of Rev. Mr. Van Zandt*, 2–4.

40. Kerr, *Several Trials*, iv.

41. Weeks, *Trial of Rev. Joy Hamlet Fairchild*, 14–15.

42. Reynolds, *Beneath the American Renaissance*, 260–62, 290, 476; see also Gedge, *Without Benefit of Clergy*, 80–85.

43. Sampson, *Trial of Mr. William Parkinson*, 80–84.

44. Brekus, *Strangers and Pilgrims*, 194–231.

45. The literature on the rise of women's activism in Protestant churches in the first half of the nineteenth century is voluminous; some of the most important and influential works include Jeffrey, *Great Silent Army of Abolitionism*; Hewitt, *Women's Activism and Social Change*; Ryan, *Cradle of the Middle Class*; Smith-Rosenberg, *Religion and the Rise of the American City*.

46. Heyrman, *Southern Cross*, 18–21, 145–46; Najar, *Evangelizing the South*, 65–88; Rhys Isaac, "Evangelical Revolt: The Nature of the Baptists' Challenge to the Traditional Order in Virginia, 1765 to 1775," *William and Mary Quarterly* 31, no. 3 (1974): 346–68; Janet Moore Lindman, *Bodies of Belief: Baptist Community in Early America* (Philadelphia: University of Pennsylvania Press, 2008).

47. Hatch, *Democratization of American Christianity*, 3. For a full view of Methodist growth, see Wigger, *Taking Heaven by Storm*.

48. Dee Andrews, *The Methodists and Revolutionary America, 1760–1800: The Shaping of an Evangelical Culture* (Princeton, NJ: Princeton University Press, 2010), 99–122; Brekus, *Strangers and Pilgrims*, 8, 119, 127, 128, 132, 133, 136–37, 145–46, 151–54, 160–61, 223, 227–31, 268–69.

49. McLoughlin, "Untangling the Tiverton Tragedy," 75–84. Thirteen of the texts are listed in Gedge, *Without Benefit of Clergy*, 261–62; one additional text not included in Gedge is Aristides, *Strictures on the Case of Ephraim K. Avery, Originally Published in the Republican Herald, Providence, R.I.: With Corrections, Revisions, and Additions* (Providence, RI: William Simons, Jr., Herald Office, 1833).

50. Reynolds, *Beneath the American Renaissance*, 260–62.

51. James D. Bratt, "Religious Anti-Revivalism in Antebellum America," *Journal of the Early Republic* 24, no. 1 (Spring 2004): 65–106; see also Marsden, *Evangelical Mind*, 1–87; Noll, *America's God*, 293–329; McLoughlin, *Modern Revivalism*, 125–36; Hessinger, *Seduced, Abandoned, and Reborn*, 99–102, 111–14.

52. This is not to suggest that sexual scandal alone caused the collapse of the Second Great Awakening, but its role has been underappreciated; other explanations have included the routinization of the New Measures, the Panic of 1837, the failure of William Miller's prophecies, the contentions caused by reform, the rise of bourgeois standards of comportment, and a renewed emphasis on denominationalism. See Curtis D. Johnson, "The Protracted Meeting Myth: Awakenings, Revivals, and New York State Baptists, 1789–1850," *Journal of the Early Republic* 34, no. 3 (Fall 2014): 349–83; Brekus, *Strangers and Pilgrims*, 267–306; Marsden, *Evangelical Mind*, 59–141; Abzug, *Cosmos Crumbling*; Eric Leigh Schmidt, *Holy Fairs: Scotland and the Making of American Revivalism*, 2nd ed. (Grand Rapids, MI: Wm. B. Eerdmans, 2001), chap. 4; David Hempton, *Evangelical Disenchantment: Nine Portraits of Faith and Doubt* (New Haven, CT: Yale University Press, 2008), 70–91; Cross, *Burned-Over District*, 252–321.

53. For a biography of Williams, including her religious background, see Patricia Caldwell's introduction to Oxford University Press's 1993 edition of *Fall River*.

54. Williams, *Fall River*, 197.

55. McLaughlin, "Untangling the Tiverton Tragedy," 80–83; Bratt, "Religious Anti-Revivalism," 65–106; Brekus, *Strangers and Pilgrims*, 67–106.

56. Williams, *Fall River*, 136.

57. Williams, *Fall River*, 138.

58. Williams, *Fall River*, 47, 5.

59. Williams, *Fall River*, 4.

60. Maffitt and Buckingham, *Trial*, 6; see also "Article 2—for the Inquirer," 36.

61. Williams, *Fall River*, 88.

62. Williams, *Fall River*, 5.

63. Williams, *Fall River*, 144–45, 157.

64. Bratt, "Religious Anti-Revivalism," 65–106; Noll, *America's God*, 293–329; Hessinger, *Seduced, Abandoned, and Reborn*, 99–102, 111–14.

65. Williams, *Fall River*, 166–68.

66. Williams, *Fall River*, 169.

67. Williams, *Fall River*, 177.

68. Williams, *Fall River*, 185, 177.

69. Williams, *Fall River*, 183–84.

70. Williams, *Fall River*, 184–85.

71. *Methodist Error; or, Friendly Christian Advice, to Those Methodists, Who Indulge in Extravagant Emotions and Bodily Exercises, by a Wesleyan Methodist* (Trenton, NJ: D. & E. Fenton, 1819), 23–24; on the alienation and differentiation between white and Black Methodists, see Dee Andrews, *Methodists and Revolutionary America*, 123–54; Nash, *Forging Freedom*, 190–202; Wigger, *Taking Heaven by Storm*, 125–50; Richard Neuman, *Freedom's Prophet: Bishop Richard Allen, the AME Church, and the Black Founding Fathers* (New York: New York University Press, 2008), 158–82.

72. Johnson and Wilentz, *Kingdom of Matthias*; Nell Irvin Painter, *Sojourner Truth: A Life, a Symbol* (New York: Norton, 1997), 48–61. As Stone himself recognizes, Matthias's ideas about marriage seemed to resemble circulating ideas of the perfectionists and Joseph Smith's emerging ideas about plural marriage. See Bushman, *Rough Stone Rolling*, 323–37; Stone, *Matthias and His Impostures*, 17, 39, 288, 316.

73. The impact of this story can be seen in the publication history of Stone's book. According to one reviewer, it sold out its seventeen hundred initial copies on the day of publication and went through four or five additional printings within the next few weeks. See C. S. Henry, "Review of Matthias," *Literary and Theological Review* 2, no. 7 (September 1835): 477.

74. See Stone, *Matthias and His Impostures*, 13, 321. The term "ultraism" is used by Whitney Cross in *Burned-Over District*, 173–210. For a short biography of Stone, see David B. Hall, *Halls of New England: Genealogical and Biographical* (Albany, NY: Joel Munsell's Sons, 1883), 56. For Wayland's role in anti-revivalism and education, see Hessinger, *Seduced, Abandoned, and Reborn*, 121, 125–26.

75. Stone, *Matthias and His Impostures*, 320, 236; see also 34, 38–39, 46, 49, 65, 141, 146.

76. Stone, *Matthias and His Impostures*, 236.

77. Johnson and Wilentz, *Kingdom of Matthias*, 28–32.

78. Stone, *Matthias and His Impostures*, 35, 49, 38.

79. Johnson and Wilentz, *Kingdom of Matthias*, 29–30; Stone, *Matthias and His Impostures*, 46–47.

80. Stone, *Matthias and His Impostures*, 35–37.

81. Stone, *Matthias and His Impostures*, 8.

82. Stone, *Matthias and His Impostures*, 13-14. On the contrast between Alexander Campbell and Joseph Smith, see Bushman, *Joseph Smith and the Beginnings of Mormonism*, 179-88; on the opening rupture between faith and reason for enthusiastic preachers as the nineteenth century unfolded, see Susan Juster, *Doomsayers: Anglo-American Prophecy in the Age of Revolution* (Philadelphia: University of Pennsylvania Press, 2003), 260-72.

83. Stone, *Matthias and His Impostures*, 21-28, quotations on 21-22.

84. On Methodist recalibration toward respectability, especially with regard to gender relations, see Brekus, *Strangers and Pilgrims*, 267-306; Heyrman, *Southern Cross*, 197-205.

85. Stone, *Matthias and His Impostures*, 39; Painter, *Sojourner Truth*, 45.

86. Stone, *Matthias and His Impostures*, 323-24; see also 50.

87. Stone, *Matthias and His Impostures*, 313-15. On the career of Burchard and his connections to Finney, see Charles G. Finney, Garth Rosell, and Richard A. G. Dupuis, *The Memoirs of Charles G. Finney: The Complete Restored Text* (Grand Rapids, MI: Academie Books, 1989); Cross, *Burned-Over District*, 188-89; McLoughlin, *Modern Revivalism*, 133-34.

88. Stone, *Matthias and His Impostures*, 313; see also 13-14, 40, 59, 313, 316-18, 324; Vale, *Fanaticism*, part 1: 73, 74, part 2: 7, 42.

89. Painter, *Sojourner Truth*, 40-41.

90. Stone, *Matthias and His Impostures*, 39-41, 110; see also 29.

91. Stone, *Matthias and His Impostures*, 129.

92. Some of the most influential interpretations of the religious marketplace in America include Bilhartz, *Urban Religion*; Hatch, *Democratization of American Christianity*; Moore, *Selling God*.

93. Stone, *Matthias and His Impostures*, 108, 112, 149.

94. Stone, *Matthias and His Impostures*, 276. This anti-Islam rhetoric can be compared to the Orientalism for the Mormons documented by Terryl Givens; see *Viper on the Hearth*, 130-37.

95. Stone, *Matthias and His Impostures*, 334, 139, 230-31.

96. Stone, *Matthias and His Impostures*, 288; see also 17, 316. This suggestion of Mormon sexual impropriety (beyond the speculation we witnessed in the *Ohio Star*) must have been one of the first in print. Richard Bushman dates sexual rumors to 1835 in *Rough Stone Rolling*, 323.

97. Stone, *Matthias and His Impostures*, 288, 297, 308-9.

98. Painter, *Sojourner Truth*, 58-59.

99. Wayland-Smith, *Oneida*, 24-35; Bushman, *Rough Stone Rolling*, 323-27.

100. "Vale, Gilbert," in *The New Encyclopedia of Unbelief*, ed. Tom Flynn (Amherst, NY: Prometheus Books, 2007), 796.

101. Vale, *Fanaticism*, part 1: 18; see also part 1: 21-22, 32-33, 38, 70, 80, 81, 82, part 2: 7, 18. Like Stone, Vale put a share of the blame for Matthias's career at the feet of Charles Finney. He said Matthias in his religious upbringing was "much excited on religious subjects," particularly when he heard "Mr. Finney . . . whose powerful preaching has driven several persons mad" (38).

102. Vale, *Fanaticism*, part 2: 7-8.

103. Vale, *Fanaticism*, part 1: 70. In highlighting how fanaticism released social constraints on sexuality, Stone's and Vale's criticism of Matthias's kingdom

anticipated a wider critique of religious communes in the nineteenth century. See Louis J. Kern, *Ordered Love*, 50–68.

104. Vale, *Fanaticism*, part 1: 82.

105. Vale, *Fanaticism*, part 1: 31–33, 48, 62, 64, 68, 69, 81, part 2: 13, 17–18, 30–32, 36, 41, 42.

106. Vale, *Fanaticism*, part 1: 48.

107. Vale, *Fanaticism*, part 2: 13.

108. Vale, *Fanaticism*, part 1: 69.

109. Vale, *Fanaticism*, part 1: 73–74, 77–79, 81.

110. Within a year of Matthias promoting spiritual unions, the perfectionist Erasmus Stone was sharing his detailed dream of spiritual mates seeking one another on Judgment Day. See Wayland-Smith, *Oneida*, 29–30.

111. Vale, *Fanaticism*, part 2: 41–42.

112. Hessinger, *Seduced, Abandoned, and Reborn*, 96–124.

5. The Sexual Containment of Perfectionism

1. Hubbard Eastman, *Noyesism Unveiled: A History of the Sect Self-Styled Perfectionists; with a Summary View of their Leading Doctrines* (Brattleboro, VT: The Author, 1849), 267.

2. Eastman, *Noyesism Unveiled*, 271.

3. Eastman, *Noyesism Unveiled*, 272.

4. Some of the most important include Robert Allerton Parker, *A Yankee Saint: John Humphrey Noyes and the Oneida Community* (New York: G. P. Putnam's Sons, 1935); Kern, *Ordered Love*; Lawrence Foster, *Religion and Sexuality*; Lawrence Foster, *Women, Family, and Utopia: Communal Experiments of the Shakers, the Oneida Community, and the Mormons* (Syracuse, NY: Syracuse University Press, 1991); Spencer Klaw, *Without Sin: The Life and Death of the Oneida Community* (New York: Penguin, 1993); Wayland-Smith, *Oneida*; Wonderly, *Oneida Utopia*; Michael Doyle, *The Ministers' War: John W. Mears, the Oneida Community, and the Crusade for Public Morality* (Syracuse, NY: Syracuse University Press, 2018).

5. Cross, *Burned-Over District*, 238–51.

6. Stone, *Matthias and His Impostures*, 40; William Hepworth Dixon, *Spiritual Wives*, vol. 2 (Leipzig: Bernard Tauchnitz, 1868), 15–18.

7. Dixon, *Spiritual Wives*, 2:37, 45–48.

8. Wayland-Smith, *Oneida*, 29–30; Dixon, *Spiritual Wives*, 2:18–19.

9. John Humphrey Noyes, "From the Liberator of April 13th, 1838," *Witness*, January 23, 1839, 50; John Humphrey Noyes, *The Berean: A Manual for the Help of Those Who Seek the Faith of the Primitive Church* (Putney, VT: Office of the Spiritual Magazine, 1847), 431–33; John Humphrey Noyes, "Bible Argument, Defining the Relations of the Sexes in the Kingdom of Heaven," in *First Annual Report of the Oneida Association: Exhibiting Its History, Principles, and Transactions to Jan. 1, 1849* (Oneida Reserve: Leonard & Company, 1849), 19, 22–24. Joseph Smith also took his cue from this passage in imagining celestial and plural marriage. See Bachman, "New Light on an Old Hypothesis," 19–32. On the wider popularity of this Pauline ideal, see Dixon, *Spiritual Wives*, 2:37, 45–48.

10. John Humphrey Noyes and George Wallingford Noyes, *Religious Experience of John Humphrey Noyes, Founder of the Oneida Community* (New York: Macmillan, 1923), 201–2; see also Cross, *Burned-Over District*, 243–44.

11. Wonderly, *Oneida Utopia*, 22–26; Cross, *Burned-Over District*, 243–44; Parker, *Yankee Saint*, 36–38; Bachman, "New Light on an Old Hypothesis," 19–32.

12. Dixon, *Spiritual Wives*, 2:148–51.

13. John Humphrey Noyes, *The Way of Holiness: A Series of Papers Formerly Published in the Perfectionist at New Haven* (Putney, VT: J. H. Noyes, 1838), 20.

14. Dixon, *Spiritual Wives*, 1:83, 2:63–64.

15. Noyes, *Religious Experience*, 192–99. This interpretation departs from Ellen Wayland-Smith, who characterizes these perfectionists as belonging to the more "raucous, more amorous branch" of perfectionism. In his religious memoirs, Noyes tried to displace sexual scandal onto these purity perfectionists, but he also admits they had been schooled in the teachings of James Latourette. Latourette urged followers to fulfill, not transcend, the law by living lives of perfect purity. See Wayland-Smith, *Oneida*, 30. On Noyes's characterizations of the two branches of perfectionism and Latourette in particular, see Noyes, *Religious Experience*, 133–34, 186, 297.

16. Noyes, *Religious Experience*, 198–99.

17. Dixon, *Spiritual Wives*, 2:30–35; for later characterizations, see Wayland-Smith, *Oneida*, 30; Wonderly, *Oneida Utopia*, 24.

18. Dixon, *Spiritual Wives*, 2:37–38.

19. Noyes, *Religious Experience*, 199, 351–54.

20. Wayland-Smith, *Oneida*, 31–32.

21. The fullest treatment of Gates's views and life remains Charles Coleman Sellers, *Theophilus the Battle-Axe: A History of the Lives and Adventures of Theophilus Ransom Gates and the Battle-Axes* (Philadelphia: Patterson & White, 1930).

22. Parker, *Yankee Saint*, 53–54.

23. Cross, *Burned-Over District*, 190; Parker, *Yankee Saint*, 39–40; Noyes, *Religious Experience*, 204–5, 298–301; Charles Coleman Sellers, *Theophilus*, 25, 27.

24. John Humphrey Noyes, "The Battle Axe Letter," *Witness*, January 23, 1839, 49.

25. John Humphrey Noyes, "From the *Advocate of Moral Reform*, Perfectionism," *Witness*, January 23, 1839, 52.

26. John Humphrey Noyes, "Letter from Mrs. H. C. Green," *Witness*, January 23, 1839, 54–55. As described by Wayland-Smith, at this juncture it was George's wife Mary, more than George, who fully embraced Noyes, but he nonetheless stood in support of his wife and was fired from his job for it. See Wayland-Smith, *Oneida*, 38–39. On the connections between perfectionism and the *Advocate of Moral Reform*, see Carol Faulkner, *Unfaithful: Love, Adultery, and Marriage Reform in Nineteenth-Century America* (Philadelphia: University of Pennsylvania Press, 2019), 24–35.

27. Noyes, "From the *Advocate of Moral Reform*, Perfectionism," 52.

28. John Humphrey Noyes, "Copy of a Letter to the Editress of the Advocate of Moral Reform," *Witness*, April 5, 1838, 26.

29. Theophilus Gates, "Finishing of the Mystery of God," *Battle-Axe and Weapons of War*, August 1837 (June 1839 reprint), 15.

30. His concern about the dangers of pregnancy were heightened when he witnessed his wife, Harriet Holton, go through four stillborn pregnancies, but coitus interruptus would have served the same end of preventing unwanted pregnancy. Wayland-Smith attributes his adoption of male continence not to theology but to his subscription to popular scientific theories, which warned of how ejaculation could drain the male body. See Wayland-Smith, *Oneida*, 78–80. Lawrence Foster and Louis Kern emphasize Noyes's concern with male self-control, as an expression of mastery. See Foster, *Religion and Sexuality*, 93–95; Kern, *Ordered Love*, 235–46. Of course, these various motivations could all reinforce one another to the same end. In fact, it is hard to imagine Noyes adopting this unusual and demanding practice without there being multiple reasons for its adoption.

31. While George Wallingford Noyes would later describe Gates's residency at *The Perfectionist* as a sort of coup, an attempt to sack perfectionism from the inside, a comparison of the views of Noyes and Gates at the time of the Battle-Axe letter shows a deep consistency in theology. The fact that Gates was widely admired as a leader by Boyle and other perfectionists suggests a basis for the rivalry between Gates and Noyes. See Noyes, *Religious Experience*, 204–5, 298–301, Weld quotation on 205.

32. Noyes, "Copy of a Letter to the Editress," 26.

33. Noyes, *Way of Holiness*, 9.

34. Noyes, "Copy of a Letter to the Editress," 26.

35. Noyes, *Way of Holiness*, 10.

36. See Noyes, *Religious Experience*, 205.

37. Theophilus Gates, "The Order of God," *Battle-Axe and Weapons of War*, July 1837, 1, 3.

38. Gates, "Finishing of the Mystery of God," 11.

39. Gates, "From the Battle Axe, dated August, 1837," *Witness*, January 23, 1839, 49.

40. Gates, "To the Readers of the Second Edition," *Battle-Axe and Weapons of War*, August 1837 (June 1839 reprint), 9.

41. Wonderly, *Oneida Utopia*, 32; Wayland-Smith, *Oneida*, 33–34.

42. Noyes, "From J. H. Noyes to H. A. Holton," *Witness*, January 23, 1839, 56.

43. Wonderly, *Oneida Utopia*, 32–33.

44. Wonderly, *Oneida Utopia*, 41–48; Wayland-Smith, *Oneida*, 44–45.

45. Wayland-Smith, *Oneida*, 56–57.

46. "Perfectionists," *Vermont Phoenix* (Brattleboro), December 31, 1847, 2. Hubbard Eastman attributes the articles to O. H. Platt, editor of the paper, but they are not directly attributed to him within the paper itself. With the extent of research involved, I suspect they were jointly researched and composed. See Hubbard, *Noyesism Unveiled*, xi.

47. "Perfectionists," *Vermont Phoenix*, January 7, 1848, 2.

48. "Perfectionists," *Vermont Phoenix*, January 7, 1848, 2.

49. See Wonderly, *Oneida Utopia*, 46; Wayland-Smith, *Oneida*, 56–7.

50. "Perfectionists," *Vermont Phoenix*, January 7, 1848, 2.

51. "Perfectionists," *Vermont Phoenix*, January 7, 1848, 2.

52. "Perfectionists," *Vermont Phoenix*, December 31, 1847, 2.

53. "Marriage—Perfectionism," *Liberator*, November 26, 1841, 191.

54. "Perfectionists," *Vermont Phoenix*, December 31, 1847, 2.

55. "Perfectionists," *Vermont Phoenix*, January 7, 1848, 2.

56. Wayland-Smith, *Oneida*, 60–62.

57. Eastman, *Noyesism Unveiled*, 15, 287, 25.

58. Eastman, *Noyesism Unveiled*, 64, 87–88, 123, 265.

59. Eastman, *Noyesism Unveiled*, 50; see also 182–84, 300–303, 366–67, 401.

60. Eastman, *Noyesism Unveiled*, 182–83.

61. Eastman, *Noyesism Unveiled*, 298–99, 268.

62. Eastman, *Noyesism Unveiled*, 286, 62.

63. Parker, *Yankee Saint*, 124–28; George Wallingford Noyes and Lawrence Foster, eds., *Free Love in Utopia: John Humphrey Noyes and the Origin of the Oneida Community* (Urbana: University of Illinois Press, 2001), 17–18.

64. Eastman, *Noyesism Unveiled*, 410–416.

65. "For the Vermont Phoenix," *Vermont Phoenix*, January 28, 1848, 2; "Perfectionism and Fourierism," *Vermont Phoenix*, February 4, 1848, 2; "For the Vermont Phoenix," *Vermont Phoenix*, February 11, 1848, 2.

66. Wayland-Smith, *Oneida*, 64–65.

67. Lawrence Foster, *Religion and Sexuality*, 90.

68. *First Annual Report*, 41.

69. *First Annual Report*, 19, 21.

70. *First Annual Report*, 24.

71. Wayland-Smith, *Oneida*, 104–20.

72. Lawrence Foster, *Religion and Sexuality*, 93–100, 107–10; Wonderly, *Oneida Utopia*, 104–6; Wayland-Smith, *Oneida*, 104–20.

73. *First Annual Report*, 22. He did not here broach the topic of incest, but Ellen Wayland-Smith has shown that he did think about it, suggesting it might even represent a higher form of unity. See Wayland-Smith, *Oneida*, 56, 127–28.

74. See Taysom, *Shakers, Mormons, and Religious Worlds*, 4–50. This is reminiscent of Edmund Morgan's classic description of the distinction between the Pilgrims and the Puritans. See Morgan, *Visible Saints: The History of a Puritan Idea* (New York: New York University Press, 1963).

75. *First Annual Report*, 17.

76. Lawrence Foster, *Religion and Sexuality*, 103.

77. Wonderly, *Oneida Utopia*, 64.

78. Noyes and Foster, *Free Love in Utopia*, 28.

79. Wonderly, *Oneida Utopia*, 72–75; Noyes and Foster, *Free Love in Utopia*, xxviii–xxix, 94–96, 136–45.

80. "Perfectionism and Polygamy," *New York Observer and Chronicle*, January 22, 1852, 2.

81. "The Perfectionists Retracting," *New York Observer and Chronicle*, March 18, 1852, 90.

82. Noyes and Foster, *Free Love in Utopia*, 178.

83. Wonderly, *Oneida Utopia*, 73–74; Noyes and Foster, *Free Love in Utopia*, 183–84.

84. Lawrence Foster has argued that this six-month pause in complex marriage played an important internal function for the community, allowing it

to regain its moorings after having to deal with internal tensions, including conflict between Noyes and George Cragin over Mary Cragin. See Lawrence Foster, "The Rise and Fall of Utopia," in *Women, Family, and Utopia*, esp. 103–14.

Conclusion

1. Peter Cartwright and W. P. Strickland, *Autobiography of Peter Cartwright, the Backwoods Preacher* (New York: Carlton & Porter, 1856); on his lamentations about the direction of the church, see esp. chaps. 7, 30–31, 33–34.

2. Cartwright and Strickland, *Autobiography of Peter Cartwright*, 244–47.

3. Cartwright and Strickland, *Autobiography of Peter Cartwright*, 144–45.

4. Cartwright and Strickland, *Autobiography of Peter Cartwright*, 146.

5. Cartwright and Strickland, *Autobiography of Peter Cartwright*, 316–17.

6. Cartwright and Strickland, *Autobiography of Peter Cartwright*, 523–24.

7. Cartwright and Strickland, *Autobiography of Peter Cartwright*, 517–18.

8. In the early years of Methodism, there was a valorization of single preachers but never an outright ban on marriage for the clergy. See Heyrman, *Southern Cross*, 113–15.

9. Cartwright and Strickland, *Autobiography of Peter Cartwright*, 341–46, 356–57, 400–404.

10. Abzug, *Cosmos Crumbling*, 125–229.

11. The concept of the "sacred world" for African Americans is developed in Lawrence Levine, *Black Culture and Black Consciousness: Afro-American Thought from Slavery to Freedom* (New York: Oxford University Press, 1977); on its enduring relevance in the context of the North, see Nash, *Forging Freedom*, 190–202.

12. John Stauffer, *The Black Hearts of Men: Radical Abolitionists and the Transformation of Race* (Cambridge, MA: Harvard University Press, 2002), 18–20, 58–60, 110–13, 278–81; David W. Blight, *Frederick Douglass, Prophet of Freedom* (New York: Simon & Schuster, 2018), 228–51, 280–90.

BIBLIOGRAPHY

Abzug, Robert H. *Cosmos Crumbling: American Reform and the Religious Imagination*. New York: Oxford University Press, 1994.

Address of the Lay Trustees to the Congregation of St. Mary's Church, on the Subject of the Approaching Election. Philadelphia: Robert Desilver, 1822.

An Admirer of Fenelon. *A Letter to the Rev. William Vincent Harold, of the Order of Dominican Friars on Reading His Late Reply to a "Catholic Layman."* Philadelphia: Robert Desilver, 1822.

Agonito, Joseph. *The Building of an American Catholic Church: The Episcopacy of John Carroll*. New York: Garland, 1988.

Andrews, Dee. *The Methodists and Revolutionary America, 1760–1800: The Shaping of an Evangelical Culture*. Princeton, NJ: Princeton University Press, 2010.

Andrews, Edward Deming. *The People Called Shakers: A Search for the Perfect Society*. New York: Oxford University Press, 1953.

Andrews, Edward Deming, and Faith Andrews. *Visions of the Heavenly Sphere: A Study in Shaker Religious Art*. Charlottesville: Henry Francis du Pont Winterthur Museum and University Press of Virginia, 1969.

Aristides. *Strictures on the Case of Ephraim K. Avery, Originally Published in the Republican Herald, Providence, R.I.; with Corrections, Revisions, and Additions*. Providence, RI: William Simons, Jr., Herald Office, 1833.

Arrington, Leonard J., and Jon Harupt. "Intolerable Zion: The Image of Mormonism in Nineteenth-Century American Literature." *Western Humanities Review* 22 (Summer 1968): 243–60.

Bachman, Daniel W. "New Light on an Old Hypothesis: The Ohio Origins of the Revelation on Eternal Marriage." *Journal of Mormon History* 5 (1978): 19–32.

Barker-Benfield, G. J. *The Culture of Sensibility: Sex and Society in Eighteenth-Century Britain*. Chicago: University of Chicago Press, 1992.

The Battle of St. Mary's, A Seriocomic Ballad, with Desultory Remarks on the Dissension in That Church by an Observer, Wholly Unconnected with the Parties, but Wishing Well to Liberty and Peace. Philadelphia, 1822.

Bauer, Cheryl, and Rob Portman. *Wisdom's Paradise: The Forgotten Shakers of Union Village*. Wilmington, Ohio: Orange Frazer Press, 2004.

Belisle, Orvilla. *The Prophets or Mormonism Unveiled*. Philadelphia: William White Smith, 1855.

Bell, Alfreda Eva. *Boadicea, The Mormon Wife: Life Scenes in Utah*. Edited by Kent Bean. Book Verve E-Books. Baltimore, MD: A. R. Orton, 2014, Kindle edition.

Beneke, Chris. *Beyond Toleration: The Religious Origins of American Pluralism*. New York: Oxford University Press, 2006.

Bennett, John C. *The History of the Saints, or, An Exposé of Joe Smith and Mormonism*. 3rd ed. Urbana: University of Illinois Press, 2000.

Benson, RoseAnn. "Alexander Campbell: Another Restorationist." *Journal of Mormon History* 41, no. 4 (October 2015): 1–42.

Bilhartz, Terry. *Urban Religion and the Second Great Awakening: Church and Society in Early National Baltimore*. Rutherford, NJ: Fairleigh Dickinson University Press, 1986.

Billington, Ray Allen. *The Protestant Crusade, 1800–1860: A Study of the Origins of American Nativism*. Chicago: Quadrangle Books, 1964.

Bixby, Brian. "Seeing Shakers: Two Centuries of Visitors to Shaker Villages." PhD diss., University of Massachusetts Amherst, 2010.

Blight, David W. *Frederick Douglass, Prophet of Freedom*. New York: Simon & Schuster, 2018.

Bloch, Ruth H. "American Feminine Ideals in Transition: The Rise of the Moral Mother, 1785–1815." *Feminist Studies* 4, no. 2 (June 1978): 100–126.

Block, Sharon. *Rape and Sexual Power in Early America*. Chapel Hill: University of North Carolina Press, 2006.

Boles, John E. *The Great Revival: The Beginnings of the Bible Belt*. Lexington: University Press of Kentucky, 1972.

Boydston, Jeanne. "The Woman Who Wasn't There: Women's Market Labor and the Transition to Capitalism in the United States." *Journal of the Early Republic* 16, no. 2 (Summer 1996): 183–206.

Boylan, Anne. *Sunday School: The Formation of an American Institution, 1790–1880*. New Haven, CT: Yale University Press, 1988.

Branson, Susan. *Dangerous to Know: Women, Crime, and Notoriety in the Early Republic*. Philadelphia: University of Pennsylvania Press, 2008.

——. *These Fiery Frenchified Dames: Women and Political Culture in Early National Philadelphia*. Philadelphia: University of Pennsylvania Press, 2001.

Bratt, James D. "Religious Anti-Revivalism in Antebellum America." *Journal of the Early Republic* 24, no. 1 (Spring 2004): 65–106.

Brekus, Catherine. *Strangers and Pilgrims: Female Preaching in America, 1740–1845*. Chapel Hill: University of North Carolina Press, 1998.

Brodie, Fawn M. *No Man Knows My History: The Life of Joseph Smith*. New York: Vintage Books, 1995.

Brooke, John L. *The Refiner's Fire: The Making of Mormon Cosmology, 1644–1844*. New York: Cambridge University Press, 1996.

Bushman, Richard Lyman. *Joseph Smith and the Beginnings of Mormonism*. Chicago: University of Illinois Press, 1987.

——. *Joseph Smith: Rough Stone Rolling: A Cultural Biography of Mormonism's Founder*. New York: Vintage Books, 2005.

Caldwell, Patricia. "Introduction." In Catherine Williams, *Fall River: An Authentic Narrative*, edited by Patricia Caldwell, xi–xxii. New York: Oxford University Press, 1993.

Campbell, Alexander. *Delusions: An Analysis of the Book of Mormon; with an Examination of Its Internal and External Evidences, and a Refutation of Its Pretenses to Divine Authority*. Boston: Benjamin H. Green, 1832.

Carey, Matthew. *Address to the Right Rev. Bishop Conwell and the Members of St. Mary's Congregation*. Philadelphia, 1821.

——. *Address to the Right Rev. the Bishop of Pennsylvania, and the Members of St. Mary's Congregation*. Philadelphia, 1820.

——. *Address to the Right Reverend the Bishop of Pennsylvania, the Catholic Clergy of Philadelphia, and the Congregation of St. Mary's in This City*. Philadelphia: H. C. Carey & I. Lea, 1822.

——. *Brief Address to the Roman Catholic Congregation Worshipping at St. Mary's, on the Approaching Election for a Board of Trustees*. Philadelphia, 1822.

——. *A Desultory Examination of the Reply of the Rev. W. V. Harold to a Catholic Layman's Rejoinder*. Philadelphia: H. C. Carey & I. Lea, 1822.

——. *Rejoinder to the Reply of the Rev. Mr. Harold, to the Address to the Right Rev. the Catholic Bishop of Pennsylvania, the Catholic Clergy of Philadelphia, and the Congregation of St. Mary's*. Philadelphia: H. C. Carey & I. Lea, 1822.

——. *Review of Three Pamphlets Lately Published by the Rev. W. V. Harold*. Philadelphia: H. C. Carey & I. Lea, 1822.

——. *To the Congregation of St. Mary's, "On the Banks of the Rubicon."* Philadelphia, 1821.

Carey, Patrick W. *An Immigrant Bishop: John England's Adaptation of Irish Catholicism to American Republicanism*. Yonkers, NY: US Catholic Historical Society, 1982.

——. *People, Priests, and Prelates: Ecclesiastical Democracy and the Tensions of Trusteeism*. Notre Dame, IN: University of Notre Dame Press, 1987.

——. "Republicanism within American Catholicism, 1785–1860." *Journal of the Early Republic* 3, no. 4 (Winter 1983): 413–37.

——. "William Hogan." In *American National Biography*, edited by John A. Garraty and Mark C. Carnes, vol. 11, 8–9. New York: Oxford University Press, 1999.

Carr, Mary Clark. *A Compendious Trial of the Rev. William Hogan, Pastor of the Roman Catholic Church of St. Mary's on an Indictment for an Assault and Battery on the Person of Mary Connell*. Philadelphia, 1822.

Carson, Ann, and Mary Clarke. *The Memoirs of the Celebrated and Beautiful Mrs. Ann Carson; 2nd Edition, Revised, Enlarged, and Continued till Her Death, by Mrs. M. Clarke, in Two Volumes*. New York, 1838.

Carter, Michael S. "Under the Benign Sun of Toleration: Mathew Carey, the Douai Bible, and Catholic Print Culture, 1789–91." *Journal of the Early Republic* 27, no. 3 (Fall 2007): 437–69.

Cartwright, Peter, and W. P. Strickland. *Autobiography of Peter Cartwright, the Backwoods Preacher*. New York: Carlton & Porter, 1856.

Carwardine, Richard. "The Second Great Awakening in the Urban Centers: An Examination of Methodism and the 'New Measures.'" *Journal of American History* 59, no. 2 (September 1972): 327–40.

Catholic Church, Diocese of Philadelphia (Pa.). *A Pastoral Charge Delivered by the Right Revd. Henry, Bishop of Philadelphia, February 11th, 1821*. Philadelphia, 1821.

Chapman, Eunice. *An Account of the Conduct of the People Called the Shakers*. Albany, 1817.

——. *An Account of the Conduct of the Shakers, in the Case of Eunice Chapman & Her Children*. Lebanon, Ohio: Van Vleet & Camron, 1818.

——. *No. 2, being an Additional Account of the Conduct of the Shakers, in the Case of Eunice Chapman and Her Children.* Albany: I. W. Clark, 1818.

Chudacoff, Howard P. *How Old Are You? Age Consciousness in American Culture.* Princeton, NJ: Princeton University Press, 1989.

Cohen, Daniel A. "The Respectability of Rebecca Reed: Genteel Womanhood and Sectarian Conflict in Antebellum America." *Journal of the Early Republic* 16, no. 3 (Autumn 1996): 419–61.

Cohen, Patricia Cline. "Ministerial Misdeeds: The Onderdonk Trial and Sexual Harassment in the 1840s." *Journal of Women's History* 7, no. 3 (1995): 34–57.

——. *The Murder of Helen Jewett: The Life and Death of a Prostitute in Nineteenth-Century New York.* New York: Knopf, 1998.

Conkin, Paul K. *Cane Ridge: America's Pentecost.* Madison: University of Wisconsin Press, 1990.

Cott, Nancy. *Bonds of Womanhood: "Woman's Sphere" in New England, 1780–1835.* New Haven, CT: Yale University Press, 1977.

——. "Passionlessness: An Interpretation of Victorian Sexual Ideology, 1790–1850." *Signs* 4, no. 2 (1978): 219–36.

——. *Public Vows: A History of Marriage and the Nation.* Cambridge, MA: Harvard University Press, 2002.

Cross, Whitney. *The Burned-Over District: The Social and Intellectual History of Enthusiastic Religion in Western New-York, 1800–1850.* Ithaca, NY: Cornell University Press, 1950.

Davis, David Brion. "Some Themes of Counter-Subversion: An Analysis of Anti-Masonic, Anti-Catholic, and Anti-Mormon Literature." *Mississippi Valley Historical Review* 47, no. 2 (September 1960): 205–24.

DeWolfe, Elizabeth A. *Shaking the Faith: Women, Family, and Mary Marshall Dyer's Anti-Shaker Campaign, 1815–1867.* New York: Palgrave, 2002.

Dignan, Patrick J. *A History of the Legal Incorporation of Catholic Church Property in the United States, 1784–1932.* New York: P. J. Kenedy and Sons, 1935.

Ditz, Toby L. "Shipwrecked; or, Masculinity Imperiled: Mercantile Representations of Failure and the Gendered Self in Eighteenth-Century Philadelphia." *Journal of American History* 81, no. 1 (January 1994): 51–80.

Dixon, William Hepworth. *Spiritual Wives.* Leipzig: Bernard Tauchnitz, 1868.

Dolan, Jay P. *The American Catholic Experience: A History from Colonial Times to the Present.* Garden City, NJ: Doubleday, 1985.

——. *Catholic Revivalism: The American Experience, 1830–1900.* Notre Dame, IN: University of Notre Dame Press, 1978.

——. *In Search of American Catholicism: A History of Religion and Culture in Tension.* New York: Oxford University Press, 2002.

Dorsey, Bruce. "'Making Men What They Should Be': Male Same-Sex Intimacy and Evangelical Religion in Early Nineteenth-Century New England." *Journal of the History of Sexuality* 24, no. 3 (2015): 345–77.

——. *Reforming Men and Women: Gender in the Antebellum City.* Ithaca, NY: Cornell University Press, 2002.

Douglas, Ann. *The Feminization of American Culture.* New York: Knopf, 1977.

Dowling, Joseph A. *The Trial of the Rev. William Hogan, Pastor of St. Mary's Church, for an Assault and Battery on Mary Connell. Tried before the Mayor's Court in and for the City of Philadelphia.* Philadelphia: R. Desilver, 1822.

Doyle, Michael. *The Ministers' War: John W. Mears, the Oneida Community, and the Crusade for Public Morality.* Syracuse, NY: Syracuse University Press, 2018.

Doyle, Nora. "'The Highest Pleasure of Which Woman's Nature Is Capable': Breast-Feeding and the Sentimental Maternal Ideal in America, 1750–1860." *Journal of American History* 97, no. 4 (March 2011): 958–73.

Dyer, Mary Marshall. *A Brief Statement of the Sufferings of Mary Dyer Occasioned by the Society Called Shakers.* Boston: William S. Spear, 1818.

——. *The Rise and Progress of the Serpent from the Garden of Eden, to the Present Day: With a Disclosure of Shakerism.* Concord, NH: By the Author, 1847.

Eastman, Hubbard. *Noyesism Unveiled: A History of the Sect Self-Styled Perfectionists; with a Summary View of Their Leading Doctrines.* Brattleboro, VT: The Author, 1849.

Ellis, John Tracy. *American Catholicism.* Chicago: University of Chicago Press, 1956.

Ellis, Markman. *The Politics of Sensibility: Race, Gender, and Commerce in the Sentimental Novel.* Cambridge: Cambridge University Press, 1996.

Ennis, Arthur J. "Henry Conwell, Second Bishop of Philadelphia." In *The History of the Archdiocese of Philadelphia*, edited by James F. Connelly, 83–104. Philadelphia: Archdiocese of Philadelphia, 1976.

Eslinger, Ellen. *Citizens of Zion: The Social Origins of the Camp Meeting Revival.* Knoxville: University of Tennessee Press, 1999.

Faulkner, Carol. *Unfaithful: Love, Adultery, and Marriage Reform in Nineteenth-Century America.* Philadelphia: University of Pennsylvania Press, 2019.

Finney, Charles G., Garth Rosell, and Richard A. G. Dupuis. *The Memoirs of Charles G. Finney: The Complete Restored Text.* Grand Rapids, MI: Academie, 1989.

First Annual Report of the Oneida Association: Exhibiting Its History, Principles, and Transactions to Jan. 1, 1849. Oneida Reserve: Leonard & Company, 1849.

Flake, Lawrence R. "A Shaker View of a Mormon Mission." *BYU Studies Quarterly* 20, no. 1 (Fall 1979): 94–99.

Fliegelman, Jay. *Prodigals and Pilgrims: The American Revolution against Patriarchal Authority, 1750–1800.* New York: Cambridge University Press, 1982.

Fluhman, J. Spencer. *"A Peculiar People": Anti-Mormonism and the Making of Religion in Nineteenth-Century America.* Chapel Hill: University of North Carolina Press, 2012.

Flynn, Tom, ed. *The New Encyclopedia of Unbelief.* Amherst, NY: Prometheus Books, 2007.

Foster, Lawrence. *Religion and Sexuality: The Shakers, the Mormons, and the Oneida Community.* Urbana: University of Illinois Press, 1984.

——. *Women, Family, and Utopia: Communal Experiments of the Shakers, the Oneida Community, and the Mormons.* Syracuse, NY: Syracuse University Press, 1991.

Foster, Thomas A. *Sex and the Eighteenth-Century Man: Massachusetts and the History of Sexuality in America.* Boston: Beacon Press, 2006.

Foucault, Michel. *The History of Sexuality*, vol. 1: *An Introduction*. Translated by Robert Hurley. New York: Vintage Books, 1990.

Franchot, Jenny. *Roads to Rome: The Antebellum Protestant Encounter with Catholicism*. Berkeley: University of California Press, 1994.

Freeman, Joanne B. *Affairs of Honor: National Politics in the New Republic*. New Haven, CT: Yale University Press, 2002.

French, Kara M. *Against Sex: Identities of Sexual Restraint in Early America*. Chapel Hill: University of North Carolina Press, 2021.

——. "Prejudice for Profit: Escaped Nun Stories and American Catholic Print Culture." *Journal of the Early Republic* 39, no. 3 (Fall 2019): 503–35.

Fuller, Metta Victoria. *Mormon Wives: A Narrative of Facts Stranger than Fiction*. New York: Derby & Jackson, 1856.

Gedge, Karin E. *Without Benefit of Clergy: Women and the Pastoral Relationship in Nineteenth-Century American Culture*. New York: Oxford University Press, 2003.

Ginzberg, Lori D. *Women and the Work of Benevolence: Morality, Politics, and Class in the Nineteenth-Century United States*. New Haven, CT: Yale University Press, 1990.

Givens, Terryl L. *Viper on the Hearth: Mormons, Myths, and the Construction of Heresy*. New York: Oxford University Press, 1997.

Glenn, Myra C. *Campaigns against Corporal Punishment: Prisoners, Sailors, Women, and Children in Antebellum America*. Albany: State University of New York Press, 1984.

Goodwillie, Christian, ed. *Writings of Shaker Apostates and Anti-Shakers, 1782–1850*. Vol. 1, *1782–1811*. London: Pickering & Chatto, 2013.

Gordon, Sarah Barringer. "The Liberty of Self-Degradation: Polygamy, Woman Suffrage, and Consent in Nineteenth-Century America." *Journal of American History* 83, no. 3 (December 1996): 815–47.

——. *The Mormon Question: Polygamy and Constitutional Conflict in Nineteenth Century America*. Chapel Hill: University of North Carolina Press, 2002.

——. " 'Our National Hearthstone': Anti-Polygamy Fiction and the Sentimental Campaign against Moral Diversity in Antebellum America." *Yale Journal of Law and the Humanities* 8, no. 2 (1996): 295–350.

Gordon, Sarah Barringer, and Jan Shipps. "Fatal Convergence in the Kingdom of God: The Mountain Meadows Massacre in American History." *Journal of the Early Republic* 37, no. 2 (2017): 307–47.

A Graphic Account of the Alarming Riots at St Mary's Church, in April of 1822, together with the Most Important Extracts from the Decisions of Chief Justices Tilghman, Duncan and Gibson, Relative to the Charter of Said Church, Including Letters from Hon. J. R. Ingersol & Thos. Kittera, Esq. Philadelphia, 1844.

Green, James. *Mathew Carey: Publisher and Patriot*. Philadelphia: Library Company of Philadelphia, 1985.

Griffin, Martin I. J. "Life of Bishop Conwell of Philadelphia." *Records of the American Catholic Historical Society of Philadelphia*, edited by Lemuel B. Norton, vols. 24–25, pp. 1913–14.

Hall, David B. *Halls of New England: Genealogical and Biographical*. Albany, NY: Joel Munsell's Sons, 1883.

Halttunen, Karen. "Humanitarianism and the Pornography of Pain in Anglo-American Culture." *American Historical Review* 100, no. 2 (April 1995): 303–34.

Hambrick-Stowe, Charles E. *Charles G. Finney and the Spirit of American Evangelicalism.* Grand Rapids, MI: Wm. B. Eerdmans, 1996.

Hanks, Maxine, ed., *Women and Authority: Re-Emerging Mormon Feminism.* Salt Lake City: Signature Books, 1992.

Hardy, B. Carmon. "Lords of Creation: Polygamy, the Abrahamic Household, and Mormon Patriarchy." *Journal of Mormon History* 20, no. 1 (Spring 1994): 119–52.

Harold, Rev. William Vincent. *An Address to the Roman Catholics of Philadelphia.* Philadelphia: Printed for the Trustee of Harriet and Jane Dornin, 1823.

Hatch, Nathan. "The Christian Movement and the Demand for a Theology of the People." *Journal of American History* 67, no. 3 (December 1980): 545–67.

——. *Democratization of American Christianity.* New Haven, CT: Yale University Press, 1989.

Haulman, Kate. "Fashion and the Culture Wars of Revolutionary Philadelphia." *William and Mary Quarterly* 62, no. 4 (October 2005): 625–62.

Hempton, David. *Evangelical Disenchantment: Nine Portraits of Faith and Doubt.* New Haven, CT: Yale University Press, 2008.

Hessinger, Rodney. *Seduced, Abandoned, and Reborn: Visions of Youth in Middle-Class America, 1780–1850.* Philadelphia: University of Pennsylvania Press, 2005.

Hewitt, Nancy A. *Women's Activism and Social Change: Rochester, New York, 1822–1872.* Ithaca, NY: Cornell University Press, 1984.

Heyrman, Christine Leigh. *Doomed Romance: Broken Hearts, Lost Souls, and Sexual Tumult in Nineteenth-Century America.* New York: Knopf, 2021.

——. *Southern Cross: The Beginnings of the Bible Belt.* Chapel Hill: University of North Carolina Press, 1997.

Hogan, William. *An Address to the Congregation of St. Mary's Church, Philadelphia.* Philadelphia, 1820.

——. *Continuation of an Address to the Congregation of St. Mary's Church, Philadelphia.* Philadelphia, 1821.

——. *Popery! As It Was and Is; also, Auricular Confessions and Popish Nunneries.* Hartford, CT: Silas Andrus & Son, 1853.

——. *Strictures on a Pamphlet Written by William Vincent Harold Entitled Reply to a Catholic Layman.* Philadelphia: Robert Desilver, 1822.

Holbrook, Kate. *Women and Mormonism: Historical and Contemporary Perspectives.* Salt Lake City: University of Utah Press, 2016.

Horowitz, Helen Lefkowitz. *Rereading Sex: Battles over Sexual Knowledge and Suppression in Nineteenth-Century America.* New York: Knopf, 2002.

Howe, Daniel Walker. *What Hath God Wrought: The Transformation of America, 1815–1848.* New York: Oxford University Press, 2007.

Humez, Jean M. "'Ye Are My Epistles': The Construction of Ann Lee Imagery in Early Shaker Sacred Literature." *Journal of Feminist Studies in Religion* 8, no. 1 (Spring 1992): 83–103.

Hyde, John, Jr. *Mormonism: Its Leaders and Designs.* New York: W. P. Fetridge, 1857.

Iannaccone, Laurence R. "Why Strict Churches Are Strong." *American Journal of Sociology* 99, no. 5 (March 1994): 1180–1211.

An Irish Catholic. *A Short Address to the Roman Catholic Congregation of St. Mary's Church, on the Approaching Election for Trustees.* Philadelphia: Bernard Dornin, 1822.

Isaac, Rhys. "Evangelical Revolt: The Nature of the Baptists' Challenge to the Traditional Order in Virginia, 1765 to 1775." *William and Mary Quarterly* 31, no. 3 (1974): 346–68.

Isenberg, Nancy. *Sex and Citizenship in Antebellum America.* Chapel Hill: University of North Carolina Press, 1998.

Jabour, Anya. *Marriage in the Early Republic: Elizabeth and William Wirt and the Companionate Ideal.* Baltimore, MD: Johns Hopkins University Press, 1998.

Jeffrey, Julie Roy. *The Great Silent Army of Abolitionism: Ordinary Women in the Antislavery Movement.* Chapel Hill: University of North Carolina Press, 1998.

Johnson, Curtis D. "The Protracted Meeting Myth: Awakenings, Revivals, and New York State Baptists, 1789-1850." *Journal of the Early Republic* 34, no. 3 (Fall 2014): 349–83.

Johnson, Paul E. *A Shopkeeper's Millennium: Society and Revivals in Rochester, New York, 1815–1837.* New York: Hill & Wang, 1978.

Johnson, Paul E., and Sean Wilentz. *The Kingdom of Matthias: A Story of Sex and Salvation in 19th-Century America.* New York: Oxford University Press, 1994.

Jorgensen, Lynne Watkins. "John Hyde, Jr., Mormon Renegade." *Journal of Mormon History* 17 (1991): 120–44.

Juster, Susan. *Doomsayers: Anglo-American Prophecy in the Age of Revolution.* Philadelphia: University of Pennsylvania Press, 2003.

Keller, Karl, and John Wickliffe Rigdon. "'I Never Knew a Time When I Did Not Know Joseph Smith': A Son's Record of the Life and Testimony of Sidney Rigdon." *Dialogue: A Journal of Mormon Thought* 1, no. 4 (Winter 1966): 14–42.

Kelley, Mary. *Learning to Stand and Speak: Women, Education and Public Life in America's Republic.* Chapel Hill: OIEAHC/University of North Carolina Press, 2006.

Kennedy, Kathleen. "A Charge Never Easily Made: The Meaning of Respectability and Women's Work in the Trial of the Reverend William Hogan, 1822." *American Nineteenth Century History* 7, no. 1 (March 2006): 29–62.

Kern, Louis J. *An Ordered Love: Sex Roles and Sexuality in Victorian Utopias—the Shakers, the Mormons, and the Oneida Community.* Chapel Hill: University of North Carolina Press, 1981.

Kerner, Cynthia. *Beyond the Household: Women's Place in the Early South, 1700–1835.* Ithaca, NY: Cornell University Press, 1998.

Kerr, Jacob. *Several Trials of the Reverend David Barclay before the Presbytery of New Brunswick with Their Judgment at Oxford.* Elizabeth Town, NJ: R. & P. Canfield, 1814.

Kirschner, Ann. "At the Gate of Heaven: Early Shaker Dreams and Visions." In Morin, *Heavenly Visions*, 169–78.

Klaw, Spencer. *Without Sin: The Life and Death of the Oneida Community.* New York: Penguin Books, 1993.

Klepp, Susan E. "Revolutionary Bodies: Women and the Fertility Transition in the Mid-Atlantic Region, 1760–1820." *Journal of American History* 85, no. 3 (December 1998): 910–45.

——. *Revolutionary Conceptions: Women, Fertility, and Family Limitation in America, 1760–1820.* Chapel Hill: OIEACH/University of North Carolina, 2009.

Knott, Sarah. *Mother Is a Verb: An Unconventional History.* New York: Sarah Crichton Books, 2019.

——. *Sensibility and the American Revolution.* Chapel Hill: OIEAHC/University of North Carolina Press, 2009.

Lawrence, Christopher. "The Nervous System and Society in the Scottish Enlightenment." In *Natural Order: Historical Studies of Scientific Culture*, edited by Barry Barnes and Steven Shapin, 19–40. Beverly Hills, CA: Sage, 1979.

Layman of St. Mary's Congregation. *An Address to the Roman Catholics of the United States.* Philadelphia, 1821.

Layman of the Congregation. *An Inquiry into the Causes Which Led to the Dissentions Actually Existing in the Congregation of St. Mary's; and Observations on the Mode Best Calculated to Prevent Its Increase.* Philadelphia, 1821.

Letter to Henry, Bishop of Philadelphia, by a Lady. Philadelphia: Printed for the author, 1821.

Levine, Lawrence. *Black Culture and Black Consciousness: Afro-American Thought from Slavery to Freedom.* New York: Oxford University Press, 1977.

Levy, Barry. "Girls and Boys: Poor Children and the Labor Market in Colonial Massachusetts." In "Empire, Society and Labor: Essays in Honor of Richard S. Dunn," edited by Nicholas Canny, Joseph E. Illick, Gary B. Nash, and William Pencak, special issue, *Pennsylvania History* 64 (Summer 1997): 287–307.

Lewis, Jan. "The Republican Wife: Virtue and Seduction in the Early Republic." *William and Mary Quarterly* 44, no. 4 (October 1987): 689–721.

Light, Dale. *Rome and the New Republic: Conflict and Community in Philadelphia Catholicism between the Revolution and the Civil War.* Notre Dame, IN: University of Notre Dame Press, 1996.

Lincoln, Bruce. *Holy Terrors: Thinking about Religion after September 11.* Chicago: University of Chicago Press, 2006.

Lindman, Janet Moore. *Bodies of Belief: Baptist Community in Early America.* Philadelphia: University of Pennsylvania Press, 2008.

Lusignan, Nancy Schultz. *Fire and Roses: The Burning of the Charlestown Convent, 1834.* New York: Free Press, 2000.

Lyons, Clare. *Sex among the Rabble: An Intimate History of Gender and Power in the Age of Revolution, Philadelphia, 1730–1830.* Chapel Hill: OIEAHC/University of North Carolina Press, 2006.

Maffitt, John. *Report of the Trial of Mr. John N. Maffitt: Before a Council of Ministers of the Episcopal Church.* Boston: True & Greene, 1823.

Maffitt, John Newland, and Joseph T. Buckingham. *Trial: Commonwealth vs. J. T. Buckingham, on an Indictment for a Libel, before the Municipal Court of the City of Boston, December Term, 1822.* Boston: New England Galaxy, 1822.

Marsden, George M. *The Evangelical Mind and the New School Presbyterian Experience: A Case Study of Thought and Theology in Nineteenth-Century America.* New Haven, CT: Yale University Press, 1970.

Martin, John Hill. *Martin's Bench and Bar of Philadelphia*. Philadelphia: R. Welsh, 1883.

McAvoy, Thomas T. *A History of the Catholic Church in the United States*. Notre Dame, IN: University of Notre Dame Press, 1969.

McGreevy, John T. *Catholicism and American Freedom: A History*. New York: Norton, 2003.

McKiernan, F. Mark. "The Conversion of Sidney Rigdon to Mormonism." *Dialogue: A Journal of Mormon Thought* 5, no. 2 (Summer 1970): 71–78.

McLoughlin, William. *Modern Revivalism: Charles Grandison Finney to Billy Graham*. Eugene, OR: Wipf & Stock, 2004.

——. "Untangling the Tiverton Tragedy: The Social Meaning of the Terrible Haystack Murder of 1833." *Journal of American Culture* 7, no. 4 (1984): 75–84.

McMahon, Lucia. *Mere Equals: The Paradox of Educated Women in the Early Republic*. Ithaca, NY: Cornell University Press, 2012.

McNamara, Robert F. "Trusteeism in the Atlantic States, 1785–1863." *Catholic Historical Review* 30, no. 2 (July 1944): 135–54.

McNemar, Richard. *The Other Side of the Question in Three Parts*. Cincinnati: Looker, Reynolds, 1819.

Meade, Richard W. *An Address to the Roman Catholics of the City of Philadelphia, in Reply to Mr. Harold's Address*. Philadelphia, 1823.

Methodist Error, or, Friendly, Christian Advice, to Those Methodists, Who Indulge in Extravagant Emotions and Bodily Exercises, by a Wesleyan Methodist. Trenton, NJ: D. & E. Fenton, 1819.

Moore, R. Laurence. "How to Become a People: The Mormon Scenario." In *Religious Outsiders and the Making of Americans*, 25–47. New York: Oxford University Press, 1986.

——. *Selling God: American Religion in the Marketplace of Culture*. New York: Oxford University Press, 1994.

Morgan, Edmund S. *Visible Saints: The History of a Puritan Idea*. New York: New York University Press, 1963.

Morin, France, curator. *Heavenly Visions: Shaker Gift Drawings and Gift Songs*. New York: Drawing Center; Los Angeles: UCLA Hammer Museum; Minneapolis: University of Minnesota Press, 2001.

Murdock, Sophia, and Washington Van Zandt. *The Trial of the Rev. Van Zandt, Rector of Grace Church, Rochester, N.Y., for the Seduction of Miss Sophia Murdock, a Young and Beautiful Member of His Church*. Philadelphia, 1842.

Najar, Monica. *Evangelizing the South: A Social History of Church and State in Early America*. New York: Oxford University Press, 2008.

Nash, Gary. *Forging Freedom: The Formation of Philadelphia's Black Community*. Cambridge, MA: Harvard University Press, 1988.

Neuman, Richard. *Freedom's Prophet: Bishop Richard Allen, the AME Church, and the Black Founding Fathers*. New York: New York University Press, 2008.

Newell, Linda King, and Valeen Tippets Avery. *Mormon Enigma: Emma Hale Smith*. New York: Doubleday, 1984.

Noll, Mark A. *America's God: From Jonathan Edwards to Abraham Lincoln*. New York: Oxford University Press, 2002.

Norris, Richard Jr. *The Song of Songs: Interpreted by Early Christian and Medieval Commentators*. Grand Rapids, MI: Wm. B. Eerdmans, 2003.

Noyes, George Wallingford, and Lawrence Foster, eds. *Free Love in Utopia: John Humphrey Noyes and the Origin of the Oneida Community*. Urbana: University of Illinois Press, 2001.

Noyes, John Humphrey. *The Berean: A Manual for the Help of Those Who Seek the Faith of the Primitive Church*. Putney, VT: Office of the Spiritual Magazine, 1847.

——. "Bible Argument, Defining the Relations of the Sexes in the Kingdom of Heaven." In *First Annual Report of the Oneida Association*.

——. *The Way of Holiness: A Series of Papers Formerly Published in the Perfectionist at New Haven*. Putney, VT: J. H. Noyes, 1838.

Noyes, John Humphrey, and George Wallingford Noyes. *Religious Experience of John Humphrey Noyes, Founder of the Oneida Community*. New York: Macmillan, 1923.

O'Toole, James. *The Faithful: A History of Catholics in America*. Cambridge, MA: Belknap Press of Harvard University Press, 2008.

Pagliarini, Marie Anne. "The Pure American Woman and the Wicked Catholic Priest: An Analysis of Anti-Catholic Literature in Antebellum America." *Religion and American Culture* 9, no. 1 (1999): 97–128.

Painter, Nell Irvin. *Sojourner Truth: A Life, a Symbol*. New York: Norton, 1997.

Parker, Robert Allerton. *A Yankee Saint: John Humphrey Noyes and the Oneida Community*. New York: G. P. Putnam's Sons, 1935.

Parsons, Tyler. *Mormon Fanaticism Exposed: A Compendium of the Book of Mormon, or Joseph Smith's Golden Bible*. Boston: Printed for the Author, 1841.

Pastoral Charges Delivered by the Right Rev. Bishop Henry in St. Mary's Church on the 2d of Nov. 1820 & 11th of Feb. 1821 in the Presence of Two Thousand Persons. Philadelphia: Robert Desilver, 1821.

Potter, Ray. *Admonitions from the Depths of the Earth: or the Fall of Ray Potter; in Twenty-Four Letters; Written by Himself to His Brother, Nicholas G. Potter*. Pawtucket, RI: R. Sherman, 1838.

Procter-Smith, Marjorie. "'In the Line of the Female': Shakerism and Feminism." In *Women's Leadership in Marginal Religions: Explorations Outside the Mainstream*, edited by Catherine Wessinger, 23–40. Urbana: University of Illinois Press, 1993.

Public Discussion of the Issues between the Reorganized Church of Jesus Christ of Latter-day Saints and the Church of Christ [Disciples], Held in Kirtland, Ohio, Beginning February 12th, and Closing March 8th, 1884, between E. L. Kelley, of the R.C. of J.C. of Latter-day Saints, and Clark Braden, of the Church of Christ. St. Louis: Christian Publishing, ca. 1884.

Remer, Rosalind. *Printers and Men of Capital: Philadelphia Book Publishers in the New Republic*. Philadelphia: University of Pennsylvania Press, 1996.

Reynolds, David S. *Beneath the American Renaissance: The Subversive Imagination in the Age of Emerson and Melville*. Cambridge, MA: Harvard University Press, 1988.

Roediger, David R. *Wages of Whiteness: Race and the Making of the American Working Class*. 2nd ed. New York: Verso, 1999.

Rollman, Hans. "The Early Baptist Career of Sidney Rigdon in Warren, Ohio." *Brigham Young University Studies* 21, no. 1 (Winter 1981): 37–50.

Roloff, Francis. *Last Appeal to the Congregation of St. Mary's Church*. Philadelphia, 1821.

——. *The True Sentiments of the Writer of the Last Appeal to the Congregation of St. Mary's Church*. Philadelphia: Bernard Dornin, 1821.

Rorabaugh, W. J. "'I Thought I Should Liberate Myself from the Thraldom of Others': Apprentices, Masters, and the Revolution." In *Beyond the American Revolution: Explorations in the History of American Radicalism*, edited by Alfred F. Young, 185–217. DeKalb: Northern Illinois University Press, 1993.

Rothman, Ellen. *Hands and Hearts: A History of Courtship in America*. New York: Basic Books, 1984.

Ryan, Mary. *Cradle of the Middle Class: The Family in Oneida County, New York, 1790–1865*. New York: Cambridge University Press, 1981.

——. *Women in Public: Between Banners and Ballots, 1825–1880*. Baltimore: Johns Hopkins University Press, 1990.

Ryder, Charles H. "History of Hiram." 1864. Hiram History Narratives box 2/A/1/a, Hiram College Archives, Hiram, Ohio.

St. Mary's Church (Philadelphia, Pa.). *Address of the Committee of Saint Mary's Church of Philadelphia to Their Brethren of the Roman Catholic Faith throughout the United States of America on the Subject of a Reform of Sundry Abuses in the Administration of Our Church Discipline*. New York: Kingsland, 1821.

——. *Sundry Documents, Submitted to the Consideration of the Pewholders of St. Mary's Church, by the Trustees of That Church*. Philadelphia: Lydia R. Bailey, 1812.

Sampson, William. *Trial of Mr. William Parkinson, Pastor of the First Baptist Church in the City of New-York, on an Indictment for Assault and Battery upon Mrs. Eliza Wintringham*. New York: Largin & Thompson, 1811.

Schaaf, Jennifer, "'With a Pure Intention of Pleasing and Honouring God': How the Philadelphia Laity Created American Catholicism, 1785–1850." PhD diss., University of Pennsylvania, 2013, https://repository.upenn.edu/edissertations/925.

Schiebinger, Londa. "Why Mammals Are Called Mammals: Gender Politics in Eighteenth-Century Natural History." *American Historical Review* 98, no. 2 (April 1993): 382–411.

Schmidt, Leigh Eric. *Holy Fairs: Scotland and the Making of American Revivalism*. 2nd ed. Grand Rapids, MI: Wm. B. Eerdmans, 2001.

Sellers, Charles Coleman. *Theophilus the Battle-Axe: A History of the Lives and Adventures of Theophilus Ransom Gates and the Battle-Axes*. Philadelphia: Patterson & White, 1930.

Sellers, Charles G. *The Market Revolution: Jacksonian America, 1815–1846*. New York: Oxford University Press, 1991.

Shields, Steven L. "Joseph Smith and Sidney Rigdon: Co-Founders of a Movement." *Dialogue: A Journal of Mormon Thought* 52, no. 3 (Fall 2019): 1–18.

Smith, Agnes. "Folklore and History in the Mormon Encounter with the Disciples of Christ at Hiram, OH, March 1832." August 1966. Hiram Archives, 3/C Mormons, Hiram Library Archives, Hiram, Ohio.

Smith, Andrew F. *The Saintly Scoundrel: The Life and Times of Dr. John Cook Bennett.* Urbana: University of Illinois Press, 1997.

Smith, James. "An Attempt to Develop Shakerism." In *Writings of Shaker Apostates and Anti-Shakers, 1782–1850*, vol. 1, *1782–1811*, edited by Christian Goodwillie, 181–85. London: Pickering & Chatto, 2013.

Smith, James. "Remarkable Occurrences, Lately Discovered among the People Called Shakers." In Goodwillie, *Writings of Shaker Apostates*, 189–99.

Smith, Joseph, Jr. *History of the Church of Jesus Christ of Latter-day Saints*, vol. 1. Salt Lake City: Deseret Book Company, 1951.

Smith-Rosenberg, Carroll. *Religion and the Rise of the American City: The New York City Mission Movement, 1812–1870.* Ithaca, NY: Cornell University Press, 1971.

Smith-Rosenberg, Carroll, and Wai Chee Dimock. "Domesticating Virtue: Coquettes and Revolutionaries in Young America." In *American Literary Studies: A Methodological Reader*, edited by Michael A. Elliott and Claudia Stokes, 19–40. New York: New York University Press.

Stauffer, John. *The Black Hearts of Men: Radical Abolitionists and the Transformation of Race.* Cambridge, MA: Harvard University Press, 2002.

Stein, Stephen J. *The Shaker Experience in America: A History of the United Society of Believers.* New Haven, CT: Yale University Press, 1994.

Stephanson, Raymond. "Richardson's 'Nerves': The Physiology of Sensibility in *Clarissa.*" *Journal of the History of Ideas* 49, no. 2 (April-June 1988): 267–85.

Stone, William Leete. *Matthias and His Impostures; Or the Progress of Fanaticism.* 3rd ed. New York: Harper & Brothers, 1835.

Swan, Joseph R., ed. *Statutes of the State of Ohio.* Cincinnati: H. W. Derby, 1854.

Taysom, Stephen. *Shakers, Mormons, and Religious Worlds: Conflicting Visions, Contested Boundaries.* Bloomington: University of Indiana Press, 2011.

Thurman, Suzanne. "'Dearly Loved Mother Eunice': Gender, Motherhood, and Shaker Spirituality." *Church History* 66, no. 4 (1997): 750–61.

——. "The Seat of Sin, the Site of Salvation: The Shaker Body and the Nineteenth-Century American Imagination." *Nineteenth Century Studies* 15 (2001): 1–18.

Tobey, Kristen. *Plowshares: Protest, Performance, and Religious Identity in the Nuclear Age.* University Park: Pennsylvania State University Press, 2016.

Tourscher, Francis E. *The Hogan Schism and Trustee Troubles in St. Mary's Church Philadelphia, 1820–1829.* Philadelphia: Peter Reilly, 1930.

Trisco, Robert F. "Bishops and Their Priests in the United States." In *The Catholic Priest in the United States: Historical Investigations*, ed. John Tracy Ellis, 111–292. Collegeville, MN: Saint John's University Press, 1971.

Ulrich, Laurel Thatcher. *A House Full of Females: Plural Marriage and Women's Rights in Early Mormonism, 1835–1870.* New York: Knopf, 2017.

——. "Runaway Wives, 1830-60." *Journal of Mormon History* 42, no. 2 (April 2016): 1–26.

Vale, G. *Fanaticism: Its Source and Influence, Illustrated by the Simple Narrative of Isabella, in the Case of Matthias, Mr. and Mrs. Folger, M. Pierson, Mr. Mills, Catherine, Isabella, &c. &c.; A Reply to W. L. Stone.* In 2 Parts. New York: G. Vale, 1835.

Van Wagoner, Richard S. *Sidney Rigdon: A Portrait of Religious Excess*. Salt Lake City: Signature Books, 1994.

Varon, Elizabeth. *We Mean to Be Counted: White Women and Politics in Antebellum Virginia*. Chapel Hill: University of North Carolina Press, 1998.

Waldstreicher, David. *In the Midst of Perpetual Fetes: The Making of American Nationalism, 1776–1820*. Chapel Hill: OIEACH/University of North Carolina Press, 1997.

Waln, Robert. *The Hermit in America on a Visit to Philadelphia*. 2nd ed. Philadelphia: M. Thomas, 1819.

Ward, Maria. *Female Life among the Mormons: A Narrative of Many Years' Personal Experience; by the Wife of a Mormon Elder, Recently from Utah*. New York: Derby & Jackson, 1855, 1860.

Warner, Michael. *The Letters of the Republic: Publication and the Public Sphere in Eighteenth-Century America*. Cambridge, MA: Harvard University Press, 1990.

Warner, William W. *At Peace with All Their Neighbors: Catholics and Catholicism in the National Capital, 1787–1860*. Washington, DC: Georgetown University Press, 1994.

Wayland-Smith, Ellen. *Oneida: From Free-Love Utopia to the Well-Set Table*. New York: Picador, 2016.

Weeks, W. E. P. *Trial of Rev. Joy Hamlet Fairchild on a Charge of Adultery with Miss Rhoda Davidson*. Boston: Published at the "Times" Office, 1845.

Wells, Seth Y., ed. *Testimonies Concerning the Character and Ministry of Mother Ann Lee and the First Witnesses of the Gospel of Christ's Second Appearing, Given by Some of the Aged Brethren and Sisters of the United Society*. Albany, NY: Packard & Van Benthuysen, 1827.

Wergland, Glendyne. *One Shaker Life: Isaac Newton Youngs, 1793–1865*. Amherst: University of Massachusetts Press, 2006.

——. *Sisters in the Faith: Shaker Women and Equality of the Sexes*. Amherst: University of Massachusetts Press, 2011.

Wheeler, Harvey. *Trial of Rev. Issachar Grosscup for the Seduction of Roxana L. Wheeler, Comprising the Testimony in the Case, and Also a Sketch of the Arguments Addressed to the Jury*. Canandaigua, NY, 1848.

Wigger, John. *Taking Heaven by Storm: Methodism and the Rise of Popular Christianity in America*. New York: Oxford University Press, 1998.

Williams, Catherine. *Fall River: An Authentic Narrative*. Providence, RI: Marshall, Brown, 1833.

Wilson, James Grant, and James Fiske. "Reed, Joseph." In *Appletons' Cyclopaedia of American Biography*, edited by James Grant Wilson and James Fiske, 208–9. New York: D. Appleton, 1888.

Wilson, Lisa. *Ye Heart of a Man: The Domestic Life of Men in Colonial New England*. New Haven, CT: Yale University Press, 1999.

Winiarski, Douglas L. "Seized by the Jerks: Shakers, Spirit Possession, and the Great Revival." *William and Mary Quarterly* 76, no. 1 (January 2019): 111–50.

Wonderly, Anthony. *Oneida Utopia: A Community Searching for Human Happiness and Prosperity*. Ithaca, NY: Cornell University Press, 2017.

Woo, Ilyon. *The Great Divorce: A Nineteenth-Century Mother's Extraordinary Fight against Her Husband, the Shakers, and Her Times.* New York: Atlantic Monthly, 2010.

Wyatt-Brown, Bertram. *Southern Honor: Ethics and Behavior in the Old South.* New York: Oxford University Press, 1982.

Youngs, Benjamin Seth. *Transactions of the Ohio Mob, Called in the Public Papers, "An Expedition against the Shakers."* Ohio, 1810.

Zagarri, Rosemarie. "Politics and Civil Society: A Discussion of Mary Kelley's Learning to Stand and Speak." *Journal of the Early Republic* 28, no. 1 (Spring 2008): 61–73.

——. *Revolutionary Backlash: Women and Politics in the Early American Republic.* Philadelphia: University of Pennsylvania Press, 2007.

INDEX

Note: Page numbers in **bold** refer to images.

Buckingham, J. T., 108
Burchard, Jedediah, 116
Burned-Over District, The (Cross), 9
Bushman, Richard L., 17, 183n96

Campbell, Alexander, 2, 3, 18, 38, 157n2, 162n21
Campbell, Thomas, 18
camp meetings, 107, **109,** 110–12, 152–53
Canton, Sarah, 98
Carey, Mathew, 43, 45–46
Carr, Mary Clarke, 52–53
Cartwright, Peter, 151–53, 154
castration, 14, 16, 24
Catholicism, 7, 11–12, 39–67, 154–55, 169n15
  anti-Catholic writings, 64–67
  classification of, 8–9
  colonial status of American church, 51
  compared with Shakerism, 80
  and democratization, 40–41, 50–52, 67
  Hogan trial for assault of Mary Connell, 39–40, 41–42, 53–63
  and pamphlet warfare, 41, 46–47, 51–53
  trusteeism in, 40, 41, 50–51, 64
celestial marriage, 33
celibacy/chastity, 4
  in Catholicism, 66–67
  in Hogan trial, 57, 65
  and perfectionism, 126–28
  and Shakerism, 69, 72, 127–28, 175n6
Chapman, Eunice, 70, 73–74, 75–76, 77, 79–80
children
  danger of losing, 68, 69, 77–81, 107–8, 140, 142–43, 152–3
  treatment of, 73–76, 77–81, 83–84
Church of Jesus Christ of Latter-day Saints. *See* Mormonism
class
  in Hogan trial, 54, 63, 168n8
  and religious enthusiasm, 112, 115, 155
Clinton, DeWitt, 92, 103
Cogswell, Hannah, 87
Cohoon, Hannah, 85, **86,** 88–**89**
coitus interruptus (withdrawal method), 133–34, 186n30
coitus reservatus (male continence), 134, 146, 186n30
Collins, Polly, 88, **90**
communalism, 3, 69, 137

communism, sexual. *See* complex marriage
complex marriage, 7, 12–13, 124–25, 144–48, 150
confession, Catholic, 65–67
Connell, Mary, 39, 40, 54, 55. *See also* Hogan trial
consent, 11, 27, 35–37, 38, 96
conversion. *See also* proselytism
  as sexually loaded, 17, 35, 37, 38, 152
Conwell, Henry, 40–41, 45–46, 47–48, 49, 52–53
Copley, Leman, 3, 4–6
Cornell, Sarah, **105,** 106, 107–8
Cowdery, Oliver, 4, 20, 21
Cragin, George, 132, 137, 185–86n26
Cragin, Mary, 132, 137, 185–86n26
Cross, Whitney, 9

Dallas, George, 53–54, 57–58
Darrow, David, 77
Davidson, Rhoda, 98
democratization, and Catholicism, 12, 40–41, 50–52, 67
Disciples of Christ movement, 2–3, 22–23, 161n15
divorce, 26, 77, 79–80
Dixon, William Hepworth, 127, 130
Doctrine and Covenants 49 (Smith), 3–4
domestic abuse, 30–31
Douglas, Ann, 67
Douglass, Frederick, 155
Doyle, Nora, 76
drinking (alcohol use), 59–60
Dyer, Mary Marshall, 68, 70, 73, 74–75, 76, 77

Eastman, Hubbard, 122–23, 141–43, 186n46
enthusiastic religion. *See* religious enthusiasm
evangelicalism. *See also* proselytism; religious enthusiasm
  as category, 8
  and enthusiasm as out of control, 114–15, 154
  and female-pastoral relations, 99–100
  and motherhood, 70
  and respectability, 110–11
  and women's power in the church, 94, 104
expediency, 131, 136–37, 143–44

Vale, Gilbert, 113, 118–20, 183n101
Van Zandt, Washington, 99, 102
vegetarianism, 4, 115
Vermont Phoenix, 137–40, 141, 150,
    186n46
violence. *See* mob attacks; sexual assault

Wallace, George B., 29–30
Waln, Robert, 49
Ward, Maria, 25, 27, 29, 30, 31, 32, 35,
    36–37, 165n63
Wayland, Francis, 113
Wayland-Smith, Ellen, 124, 185n15,
    185n26, 186n30, 187n73
Weld, Charles, 134
Wells, Seth, 82
Wheeler, Roxana, 98
Williams, Catherine, 105, 106–7
Wintringham, Eliza
    character of, 92
    on Parkinson's conduct, 100
    relationship to Parkinson, 98–99
    religious activities of, 95–96
    sexual comportment of, 96–97
    trial for sexual assault of, 92–94, 95–97,
        98–99, 100–102
The Witness (publication), 133, 135, 137, 138
women. *See also* women's political
    involvement in church affairs
    in Ann Lee's rendering, 86

and breastfeeding, 72, 76, 97
and changing conceptions of
    motherhood, 70–72
in civil society, 40
defense of Shakerism, 80
and enthusiastic religion, 111–12,
    113–14
and Mormonism, 25–27, 35–37
as preachers, 105, 111–12, 153–54
relationship between ministers and,
    99–100, 108, 152–53
suffrage for, 26
women's political involvement in
    church affairs
    and fear of reverend rakes, 104
    and Hogan Schism, 39–40, 41,
        56–57, 63, 65
    and Mormonism, 33
    and Parkinson trial, 94, 95, 104
    and religious marketplace, 10
Wonderly, Anthony, 124, 149
Wood, Aaron, 85
Wright, Frances, 133
Wright, Lucy, 11, 77, 81

Yarrington, S. B., 122–23
Young, Brigham, 17, 36
Youngs, Benjamin Seth, 78–79

Zagarri, Rosemarie, 25, 40, 174n74

CPSIA information can be obtained
at www.ICGtesting.com
Printed in the USA
LVHW040045021222
734313LV00018B/451/J